WHAT WE STAND FOR

WHAT WE STAND FOR

A Program for Progressive Patriotism

The New Democracy Project

Edited by Mark Green

Newmarket Press • New York

To my children Jenya and Jonah—because
it's their America we're creating.

This book is published in the United States of America.

First Edition

10 9 8 7 6 5 4 3 2 1

Library of Congress Cataloging-in-Publication Data available upon request.

ISBN 1-55704-613-1

QUANTITY PURCHASES

Companies, professional groups, clubs, and other organizations may qualify for special terms when ordering quantities of this title. For information, write Special Sales Department, Newmarket Press, 18 East 48th Street, New York, NY 10017; call (212) 832-3575; fax (212) 832-3629; or e-mail mailbox@newmarketpress.com.

www.newmarketpress.com

Manufactured in the United States of America.

Acknowledgments

An anthology is a quilt knit by many hands but based on a common design. So I'd like to thank all the extraordinary individual authors of *What We Stand For* who contributed their talent and time to this common design of a stronger democracy. All came together in the spirit of change, for good—in the spirit of Johnny Mercer's lyrics to "ac-cen-tu-ate the positive."

This volume would not exist without the editorial and research assistance of the always-resourceful Jenny Stepp, research director at the New Democracy Project—and the substantive suggestions of five close friends in particular: Katrina vanden Heuvel, Michael Waldman, Ellen Chesler, John Siegal, and Deni Frand (who doubles as my wife). Thanks also to the other staff of the New Democracy Project for helping shepherd this book to completion—Leora Hanser, Patrick Low, and Heather Austin.

Last we could never have completed this book—or the national conference based on it in May 2004 at New York University—without the generous support of many allies. We thank Chuck Blitz, Jerry Colonna, Barbara Fife, Gail Furman, Matt Gohd, Danny Goldberg & Rosemary Carroll, Stephen & Nancy Green, Frances & Isabelle Greenberger, Fern Hurst, Anne Hess & Craig Kaplan, Nancy Konipol & Adam Townsend, Charles Kushner, Randy Lee, Ken Lerer & Katherine Sailer, Will Little Jr., Jeffrey Lynford, Dal La Magna, Frank Mercado-Valdes, Danny Meyer, Paul L. Newman, Andrew Rasiej, Bernard & Irene Schwartz, David E. Shaw, Samuel Simon, Michael Sonnenfeldt, and David & Sylvia Steiner. Institutional support came from New York Community Trust; Open Society Institute; Rockefeller Foundation; Retail, Wholesale and Department Store Union and Stuart Appelbaum; Schumann Center for Media and Democracy; SEIU Local 32-BJ and Michael Fishman; Tides Foundation and Drummond Pike; UNITE! and Bruce Raynor & Edgar Romney; United Federation of Teachers and Randi Weingarten.

This is their book, too.

Mark Green
President, New Democracy Project
April 5, 2004

Contents

Introduction: Patriotic Progressives Enlist in the War of Ideas
—Mark Green xi

INTERNATIONAL POLICY: TOWARD A SAFER AMERICA

1. **Power and Authority: America's International Path Ahead**
   —Samuel R. Berger 1

2. **Containing Nuclear Proliferation**—Jonathan Schell 13

3. **A New Global Bargain**—Anne-Marie Slaughter 28

4. **National Security in the Age of Terrorism**
   —Gary Hart. 40

ECONOMY: TOWARD A MORE PROSPEROUS AMERICA

5. **An Economy, Not an Empire: A Program for Growth and
   Jobs *After* the Election**—James K. Galbraith 53

6. **A Broken Federal Fiscal Policy. . . and How to Fix It**
   —Robert Greenstein and Peter Orszag 68

7. **Corporate Accountability: Bolster the SEC and Litigation**
   —Joel Seligman 87

DOMESTIC AFFAIRS: TOWARD A FAIRER AMERICA

8. **Out of the Quagmire: A Human Investment Strategy for
   Federal Education Policy**—Richard F. Elmore 101

9. **Making Health Care Affordable and Accessible**
   —Ron Pollack 118

10. **Stop Environmental Darwinism: A Program for a
    Renewable Economy**—Carl Pope 135

11. **A Progressive Agenda for Metropolitan America**
    —Bruce Katz 150

JUSTICE: TOWARD A MORE JUST AMERICA

12. Terrorism and the Rule of Law: Maintaining Security and Liberty—David Cole. 167

13. From Affirmative Action to Affirmative Opportunity—Christopher Edley Jr. 183

14. A Progressive Agenda for Women's Rights—Ellen Chesler. 204

15. No Compromise on Crime—Christopher Stone 219

16. Beyond Money: Making Democracy Work—Mark Schmitt. 234

Endnotes 250

Contributors

SAMUEL R. BERGER *is Chairman of Stonebridge International LLC, an international strategic advisory firm based in Washington, D.C. He served as the National Security Advisor to President Clinton (1997–2000) and before then as the Deputy National Security Advisor (1993–1996).*

ELLEN CHESLER *is a senior fellow at the Open Society Institute, where she has directed its program on reproductive health and rights. She is author of* Woman of Valor: Margaret Sanger and the Birth Control Movement in America.

DAVID COLE, *a professor at Georgetown University Law Center, is author, most recently, of* Enemy Aliens: Double Standards and Constitutional Freedoms in the War on Terrorism.

CHRISTOPHER EDLEY JR. *is a professor at Harvard Law School, Co-Director of The Civil Rights Project at Harvard, and Dean-Designate of the University of California at Berkeley Law School (Boalt Hall). He was in charge of President Clinton's Review of Federal Affirmative Action Programs.*

RICHARD F. ELMORE *is the Gregory Anrig Professor of Educational Leadership at the Graduate School of Education, Harvard University. His research and teaching focus on accountability isssues in education and on the improvement of teaching and learning in public schools.*

JAMES K. GALBRAITH *is Lloyd M. Bentsen Jr. Chair in Government/Business Relations at the Lyndon B. Johnson School of Public Affairs, the University of Texas at Austin, and Senior Scholar of the Levy Economics Institute.*

MARK GREEN *is President of the New Democracy Project. He's the former Consumer Affairs Commissioner (1990–1993) and then Public Advocate of New York City (1994–2001) and author or editor of 19 books on public affairs.*

ROBERT GREENSTEIN *is Executive Director of the Center on Budget and Policy Priorities.*

GARY HART, *a U.S. senator from Colorado (1975–1987), is a former member of the U. S. Senate Armed Services Committee. He is co-founder of the Congressional Military Reform Caucus, co-author of* America Can Win: The Case for Military Reform, *and co-chair of the U.S. Commission on National Security for the 21st Century.*

BRUCE KATZ is Vice President of the Brookings Institution and Founding Director of its Center on Urban and Metropolitan Policy. From 1993 to 1996, Mr. Katz served as Chief of Staff to Henry G. Cisneros, the Secretary of Housing and Urban Development.

PETER ORSZAG is Joseph A. Pechman Senior Fellow at the Brookings Institution and co-director of the Urban Institute-Brookings Tax Policy Center.

RON POLLACK is the Executive Director of Families USA, the national organization for health care consumers.

CARL POPE is Executive Director of the Sierra Club.

JONATHAN SCHELL is the Harold Willens Peace Fellow at the Nation Institute. He writes frequently on the nuclear question for The Nation, Foreign Affairs, and Harper's, where he is also a contributing editor.

MARK SCHMITT is Director of Policy and Research for the U.S. Programs of the Open Society Institute.

JOEL SELIGMAN is the Dean and Ethan A.H. Shepley University Professor at Washington University School of Law. He is the author or co-author of numerous books on legal issues related to securities and corporations, including the 11-volume treatise co-authored with the late Louis Loss, Securities Regulation.

ANNE-MARIE SLAUGHTER is the Dean of the Woodrow Wilson School of Public and International Affairs at Princeton University and President of the American Society of International Law.

CHRISTOPHER STONE is the Director of the Vera Institute of Justice.

PATRIOTIC PROGRESSIVES
ENLIST IN THE WAR OF IDEAS

By Mark Green*

The Historic Stakes

What We Stand For grew directly out of a dinner that the New
Democracy Project held with President Bill Clinton after the mid-term
congressional elections in December 2002. "Elections are about the differences between choices. And I realized Democrats were in big trouble when
a month before the election voters thought Republicans had an agenda but
the Democrats didn't," said the only two-term Democratic president since
FDR. Leaning forward in his chair and referring back to the agency-by-
agency policy transition book that we had published in 1992, *Changing
America: Blueprints for the New Administration,* he urged a similar volume of
positive policy in 2004. "The New Democracy Project is important
because it can publish in one place big, interesting ideas about where we
are on security issues and domestic issues."

His suggestion was a match to kindling.

First, on-the-one-hand, on-the-other-hand liberals have been timid or
cowed by perhaps-wrong-but-never-in-doubt conservatives—or at least
that's been the appearance on talk shows and op-ed pages. They lived up
to Robert Frost's mocking observation that "a liberal is a man too broad-
minded to take his own side in a quarrel."

Second, there has been a gross disparity of resources in ideological
clashes, at least ever since Richard Mellon Scaife began investing hundreds
of millions of dollars in conservative think tanks in the 1960s. The result:
large marble buildings in Washington house the American Enterprise
Institute, the Heritage Foundation, the CATO Institute, and dozens of others that often prevail in public opinion due more to volume than quality.

Third, these intensity and resource gaps are occurring precisely at a

---

* **Mark Green** *is president of the New Democracy Project. He's the former Consumer
Affairs Commissioner (1990–1993) and then Public Advocate of New York City
(1994–2001), as well as the author or editor of 19 books on public affairs.*

transformational moment in both world and domestic affairs. In the past 15 years, a historical blink of an eye really, the world has evolved from one dominated by an East-West superpowers' conflict to one with a sole hyperpower and many terrorist lilliputians—and from nation-based industrial economies to a more globalized information economy with far greater trade in goods and services.

Domestically, President Bush is pushing hard-right policies to excite his base and win a realigning election in 2004 in order to dominate politics and policies for decades. Sociologist Daniel Bell may have talked about "the end of ideology" in the 1950s, but Karl Rove and Tom DeLay weren't listening. After interviewing Rove at length and hearing him muse about a "period of dominance," *New Yorker* magazine's Nicholas Lemann concluded that the man called "Bush's brain" had the goal of "creating a Republican majority that ... would last for a generation and would wind up profoundly changing the relationship between citizen and state in this country." Majority Leader DeLay told a group of GOP activists, "For the first time in more than a century, the Republican party is in the position to reshape American politics, and, therefore, reshape American society for more than a generation." Turning a deterministic Marx on his head, DeLay went on to boldly conclude that "instead of actions being dictated by the terms of history, the terms of history will be dictated by our actions."

Other books have exposed the radical policies of Bush & Co., including *The Book on Bush: How George W. (Mis)leads America,* which I coauthored with Eric Alterman. For example, it's not mainstream but extreme:

√ to shift $9 trillion in projected federal accounts over three years—from a $5 trillion surplus over the coming decade to a $4 trillion federal deficit, due in large part to excessive tax cuts that redistribute wealth from the bottom 95 percent to the top 5 percent;

√ to run an anti-science administration on issues such as global warming and stem cells, so that 60 leading scientists, including 20 Nobel laureates, charged in February 2004 that the administration had "misrepresented scientific knowledge and misled the public about the implications of its policies";

√ to ignore 800 years of Western common law by incarcerating hundreds of profiled men without trial or lawyers—none of whom were linked to al Qaeda—in the misplaced belief that 9/11 was more important than the U.S. Constitution;

√ and to launch a largely unilateral, preventive war on false pretenses, which turned our allies into adversaries and resulted in an American occupation of an Arab country that's become a magnet for terrorists.

If one asked our enemies if they'd like to see America occupying an Arab country and becoming a debtor nation, presumably they'd say yes. It's hard to see how George W. Bush could have come up with policies to make America weaker even if he had tried.

But since "nothing succeeds like excess," the conservative movement now openly seeks the complete take-over of American politics. With their radical record after only a single presidential term, however, one wonders what President Bush would do in a second term without the restraining prospect of reelection. So the real question in this election year is whether America is headed to an 1896 or 1980, when McKinley and Reagan inaugurated eras of conservative dominance based on Social Darwinism...or 1932 and 1960, when FDR and Kennedy established the premise of liberal, activist government.

This of course is a long-standing tug of war, with many premature reports of victory. Johnson's crushing defeat of Goldwater—and 1965 legislative successes—seemed to presage an era of liberal dominance. Except that conservatives then rethought, reorganized, returned to the grassroots—and four years later won the presidency and 16 years later the federal government as well. After Reagan's election in 1980, a jubilant William Rusher, publisher of the *National Review*, triumphantly announced, "Liberalism is dead." Triumphantly and prematurely, of course, since a center-left Democrat named Bill Clinton won the presidency a decade later.

After a presidential election decided by either one vote or 537 votes (if you're counting the Supreme Court or Florida), neither polls nor trends provide much assistance in predicting future results. True, while the populations of "Red States" have grown so significantly that W's electoral college margin has risen from four to eighteen, at the same time population increases within these states have been disproportionately minority, which trend Democratic. And to confuse matters more, there's much evidence that the country, in Lloyd Free's and Hadley Cantril's useful dichotomy, is more than ever ideologically conservative but operationally liberal. There's a majority against "big government" *and* a majority for regulation to stop Enron and mad cow disease—a majority for "lower taxes" *and* a majority for spending more on environmental safety. Indeed, on issue after issue with the sole exception of national security—from education, health care, and jobs to environment, consumer justice, and reproductive rights—the country sides with progressive policies more than conservative ones. There is then a large policy gap that progressives could exploit if they developed a competing, compelling narrative to the prevailing one focused on taxes and terrorism.

One Premise, Four Goals

The answer to whether America will tip to the McKinley/Reagan philosophy or the FDR/JFK philosophy is more substantive than political. For in the chicken-and-egg of elections, ideas precede votes—indeed, determine votes. Nor is it sufficient in this "war of ideas" simply to assert that the other guys are bums—be they "Massachusetts Liberals" or "Texas Cowboys." "What counts is not just what you're against," said Governor Adlai Stevenson a half-century ago, "but what you're for."

Hence, *What We Stand For.*

Each contributor is a leading progressive author, scholar, or advocate in her or his field. Each has written an original essay answering a basic question—what kind of America do we want? What are new directions for this new era? Writers both discuss the state-of-play in their areas and propose solutions—from the practical to the visionary—that a sympathetic President and Congress could pursue in 2005 and accomplish by 2010.* Authors were also urged not to wear the blinders of current political reality. They were reminded that (a) in 1988, world affairs pivoted around the seemingly immutable U.S.S.R., Berlin Wall, East-West nuclear arms race, and apartheid—and within two years all had vanished, and (b) in June of 2002 the *New York Times* predicted in a front page article that corporate governance reform was dead for that congressional session, except that the Sarbanes-Oxley legislation passed 97-0 one month (and WorldCom) later.

So ours is a book about future programs, not today's politics. It takes off

---

* Each chapter, therefore, has a similar template: *I. The Problem, II. Recent Developments* or *The Bush Response* (occasionally, I and II are merged), and *III. Solutions* (often separated into "short term" and "long term").

from a TV ad frequently aired this year for a Viagra competitor, Cialis: "When the moment comes, will you be ready?"

On 9/11, to take the most dramatic example, an enormous tragedy occurred that released an enormous volume of unexpected civic energy, philanthropic generosity, and political will that could have been harnessed to do great things—from a real program for energy independence to a worldwide coalition against terrorism to new multilateral efforts to stem pollution, proliferation, AIDS, or slave wages. But the Bush administration was ready neither for such a cataclysmic attack nor for such a public out-pouring. Instead, Republican leaders attempted to exploit it to advance their preexisting program of tax cuts, regulatory reduction, civil liberties restrictions, nuclear energy, tort reform—and invading Iraq. This public opportunity came and went, with little to show for it other than the American occupation of Baghdad at a cost of $200 billion or so.

This volume aspires to different goals should there come another moment—whether born of political success or domestic crisis—producing a national consensus for change. Although not based on any catechism, common to all the essays is one basic premise and four core values that could guide a new government.

The premise is that patriotism—or love of country—includes, but goes beyond attacking those who attack us. If that were all it meant, how could we distinguish between a democracy and a dictatorship oppress-ing people in the name of *their* thrones or theologies? Indeed, while a with-us-or-against-us patriotism worked well in our struggle with fas-cism in World War II, it did not work so well when deployed in the Salem witch trials, the Alien and Sedition Act, and McCarthyism. This nativist strain of patriotism was given its fullest and fiercest voice recent-ly when Attorney General John Ashcroft testified before the U.S. Senate Judiciary Committee in December 2001: "Those who scare peace-lov-ing people with phantoms of lost liberty, my message is this: Your tactics only aid terrorists—for they ... give ammunition to America's enemies and pause to America's friends." An ever pithier version came from Tom DeLay when, in the context of Iraq, he referred to Democrats as "the appeasement party." But it's a cramped and strange definition of American patriotism to exclude Americans who exercise the constitu-tional rights we fight to defend.

* *Real patriotism* **must mean not only defending but also**

improving our country via dissent, debate, and elections. GE's slo-gan got it right—Progress *is* our most important product. America is not only a nation but also a notion, *viz.* that our vaunted freedoms *demand* that we keep challenging the status quo in order to do better. But because like-minded people can engage in a suffocating consensus—as Hans Christian Anderson understood brilliantly in "The Emperor's New Clothes"—the very First Amendment protects the right to speak and criticize. According to Cass Sunstein in his 2003 book *Why Societies Need Dissent,* "a high-level official during World War II, Luther Gulick, attributed the successes of the Allies, and the failures of Hitler and other Axis powers, to the greater abil-ity of citizens in democracies to scrutinize and dissent and hence to improve past and proposed courses of action."

Real patriots who love an ever-improving America should now ask whether a policy or program advances the middle class, collective security, a stronger democracy—and One America. For a quarter century of con-servative doctrine from Reagan to Bush has inflicted great harm on aver-age families and global problem-solving. Is it patriotic to say that you love your country but hate your government? To cut taxes for the super-rich during war-time while asking soldiers to risk their lives? So public policy should now focus on how to build a stronger America on these four cor-nerstones:

1. Strengthen the Middle Class. There has been an historic, largely unheralded redistribution of wealth in the past three decades from the stretched middle class to the already wealthy. It began with the incipient globalization and oil shocks of the 1970s and continued with the climbing stock market in the 1990s. It accelerated, however, as George Bush redis-tributed wealth more than George McGovern was ever accused of—except upward rather than downward. His tax cuts—on income, estates, dividends, capital gains, corporate earnings—was a program of plutocracy posing as populism. While the public rationale was economic growth and the rheto-ric was "it's your money," in effect nearly half of "our" money somehow flowed to the top 1 percent of all income earners: a person earning over a million dollars a year received an average tax rebate of $89,509; a person earning over $330,000 (definitionally the top 1 percent), got an average rebate of $20,762; absolute tax reductions were obviously larger for people with larger incomes but they were also larger in percentage terms—15 per-cent for those in the top one percent, 7 percent for the rest of us.

What's actually been happening is that President Bush has purchased some anti-tax popularity but sent the bills either to governors and mayors—who have to hike property or sales taxes or cut teachers, cops, health programs—or to future presidents. So the upper class gets tax cuts and the middle class and poor get service cuts to pay for this wealth redistribution. "I can't believe it," said one New York City businessman to the author. "After years of deducting use of my plane only for business purposes, my accountant tells me that under new tax regulations, I can actually deduct all operating expenses even if I use the plane 95 percent for personal use. I don't mind saving $100,000 a year but I sure don't need this—and what public good does it serve?"

Yet this program is occurring just as many costs are increasing for the middle class, who are often a pink slip or a paycheck away from financial ruin. Health costs are again at double-digit rates; the cost of college too. Personal bankruptcies are at or near all-time highs. While 90 percent of productivity gains in the past 30 years have gone to owners, the real income of blue-collar workers has been flat (except for the last three years of Clinton-Gore)—the result of declining unionization, temping, the Wal-Marting of wages and benefits, and the outsourcing of so many high-paying manufacturing and technology jobs. The only reason more middle-class families avoid slipping into poverty is not rising incomes but couples needing two incomes to scrape by, as described so well in *The Two Income Trap: Why Middle-Class Mothers and Fathers Are Going Broke* by Elizabeth Warren and Amelia Warren Tyagi. In effect, there's a growing number of people characterized by a kind of middle-class poverty, families who feel like they're running faster after an ever-accelerating bus.

At what point will "NASCAR dads" or "Reagan Democrats" realize that Republicans waving the bloody shirt of guns and gays and god seek to distract them from the reality that they're working harder, earning less, and tolerating a world where their children will be economically worse off? One explanation is that more people in blind taste tests say they like Pepsi, yet more people buy Coke—it's the psychological triumph of branding. A party of flags and faith have created, so far, a politically superior brand.

It's time to become liberal hawks in the class war of ideas. Instead of simply being reactivists—a little more tax equity, please—it's time for a new narrative other than plutocracy at home and preemption abroad. For the ideological debate in America today is less left-right and more up-down. The Party of CEOs versus the Party for Children—a trillion more for the top 1 percent or a trillion more for school construction, teacher recruitment, and smaller classes. Why is it called class warfare to want to go back to the tax rates of Ronald Reagan? And if the conservatives' trump card is economic growth rather than "tax-and-spend liberalism," how do they respond to the following fact: from FDR to W, the average GDP under Republican presidents has been 2.8 percent, while under Democratic presidents, 5.1 percent?

Public policy, consequently, should constantly attempt to protect the middle class from slipping into poverty and help those in poverty enter the middle class. James K. Galbraith, Bob Greenstein, Peter Orzag, Ron Pollack, and Richard Elmore discuss specific ways to strengthen the struggling middle-class, from creating a Living Wage, making health care more affordable, providing for pre-K and after-school programs, shrinking class size, and investing in job training rather than nation-building—paid for by shrinking corporate welfare and reversing the overgenerous and unproductive tax cuts for the top two percent.

2. Strengthen Collective Security. When President Bush said to great applause in his 2004 State of the Union Address, "America will never seek a permission slip to defend the security of our country," it was a near perfect example of Bill Clinton's adage that Americans prefer someone who is strong and wrong to someone who appears weak and right. At the level of rhetorical sound bite, the "permission slip" reference is a big winner. Of course America has not and will not cede its destiny to others. But at the same time, government officials had better understand the admonition of Michael Tomasky, executive editor of the *American Prospect*. "America is not an empire, it is a democracy. A democracy leads the world but it does not seek to rule it."

And the admonition of history. As World War II—the war *after* the "war to end all wars"—was drawing to a close, Roosevelt and Churchill began planning how to avoid future conflagrations. Their answer lay in the strategy of collective security, where allies would pool their resources and interests to make future threats less likely, or at least less dangerous. Victorious allies bet their futures on a world monetary system after Bretton Woods and a world peace organization, the United Nations. Collective security was built not merely on idealism but also on self-interest—countries that engaged in mutually beneficial commerce and complied with international-al law were less likely to engage in hostilities. Countries, however, that through hubris or misperceived threat did attempt occupations—England in India, France in Algeria, Israel in Lebanon—suffered prohibitive eco-nomic costs, as Professor Galbraith discusses in his essay, "An Economy, Not an Empire."

Sixty years later, collective security is an even more compelling strate-gy. True, the American military establishment is equal to the next twenty countries combined; we have nine supercarrier fleets, while our nearest rivals have none—and we have three separate types of stealth aircraft (the B-1 and B-2 bombers and F-117 fighter) with two more near production (the F-22 and F-35 fighters), while our nearest rivals have none. But as Samuel Berger, Anne-Marie Slaughter, Jonathan Schell, and Gary Hart explain, America today can surely win any army-on-army battle but even we cannot alone effectively occupy and govern another country, quell insurgencies, or force desired results in the Korean peninsula, Kashmir, Northern Ireland, or the Middle East. We can win wars but only alliances can win peaces—and only alliances, like the one put together by Bush's father in 1991, can win wars at a far lower cost in American lives and resources. Can anyone today seriously maintain that America and Iraq wouldn't be far better off if the UN had been more involved in post-war governance and reconstruction?

These examples have even more relevance in today's world of stateless evils—of shadowy terrorists carrying devastation in a backpack, of brilliant scientists selling the nuclear secrets stored in their brains, of invisible pol-lution drifting from Chernobyl to Hartford, of international financiers bet-ting against currencies—or AIDS-carrying lotharios seducing women in different countries. Older axioms that "bigger is better" and "might makes right" appear largely ineffectual to cope with such "problems without pass-ports," as U.N. Secretary General Kofi Annan aptly describes them.

In this context, the perception of America as the Lone Ranger and allies as an unquestioning Tonto is hopelessly counterproductive. Simply walking away from the ABM Treaty, Kyoto Protocol, Small Arms Agreement, International Criminal Court, Chemical and Biological Weapons Convention, and U.N. Commission on the Status of Women—as well as our bungle in Iraq—has soured the populations of nearly every nation in the world and isolated America.

"So what?" say the neoconservative intellectuals and armchair generals—Richard Cheney, Donald Rumsfeld, Paul Wolfowitz, Condoleezza Rice—who wanted to invade Iraq long before 9/11, according to former insiders Paul O'Neill and Richard Clarke. When President Bush in 2004 was asked whether holding detainees at Guantanamo without trial or access to lawyers violated international law, he contemptuously replied, "International law? Well, I better call my lawyer!"

Just as wealthy families realized that communal fire and police departments were preferable to private militia in the 1800s, collective security makes us stronger not weaker. "The most important reason for the United States to commit itself to rules," concludes Anne-Marie Slaughter in her essay, "is not because they will restrain our enemies but because they will reassure our friends—and without our friends we cannot in the end defeat our enemies." And the way to attract and keep friends, writes Sandy Berger, is "not only the example of our force but the force of our example." This phrase is built on the analysis of Joseph S. Nye, Jr., Dean of the Kennedy School of Government, in his 2004 book, *Soft Power: The Means to Success in World Politics*:

> A country may obtain the outcomes it wants in world politics because other countries—admiring its values, emulating its example, aspiring to its level of property and openness—want to follow it...The soft power of a country rests primarily on three resources: its culture (in places where it is attractive to others), and its political values (when it lives up to them at home and abroad), and its foreign policies (when they are seen as legitimate and having moral authority).

Slaughter, Berger, and Nye illuminate why the next government should recognize that all nations, great and small, are afloat on this lifeboat called Earth together.

3. Strengthen Democracy. One of the prevailing ironies of political life is how some American warriors are eager to cross oceans to fight for democracy but how uninterested—or even opposed—they are to expanding it at home. Over two centuries, it was wealthy elites, open racists, and flag-draped "patriots" who pushed for property, racial, gender, literacy, and registration barriers to voting. This is a current struggle, as measured by the contradiction between our July 4th rhetoric about freedom and democracy and the reality that, of 22 Western democracies, only Botswana has a lower turnout of eligible adults voting. While European allies such as Great Britain, France, and Germany regularly have 70 percent-plus majorities voting, only half of eligible Americans vote in presidential elections and a third in congressional.

The recent sagas of Florida and campaign finance reform portray the problem.

Florida's felony disenfranchisement laws struck 200,000 from the voting rolls, usually citizens of color and often non-felons. When combined with the celebrated snafus about butterfly ballots and hanging chads, the electoral value of the Florida governor to the Texas governor was hard to ignore. And when in response Congress in 2003 enacted HAVA, the Help America Vote Act, a Republican condition of enactment was the very mischievous provision that local election officials could require the kind of official documents that could easily be used to discourage or turn away minorities and new immigrants. "We don't want everyone to vote," admitted a candid Paul Weyrich, one of the godfathers of the conservative movement, years before. "Quite frankly, our leverage goes up as the voting population goes down."

In Washington, Republicans led by Senator Mitch McConnell (R-KY) successfully stripped any possibility of public financing of congressional elections from the McCain-Feingold bill. So money from the oil, drug, automobile, and defense industries continue to dominate oil, drug, automobile, and defense committees—and policies. When combined with the 1976 decision of *Buckley v. Valeo* that wealthy candidates could continue to self-finance their elections, America faces a continuing risk of purchased politicians or heirs or CEOs largely populating our legislatures. (In 1976, it cost an average of $87,000 to win a House seat and $609,000 a Senate seat; by 2000, those amounts grew ten-fold to $842,000 and $7.2 million, respectively.) In a few election cycles, it'll be the norm, not the exception, for local, state, federal, and even presidential campaigns to include not one but several multi-millionaires or billionaires running and winning because of $10 million or $100 million expenditures. But it's one thing for private money to buy a company, quite another for it to buy public office.

Mark Schmitt responds to this crisis of democracy by seeking to put people back in our democracy and to update Jefferson's insight that America should stand for "equal rights for all, special privileges for none."

For if the laws governing voting and contributing mean that those who govern us respond more to donors than voters, then there's little prospect of enacting needed consumer, environmental, housing, and education laws. Unless a new president and congress seek to renew our democracy, we risk evolving from a country founded on a revolution against British royalty to a country governed by an economic royalty hiding behind the rhetorical curtain of the world's greatest democracy.

4. One America. In Ric Burns's *New York*, the narrator describes our largest city in words that characterize our country as well. New York is "a continuing experiment to see if all the peoples of the world can live together in one small space." While America is surely a place divided into numerous ethnicities, races, religions and cultures, all proud of their history and heritage, each group should not live in their separate silos from where they look on others as threatening or unworthy. We are, after all, the *United* States of America.

Yet when we began the twentieth century, the great black scholar W.E.B. DuBois predicted that the new centennial, coming only 35 years after the Civil War, would be dominated by "the color line." He was right. But will it dominate not only the nineteenth and the twentieth centuries but also the twenty-first as well?

Race has been far less discussed in recent years and in the 2004 presidential election, explains law professor Christopher Edley Jr., in part because different racial constituencies are on such political hair-triggers that few politicians think it worth the risk of offending someone—or everyone. It's nonetheless urgent that we acknowledge—and try to bridge—our racial divides. Can we really afford to continue to have two-thirds of black children born out-of-wedlock? Latino families net worth averaging one-twenty-fifth of that of white families? An unemployment rate of 50 percent for African-American men ages 16-64 in New York City? Or a United States Senate with zero percent Black, Latino or Asian in a country one-fourth minority?

The next government must more resolutely stand for equality and justice because equal opportunity remains an unfulfilled promise for too many Americans merely due to their race, religion, national origin or sexual orientation. But how can a president and congress accomplish this in an era where discrimination comes not in the form of hooded vigilantes but politicians in dark suits and big smiles arguing against "reverse discrimination" and "special rights"?

Four options come to mind. We need more candidates and office-holders who can comfortably speak to and for White, Black, *and* Hispanic audiences, as Robert Kennedy did so well in the mid-1960s—and Bill Clinton 30 years later. We need other politicians to stop exploiting racial tensions by new versions of Nixon's "southern strategy." We need to face race and not act as if indifference is a solution. Last, we should look more to universal solutions based on need rather than complexion in order to mobilize majority coalitions. Better health care, public transit, public schools, and environmental regulation can simultaneously be more readily enacted and disproportionately help minorities enduring poorer schools, no health insurance, and dirty air. White and non-white politicians, there-fore, should complete an anti-discrimination agenda, argues Edley, but also go further to enact an "opportunity agenda" which in turn would require that we transcend race in order to include all in the promise of America.

A Program for Progressive Patriotism

The purpose of these essays was to go beyond the usual liberal bro-mides—and certainly beyond the blame-government-first conservatism that seeks to enter the twenty-first century via the nineteenth. So while others work for their respective candidates and parties, the authors in this volume want to contribute to the quadrennial American conversation by focusing not on *who* will govern but *how.* What are affordable, smart, pro-gressive ideas that a President, Congress, and State Capitols could rally behind to create a better America?

In 1808 Thomas Jefferson drew up plans to develop the West, and we did. In 1908, Theodore Roosevelt conceived of how to preserve our nat-ural resources, and our national parks and environmental movements were born. In the 1930s, FDR created a lattice-work of regulatory agencies that "saved capitalism from itself" and provided a safety net for people in need. Eisenhower constructed an interstate highway system that economically proved to be the Erie Canal of the 20th Century. By "throwing his hat over the wall of space," Kennedy's Apollo program forever altered the way we think of ourselves and opened possibilities as yet unrealized. And more recently, civil rights laws, consumer laws, environmental laws, the Freedom of Information Act, the Americans with Disabilities Act, the Earned Income Tax Credit, and Family and Medical Leave Act proved to be breakthroughs that made America more prosperous and just. Assume there's a new president who wants to be as strong a leader as Bush has been—for W., to his credit, converted an electoral tie into a conservative mandate. What's the next big or small progressive idea or ideas that by 2010 could similarly change America?

At today's transformational moment, there *are* a clear, confident and credible set of policies that would work to truly change and strengthen our nation. These polices build on, but don't merely rely on, earlier generations of progressive programs. Here are ten out of dozens from *What We Stand For.*

1. Recommit to a new *global bargain for collective security* whereby the United States agrees to accept some constraints on its ability to use force in return for a genuine commitment by the nations of the world to do everything possible to combat terrorism, radical (armed) fundamentalism, the threat of failed states and nuclear proliferation.

2. *Transform America's military forces* and intelligence services away from unilaterelism and preemptive invasion and toward more human intelligence and swifter troop deployments.

3. Stop investing in an empire abroad and start *publicly investing in our economy* at home by such new approaches as a Federal Infrastructure Bank, Office of Capital Investment, and Revenue Sharing to states with sustained high unemployment so they don't cut services just when they're needed.

4. *End the tax cuts* for the top 2 percent and *reinvest the savings* into deficit reduction and health care.

5. *Save Social Security* by gradually increasing the ceiling on the amount of earnings subject to the payroll tax and gradually reducing benefits to those with very high lifetime earnings.

6. Embrace an urban-suburban *metropolitan agenda* that promotes smart growth, stimulates investment in metropolitan regions, and

connects low-income families to new employment and educational opportunities.

7. Toss out the unworkable No Child Left Behind law to focus not only on testing but also on *school construction, teacher recruitment, and smaller class sizes* in earlier grades.

8. Base *health insurance on need* not family status and redraft the Medicare prescription drug benefit to allow more drug price competition to keep costs down and to increase coverage.

9. Adopt an *energy independence strategy* beginning with a 50 percent increase in auto fuel-efficiency standards over the next decade— and enforce environmental laws, again.

10. Pursue a *democracy agenda* which includes a) the public financing of congressional elections, b) restrictions on self-financing (reversing *Buckley*), c) paper trails for electronic voting, d) elimination of discriminatory felony disenfranchisement laws, e) restrictions on further media concentration—and merging Veterans Day into a Democracy Day holiday the first Tuesday every November when we pay respect to veterans who defended democracy by voting.

The agenda rejects messianic incompetence abroad and greed-is-good economics at home. It assumes that what matters is not bigger or smaller but smarter government relentlessly progressing to restrict corporate power, to encourage entrepreneurs, to expand health care, to put inspiring teachers in front of small classes, to clean up the environment. So "what we stand for" is a government advocating for—not against—middle-class families, collective security, more democracy, and One America. That's a narrative in step with Walt Whitman's description of an America that's "always becoming." That's a program for progressive patriotism worthy of our history and our future.

INTERNATIONAL POLICY:

TOWARD A SAFER AMERICA

Power and Authority:
America's International Path Ahead

SAMUEL R. BERGER[*]

Advance America's security and values by unleashing not just the example of our force but also the force of our example—to rebuild alliances, fight terrorism, pursue Middle East peace, contain weapons of mass destruction, and stabilize Iraq.

I. The Problem

September 11, 2001, transformed the way America looked at the world. In the twisted steel of the World Trade Center and the smoldering ashes of the Pentagon, our country's sense of invulnerability was shattered. From our earliest days as a nation, we had seen the world as a dangerous place to be avoided if possible—recall President Washington's warning to shun "entangling alliances." Now we saw the world as hostile, yet unavoidable. We learned that even Manhattan is not an island.

But if that terrible morning caused Americans to see the world through different eyes, in the two years that followed, the eyes of the world have seen a different America—one that performed brilliantly in war yet is struggling with its complex aftermath; one that is drawing closer to some traditional adversaries yet becoming estranged from some long-time allies; one that is exercising power around the world yet watching its popularity sink.

Four key foreign policy initiatives mark the current U.S. course. First, in the wake of 9/11, the war against terrorism became our overriding strategic priority. We defeated the Taliban. We crushed al Qaeda's training camps. And we have taken the fight to the terrorists—although the battle is far from over. Then, President Bush greatly expanded the boundaries of the fight against terrorists to encompass rogue regimes that could provide weapons of mass destruction to terror groups—linking North Korea, Iran,

---

* **SAMUEL R. BERGER** *is Chairman of Stonebridge International LLC, an international strategic advisory firm based in Washington, D.C. He served as the National Security Advisor to President Clinton (1997–2000) and before then as the Deputy National Security Advisor (1993–1996).*

and Iraq as an "axis of evil," nations that could be dealt with only by ulti-matum. Next, he elevated preemption from an option every President has reserved to a defining doctrine of American strategy. Together, these three initiatives led inexorably to the fourth. Many rationales were offered for regime change in Iraq. But the one that resonated most deeply, and the one the White House relied upon most heavily, was to prevent another 9/11, this time with deadly weapons provided by Saddam Hussein.

All four of these national security initiatives were based on a set of convictions that dominate the Bush administration: that in a Hobbesian world, American power, particularly military power, is the central force for advancing our interests; that it is more important to be feared than admired; and that "root cause" thinking is dangerous moral relativism—evil is evil and can never be justified.

Not all of that is wrong. Without question, the fight against terrorism aimed at the United States must be our central strategic priority today; in al Qaeda and other anti-American jihadists, we face a mortal enemy. Whatever grievances they exploit do not diminish the imperative of find-ing and destroying them before they destroy us. Nor can anyone deny that we have an urgent need to keep the world's deadliest weapons out of its most dangerous hands. Deterrence does not work against suicide bombers whose purpose is to cause massive bloodshed and who believe they answer only to their God.

As for Iraq, unquestionably Saddam Hussein was a brutal dictator with ongoing ambitions to dominate a vital region. After 9/11, the administra-tion saw a window to act—although it was not so narrow that we could not have gained greater international support and had in place a coherent plan for the day after.

But in important respects, the administration's vision of American leadership is misfocused and dangerously limited. The confident use of U.S. military power sometimes is necessary in this new world. It is not, howev-er, sufficient or self-justifying. And looking at where America stands near-ly three years after September 11, there is reason for serious concern about where we are headed, and how.

In 2002, leaders in Germany and South Korea—two of our closest allies—were elected in part on anti-American platforms. In the run-up to the Iraq war, despite our indisputable strength, we could not persuade even long-time friends like Chile and Mexico to support us in the United

Nations, or Turkey to help us logistically, or more than a handful of countries to put combat troops on the ground. By the summer of 2003, a major global survey conducted by the Pew Research Center found that favorable opinions of the United States had fallen in nearly every country over the past two years, and plummeted in most of the Muslim world, from the Middle East to Indonesia and Nigeria.

As the world's unrivaled power, the United States inevitably will attract resentment. Yet, rather than allay resentment, our actions are contributing to it, in at least five ways.

We are not using the full measure of our power—our moral authority as well as our military strength. For two years, we essentially walked away from the Israeli-Palestinian conflict. Finally, 2000 Palestinian and 800 Israeli deaths later, the White House accepted that the parties could not end the violence themselves. President Bush's entrance on the stage of Middle East diplomacy in June 2003 was welcome, but it turned out to be a brief guest appearance. There was little sustained U.S. follow-up to give momentum to the "roadmap" initiative.

Then we went from declaring a Century of the Americas to turning our back on our own backyard—undercutting a Mexican President who had invested his prestige in the U.S. relationship, temporizing on the near-retreat from democracy in Venezuela, giving the back of our hand to an old friend in trouble, Argentina. And while insisting that the world accept *our* priorities, we've turned away from efforts to deal with humanity's common concerns—from the Kyoto Protocol on climate change to a tougher Biological Weapons Convention.

Without offering any leadership in dealing with genuine concerns about how expanding trade and globalization can be made to benefit the many, not just the few, we've pandered to protectionist pressures on trade that matter deeply to the developing world. According to the World Bank, rich countries' trade barriers cost poor nations more than $100 billion a year, roughly double what wealthy countries provide in aid. At the same time, President Bush's AIDS relief plan and his efforts to boost foreign assistance are steps in the right direction; but both initiatives, as Lael Brainard of the Brookings Institution has cautioned, "bypass international efforts and existing aid agencies in favor of U.S. programs"—which only reinforces the perception of U.S. unilateralism.

We have diminished our enduring alliances. After September 11, NATO for the first time in its history invoked the article that declares an attack on one to be an attack on all. But rather than accept NATO's help in Afghanistan, we dismissed it. This may have served efficiency, but it squandered international solidarity and wasted the chance to give other nations the greatest stake in Afghanistan's future.

We have allowed belligerent rhetoric to create severe strains in our alliance with South Korea. As a result, many South Koreans—particularly young people—believe the North Korean nuclear program is not a threat against the South but a response by the North to a threat from us. In August 2003, the Pew Research Center reported that between 2002 and 2003, the percentage of South Korean 18–29 year olds who had a somewhat or very unfavorable opinion of the United States has shot up to 71 percent. As North Korea moves toward the nuclear brink, our leverage has been seriously undercut by the lack of solidarity with our friends.

In the aftermath of deposing Saddam Hussein, we chose control over burden and risk sharing. Instead of reaching out to NATO, Arab countries, and others to share the cost and the considerable risks of a long-term and dangerous enterprise, we declared ourselves and the British to be occupying powers. As a result, months after the fall of Saddam's regime, we remain the address for Iraqi frustration and resentment—bearing 90 percent of the cost in blood and treasure without a desirable exit strategy in sight. Meanwhile, Iraq has become the new battleground for anti-American jihadists.

The administration has embarked on a high-risk strategy—that we can fix Iraq better and faster by ourselves than with others, and that we will win the race between dramatic improvement on the ground and loss of patience by the American people as they realize we essentially are going this alone. But to succeed in Iraq, we need a strategy that is sustainable over the long run—that can gain enduring support at home, abroad and in Iraq. Consider: Of the 162,000 troops in Iraq in June 2003, 150,000 were Americans. By contrast, 34 nations remained in Kosovo after five years, and less than 10 percent of the force was American. How long will Americans bear the cost of opening schools in Baghdad while we close them in Baltimore?

The doctrine of preemption risks making us less secure, not more, by exacerbating rather than alleviating instability and proliferation. Certainly, every country reserves the right to act preemptively in unique circumstances of danger. But the Bush administration's decision to elevate preemption from an option reserved for unique circumstances to a broadly espoused doctrine is badly misguided. As legal scholar Ambassador Richard Gardner has written, "if it is intended to assert a right available to the United States alone, [it] is obviously unacceptable. If it is intended to assert a new legal principle of general application, its implications are so ominous as to justify universal condemnation." The broader the application America gives to a policy of striking first, the greater justification we give other nations, in dangerous regions like the Middle East or South Asia, to use it as a pretext for attacking enemies. And a world governed by the logic of preemptive strikes will likely be more violent, not less, as each actor in a crisis is tempted to act first, to use or lose.

Moreover, preemption, to be successful, relies on accurate intelligence. The failure, at least as of the start of 2004, to locate weapons of mass destruction (WMD) in Iraq points up how uncertain such intelligence can be. The United States cannot afford to be perceived as pursuing a foreign policy of "shoot now, ask questions later." Our credibility and authority, already tarnished, would then be completely destroyed.

There is another, exceedingly perilous consequence of preemption policy: In the name of deterring nations from going nuclear, in particular North Korea and Iran, we actually may be driving them to accelerate their nuclear programs—in effect, to draw the conclusion that Saddam's mistake was not getting his nuclear weapons fast enough to make the costs of U.S. military action against him unacceptably high.

While our priority of stopping proliferation is right, our focus is much too narrow. As former Senator Sam Nunn has said, right now "tons of poorly secured plutonium and highly enriched uranium—the raw materials of nuclear terrorism—are spread around the world." The proliferation problem is a complex, global challenge. Yet America has focused most of our energies on one state—Iraq—and with one blunt tool—military preemption.

North Korea, an established weapons merchant, could be in a position to produce six nuclear weapons by mid-2004, as many as 20 or 30 a year within the next few years—making it the world's first nuclear Wal-Mart for terror groups. In the face of this challenge—perhaps the most dangerous one we face—we have let more than a year go by since North Korea expelled international monitors. We have very little idea what North Korea has produced during that period as we fumbled over policy and focused on process.

Programs devoted to securing nuclear weapons and materials have not been given the priority they demand. Their total funding is only a fraction of 1 percent of the defense budget—despite the fact that there is enough potentially vulnerable fissile material in the former Soviet Union to make thousands of nuclear weapons.

The administration has pressed Congress for authority to explore new uses for nuclear weapons. This is not only unnecessary but it also cuts sharply against our nonproliferation goals. At a time when we have over-whelming superiority in conventional military power, why should we be giving new credibility to nuclear weapons—one of the great equalizers?

America's current reflexive opposition to international arms control treaties defies recent history. In the past two decades, international norms helped persuade Brazil, Argentina, Chile, South Africa, South Korea, Taiwan, Belarus, Ukraine, and Kazakhstan to give up their nuclear weapons programs. Agreed boundaries help build opposition to countries which step over the international line.

Finally, we're failing to match our goals with the resources we need to achieve them. In Afghanistan, the decision to limit a U.S. security presence to Kabul contributes to its reversion to warlordism and instability. And, in Iraq, if we had planned to commit the same number of troops there per capita as we did at the outset in Kosovo—where no peacekeepers have been killed—we would have had 500,000 troops on the ground to secure the peace. But we neglected the lessons—good and bad—of our five prior peacekeeping experiences over the past ten years.

Overall, the disparity between what we spend on defense and what we spend on other instruments of security—like diplomacy and develop-ment—is growing. The entire budget of the State Department and our development agencies today is only about 1 percent of our federal budg-et—one-sixteenth of Pentagon spending—which is one reason the Pentagon often dominates the State Department in driving American for-eign policy.

Meanwhile, at home, we simply have not sustained an urgent focus on homeland security. Less than 5 percent of cargo containers that enter the United States today are inspected. The Coast Guard has said it needs more than $4 billion to secure our ports; yet only $463 million had been appro-priated by mid-2003. Frontline first responders still lack essential resources and training. Much of our critical infrastructure remains vulnerable. Terrorism is not on the run, but homeland security still is in a crawl.

II. Solutions

It is time for concerted action in five priority areas to advance both the safety and security of our people and the reach of our values—democracy, tolerance, and peace—in the short term and by 2010.

1. We must finish what we started in Iraq.

The Iraq war did not end when the President staged his photogenic landing on the aircraft carrier. Nor did it end when American soldiers captured Saddam Hussein in his spider hole. As 2004 begins, we still are enmeshed in a guerrilla war against a self-declared American occupation. Unless we quickly reorganize this mission—both military and civilian—we will face an unpleasant choice: to endure mounting daily casualties from an increasingly resented American occupation or to take a page from the late Senator George D. Aiken on Vietnam: declare victory and come home, whether the Iraqis are ready or not. The wiser course, if it is not too late, is to end our occupation and share power, risk, and truth with our allies, Iraqis, and the American people.

If Iraq descends into chaos, it will be not just tragic but disastrous—confirming mistrust of the United States and fueling instability in the region. The essential starting point for preventing this outcome is to reduce the American face on Iraq's occupation. On the military side, we are shifting to a U.S.-commanded multinational force, endorsed by the United Nations, but we must recognize that this is not yet a peacekeeping mission; it is continuation of the war. It would be preferable to make this a NATO-led mission, if that is still possible, with a U.S. commander operating under a U.N. mandate.

On the civilian side, we must give up control for greater burden-sharing as well as greater legitimacy with the Iraqi people; they must be our allies in the battle to stop the insurgents, not their quiet supporters. We must dissolve the Coalition Provisional Authority, which now rules Iraq, and fold it into an international entity such as existed with peacekeeping missions in Bosnia, Kosovo, and Afghanistan. It should be headed by a respected and capable non-American. We will continue to play a substantial—even leading—role, but this should no longer be an "American" occupation. There will be a U.N. mandate, even though, as the Balkans and Afghanistan demonstrate, it need not be a U.N. operation.

But internationalization is not enough. Just as important is enhancing the ability of Iraqis to control their own affairs. We cannot postpone politics in Iraq while we restore order; politics is going on every day in Iraq, in the mosques and marketplaces and neighborhoods. The longer we wait to create a legitimate provisional government—not one named by us—the more likely the power vacuum will be filled by radicals and opportunists. Such a provisional government can be selected by the already-elected councils in 50 cities and regions. Authority can be transferred to the provisional government on a continuous basis as it is ready to assume it, including the enactment of a constitution and holding elections for a permanent government. That would allow us to shift control to Iraqis—function by function, week by week—conspicuously giving them a measure of sovereignty, even if not everything at once. Only when Iraqis feel ownership of their future will they take responsibility for stopping those who seek to destroy it.

2. We must be as unrelenting in the pursuit of peace in the Middle East as we were in the prosecution of war.

The continuing conflict between Israel and the Palestinians not only carries a terrible cost for people on both sides, it is a dead weight on the region's progress, permitting autocratic, corrupt governments to avoid the hard choices of economic and political reform by externalizing the cause of their problems. After more than two years of unremitting violence, most Israelis and most of the Palestinian people are exhausted. A strategy of terror by Palestinian militants has not—and cannot—work. Israel will not permit it, nor will we. Israelis are not driven to the sea by suicide bombs; they are driven to the right. Terror ultimately is a strategy of suicide for the Palestinians—as a growing number of Palestinians are coming to recognize.

At the same time, while Israel will do what it sees as necessary to protect itself, military action by itself will not bring durable security. It is not hard to understand the attractiveness in Israel of fences and trenches. On an interim basis, they can be part of a defensive posture. But no fences are high enough to keep out danger. A thousand Israeli solders were killed patrolling Southern Lebanon—a much smaller, less volatile area than the West Bank and Gaza. This scenario is a long-term war of attrition.

It will be difficult—probably impossible—for this deadly dynamic to change without active engagement and leadership from friends of Israel and of peace, particularly the United States. This is a not a self-correcting problem under current circumstances. Every American President since Richard Nixon has understood that there is nothing inconsistent with being Israel's most steadfast ally and helping build a path for Israel to a more peaceful and secure future in the region; indeed they are mutually reinforcing—the two legs we must stand on for Israel's sake, and for our own substantial stake in the region.

A flicker of hope emerged in Aqaba in June 2003, with a "roadmap" that was supposed to result in a shift toward moderate Palestinian leadership and a crackdown on extremist groups, and at the same time the dismantlement of settlement outposts by Israel to give Palestinian moderates tangible gains. Yet by fall 2003, the plan broke down, without serious efforts by the United States to prevent it.

A transition to moderate Palestinian leadership will be necessary for progress. But that is unlikely unless such forces are armed, not with terror but with a vision of the basic principles of a fair, lasting, and comprehensive solution. There already is widespread understanding of what those principles should be. President Clinton described them before leaving office. To empower moderate Palestinians to take action against those who perpetuate violence, we should work for agreement, up front, on the end state we seek to give confidence to both sides that their core concerns will be met.

Looking at the region more broadly, the United States must push authoritarian governments to reform if they hope to survive. We cannot dictate the destiny of these countries. But there is much America can do— encouraging pluralism, openness, and reform—to align ourselves with the internal physics of change in the region, not seek to impose our own.

3. We must defuse the threat of WMD more creatively and comprehensively.

This includes making clear to the North Koreans that further separation of plutonium will result in serious consequences—even military if necessary. That requires engaging in serious and direct talks with them, based on achieving a verifiable end to its nuclear weapons and missile programs, including an intrusive nationwide inspection regime. If this is achievable, we must be ready to take security, economic, and political steps involving North Korea. We must be prepared to say "yes" to a good agreement and also be ready for the consequences of "no."

It may not be possible to achieve a satisfactory agreement. North Korea may already have decided to pursue the nuclear option. But we will not know until we test Pyongyang's intentions—and unless we do so, we won't have the regional support we need to move to a more coercive posture. South Korea and China don't want a nuclear North Korea, but neither do they want the chaos of a collapsed North Korea. They will not join us in getting tough unless they are convinced we have tried negotiations in good faith and failed.

As for Iran, their support for terrorism and a nuclear weapons program are dangerous. But the internal dynamics here are both more complex and more promising than Iraq. We should initiate an "overt action" program in Iran, an open invitation to put all the issues on the table: their terrorism and weapons program, our sanctions and isolation policy. Let the Iranian leaders be the obstacle between the people and their manifest aspiration to rejoin the world.

More broadly, we need a serious, systematic counter-proliferation policy that deploys all the tools we have—better intelligence, smarter export controls, covert action, focused missile defenses, a dramatic expansion of cooperative threat reduction programs, deterrence through the threat of overwhelming and devastating retaliation if any nation uses WMD against U.S. territory, forces, or allies, and, when necessary, military action. (See chapter by Jonathan Schell.)

4. We should rebuild our alliances and treat them as an asset, not a liability.

"Coalitions of the willing" sometimes are necessary, but they are not a substitute for enduring alliances, where regular contact builds common perceptions of the dangers we all face. We should energize NATO, not just structurally but in its mission—fighting terrorism, stopping weapons proliferation, and providing muscle to peacekeeping operations. That requires us to repair the dangerous breach with South Korea, think creatively about a new architecture for cooperation in a changing Middle East, and get back in the game of shaping global arrangements that deal with global problems. We can continue to stomp away from the table where agreements like the

Kyoto Protocol are being hammered out. Or we can stay and work to address our concerns through tough and persistent negotiation. One thing is for sure: We cannot walk away from the consequences, like the danger of global warming. In this case, a rising tide will sink all the boats.

Of course, partnerships must be reciprocal. Our allies must do their part—rather than seek to constrain U.S. power or "free ride" on U.S. coattails. For others to define their role in the world in terms of constraining the United States is to miss the point: The biggest danger in a world of growing disorder may be *too little* concerted power, not too much. We should all be clear: We only strengthen our enemies when we divide ourselves.

5. We must be more creative in meeting the central challenge of our time—the fight against terrorist enemies—with a concerted effort to isolate the extremists rather than ourselves.

We should not apologize for America's strength. It has more often been harnessed to good than to ill. We must preserve it, but we need to arm ourselves with more than bunker-busters to succeed. Because while it is important to be respected, it is also important to be admired.

Particularly at a time when we are using the hard edge of our power to protect ourselves, we must lead—and be seen as leading—on the agenda of shared well-being. That is an important part of what we tried to do in the Clinton administration. We invested in the military technology that performed so well in Iraq and we doubled and tripled efforts to fight terrorism. But others around the world also saw us energetically working for peace—in Northern Ireland, the Middle East, the Balkans, and South Asia. Africans noticed when President Clinton flew half way around the world to preside over a peace conference on Burundi with Nelson Mandela, not because it would produce instant results but a lasting impression. Central and Eastern Europeans were indelibly affected when we championed NATO's expansion to new democracies. Leaders in Latin America and in Asia believed that at least they had a seat at the table on the effects of globalization when we convened the Summit of the Americas and created an architecture for dialogue in the Asia-Pacific. The whole world noticed the risks we took for our friend Mexico when the peso fell into crisis, and the way we worked to bring former adversaries Russia and China closer to the international community.

The fact is we cannot afford tunnel vision in a global world. We are more likely to earn others' support for our priorities when we pay attention to theirs. The United States is more likely to shape the outcome of events when we are in the game rather than on the sidelines. When it comes to the problems that challenge our common humanity, the more America pulls its weight, the more authority we command. To the greatest extent possible, we should use our dominant power in the world to build coalitions *around* us, not *against* us—unleashing not just the example of our force, but also the force of our example.

As we do all this, we must be clear about the true nature of the real choices. We don't have to choose between our interests and our ideals; between the willingness to act alone when we must and the will to work with others when we can; between confidence in our own ability and the conviction that alliances are an asset. These are false choices.

The real issue is what kind of leadership we will bring to a troubled world. Determined or domineering? Bold or brash? High-minded or high-handed? We do have to choose to commit the resources that are commensurate with our ambitions, or else half-hearted efforts and hasty exits will breed cynicism and chaos.

Our country must offer the world a positive vision—one around which nations who share our values can join their strength. America's greatness means standing for something larger than ourselves, to act when others can or will not, to preserve "the sacred fire of liberty," to champion hope over fear. That is the spirit and character of America.

CHAPTER TWO

Containing Nuclear Proliferation

JONATHAN SCHELL*

End the nuclear arms race by scrapping plans for new nuclear weapons, signing the Comprehensive Test-ban Treaty, renouncing the first-use of such weapons, and beginning negotiations—starting with Russia—toward their complete elimination.

"All of us have heard this term 'preventive war' since the earliest days of Hitler. I recall that is about the first time I heard it. In this day and time...I don't believe there is such a thing; and, frankly, I wouldn't even listen to anyone seriously that came in and talked about such a thing."
—President Dwight Eisenhower, 1953, upon being presented with plans to wage preventive war to disarm Stalin's Soviet Union

I. The Problem

The Bush Policies

In the spring of 2003, the United States fought a war to take weapons of mass destruction—including, of course nuclear weapons—from a country that, as it has turned out, did not have any. However, the aim of this preemptive war against war has never been only to disarm Iraq. George Bush set forth the full aim of his war policy in unmistakable terms on January 29, 2002, in his first State of the Union address. It was to stop the spread of weapons of mass destruction, not only in Iraq but everywhere in the world, through the use of military force. "We must," he said, "prevent the terrorists and regimes who seek chemical, biological, or nuclear weapons from threatening the United States and the world."

He underscored the scope of his ambition by singling out three countries—North Korea, Iran, and Iraq—for special mention, calling them an "axis of evil." Then came the ultimatum: "The United States of America will not permit the world's most dangerous regimes to threaten us with the

---

JONATHAN SCHELL is the Harold Willens Peace Fellow at the Nation Institute. He writes frequently on the nuclear question for the Nation, Foreign Affairs, and Harper's, where he is also a contributing editor.

world's most destructive weapons." Other possible war aims—to defeat al Qaeda, to spread democracy—came and went in administration pronouncements before the war, but this one remained constant. Stopping the spread of weapons of mass destruction was the reason for war given alike to the Security Council and to the American people, who were warned by the President in October 2002 not to let "the smoking gun become a mushroom cloud," and further advised in the 2003 State of the Union address to fear "a day of horror like none we have ever known."

The means whereby the United States would execute its anti-proliferation policy were first set forth on June 1, 2002, in the President's speech to the graduating class at West Point. The United States would use force, and use it preemptively. "If we wait for threats to fully materialize, we will have waited too long," he said. For "the only path to safety is the path of action. And this nation will act." Radical as the Bush administration policy was, the idea behind it was not new. Two months after the bombing of Hiroshima and Nagasaki, Gen. Leslie Groves, the Pentagon overseer of the Manhattan Project, expressed his views on controlling nuclear proliferation: "If we were truly realistic instead of idealistic, as we appear to be, we would not permit any foreign power with which we are not firmly allied, and in which we do not have absolute confidence, to make or possess atomic weapons. If such a country started to make atomic weapons we would destroy its capacity to make them before it has progressed far enough to threaten us."

The proposal was never seriously considered by President Truman and, until now, was rejected by every subsequent President. Eisenhower's views of preventive war are given in the epigraph at the beginning of this article. In 1961, during the Berlin crisis, a few of Kennedy's advisers made the surprising discovery that Russia's nuclear forces were far weaker and more vulnerable than anyone had thought. They proposed a preventive strike. Ted Sorensen, the chief White House counsel and speechwriter, was told of the plan. He shouted, "You're crazy! We shouldn't let guys like you around here." It never came to the attention of the President.

How has it happened that President Bush has revived and implemented this long-buried, long-rejected idea? The portal was September 11. The theme of the "war on terror" was from the start to strike preemptively with military force. Piece by piece, a bridge from the aim of catching Osama bin Laden to the aim of stopping proliferation on a global basis was built. First came the idea of holding whole regimes accountable in the war on terror; then the idea of "regime change" (beginning with Afghanistan); then pre-emption; then the broader claim of American global dominance. Gradually, the most important issue of the age—the rising danger from weapons of mass destruction—was subsumed as a sort of codicil to the war on terror. When the process was finished, the result was the Groves plan writ large—a reckless and impracticable idea when it was conceived, when only one hostile nuclear power (the Soviet Union) was in prospect, and a worse one today in our world of nine nuclear powers (if you count North Korea) and many scores of nuclear-capable ones.

This policy has failed—not only in Iraq but in North Korea and Iran as well. In October 2002, James Kelly, Assistant Secretary of State for East Asian and Pacific Affairs, was informed by Vice Foreign Minister Kang Sok Ju of North Korea that his country has a perfect right to possess nuclear weapons. Shortly, Secretary of State Colin Powell stated, "We have to assume that they might have one or two....that's what our intelligence community has been saying for some time." Soon North Korea announced that it had a "powerful deterrent," adding that it was terminating the Agreed Framework of 1994 under which it had shut down two reactors that produced plutonium. It ejected the U.N. inspectors who had been monitoring the agreement and then announced its withdrawal from the Nuclear Nonproliferation Treaty, under whose terms it was obligated to remain nuclear-weapon-free. Soon, it moved fuel rods from existing reactors to its plutonium reprocessing plant, and in a few months disclosed that it had completed the reprocessing. In January of 2003, it displayed to American officials what it described weapon-ready plutonium.

"We will not permit..." had been Bush's words, but North Korea went ahead and apparently produced nuclear weapons anyway. The administration now discovered that its policy of preemptively using over-whelming force had no application against a proliferator with a serious military capability, much less a nuclear power. North Korea's conventional capacity alone—it has an army of more than a million men and 11,000 artillery pieces capable of striking South Korea's capital, Seoul—imposed a very high cost; the addition of nuclear arms, in combination with missiles capable of striking not only South Korea but Japan, made it obviously prohibitive.

By any measure, totalitarian North Korea's possession of nuclear weapons is more dangerous than the mere possibility that Iraq was trying to develop them. The North Korean state, which is hard to distinguish from a cult, is also more repressive and disciplined than the Iraqi state, and has caused the death of more of its own people—through starvation. Yet in the weeks that followed the North Korean disclosure, the administration, in a radical reversal of the President's earlier assessments, sought to argue that the opposite was true. Administration spokespersons soon declared that the North Korean situation was "not a crisis" and that its policy toward that country was to be one of "dialogue," leading to "a peaceful multilateral solution," including the possibility of renewed oil shipments. But if the acquisition by North Korea of nuclear arms was not a crisis, then there never had been any need to warn the world of the danger of nuclear proliferation, or to name an axis of evil, or to deliver an ultimatum to disarm it. North Korea, fearful of American attack, demanded an ironclad security guarantee from the United States as the price of backing out of its nuclear program. In his trip through Asia in the fall of 2003, the President, sharply reversing his earlier policy, suggested that he might give one.

The North Korean debacle represented not the failure of a good policy but exposure of the futility of one that was impracticable from the start. Nuclear proliferation, when considered as the global emergency that it is, has never been, is not now and never will be stoppable by military force; on the contrary, force is likely to exacerbate the problem. The United States appeared to have forgotten what proliferation is. It is not army divisions or tanks crossing borders; it is above all technical know-how passing from one mind to another. It cannot be stopped by B-2 bombers, or even Predator drones. The case of Iraq had indeed always been an anomaly in the wider picture of nonproliferation. In the 1991 Gulf War, the U.S.-led coalition waged war to end Iraq's occupation of Kuwait. In the process it stumbled on Saddam Hussein's program for building weapons of mass destruction, and made use of the defeat to impose on him the new obligation to end the program. A war fought for one purpose led to peace terms serving another. It was a historical chain of events unlikely ever to be repeated, and offered no model for dealing with proliferation.

Events in Iran have seemed to teach a similar lesson. Iran has had a nuclear program since the late 1980s, when Shah Reza Pahlevi was still in power. With the help of Russia, Iran is building nuclear reactors that are widely believed to double as a nuclear weapons program. American threats against Iraq have failed to dissuade Iran—or for that matter, its supplier, Russia—from proceeding. Iran's path to acquiring nuclear arms, should it decide to go ahead, is clear. "Regime change" by American military action in that half-authoritarian, half-democratic country is a formula for disaster. Whatever the response of the Iraqi people might be to an American invasion, there is little question that in Iran hard-liners and democrats alike would mount bitter, protracted resistance. Nor is there evidence that democratization in Iraq or elsewhere would be a sure path to denuclearization. The world's first nuclear power, after all, was a democracy, and of nine nuclear powers now in the world, six—the United States, England, France, India, Israel, and Russia—are also democracies. Iran, within striking range of Israel, lives in an increasingly nuclearized neighborhood. In these circumstances, would the Iranian people be any more likely to rebel against nuclearization than the Indian people did—or more, for that matter, than the American people have done?

In the summer of 2002, Iran disclosed that it possessed a uranium enrichment program. In the autumn of 2003, the International Atomic Energy Agency announced that it had found traces of highly enriched uranium at Iranian facilities. It was not until a consortium of European countries engaged Iran in negotiations that Iran agreed to a program of strengthened inspections. Few believe, however, that this concession marks the end of Iran's interest in acquiring nuclear weapons.

The lesson so far? Exactly the opposite of the intended one by the Bush administration when it overthrew the government of Iraq. The lesson learned was: If you want to avoid "regime change" by the United States, build a nuclear arsenal—but be sure to do it quietly and fast. According to Mohamed El Baradei, the director general of the International Atomic Energy Agency, the United States seems to want to teach the world that "if you really want to defend yourself, develop nuclear weapons, because then you get negotiations, and not military action."

The collapse of the overall Bush policy has one more element that may be even more significant than the appearance of North Korea's arsenal or Iran's discreet march to obtaining the bomb. It has turned out that the supplier of essential information and technology for North Korea's uranium program was America's faithful ally in the war on terrorism, Pakistan, which received missile technology from Korea in return. The "father" of Pakistan's bomb, Ayub Qadeer Khan, has visited North Korea several times. This is the same Pakistan whose nuclear scientist Sultan Bashiruddin Mahood paid a visit to Osama bin Laden in Afghanistan a few months before September 11, and whose nuclear establishment even today is riddled with Islamic fundamentalists. The BBC has reported that the al Qaeda network may have succeeded at one time in building a "dirty bomb" (which may account for Osama bin Laden's claim that he possesses nuclear weapons), and Pakistan is the likeliest source for the materials involved, although Russia is also a candidate. Pakistan, in short, has proved itself to be the world's most dangerous proliferator, having recently acquired nuclear weapons itself and passed on nuclear technology to a state and, possibly, to a terrorist group.

Indeed, an objective ranking of nuclear proliferators in order of menace before the Iraq war would have placed Pakistan (a possessor of the bomb that also purveys the technology to others) first on the list, North Korea second (it peddles missiles but not, so far, bomb technology), and Iran (a country of growing political and military power with an active nuclear program) third, and Iraq, if it belonged on the list at all, fourth. (Russia, possessor of 150 tons of poorly guarded plutonium, also belongs somewhere on this list.) On the eve of the Gulf War, the Bush administration ranked them, of course, in exactly the reverse order, placing Iraq, which it planned to attack, first, and Pakistan, which it befriended and coddled, nowhere on the list. It will not be possible, however, to right this pyramid. The reason it was upside down is that it was unworkable right side up. Iraq was attacked not because it was the worst proliferator but because it was the weakest.

The *reductio ad absurdum* of the failed American war policy was illustrated by a column in the *Washington Post* by the superhawk Charles Krauthammer. He wanted nothing to do with soft measures; yet he, too, could see that the cost of using force against North Korea would be prohibitive: "Militarily, we are not even in position to bluff." He rightly understood, too, that in the climate created by pending war in Iraq, "dialogue" was scarcely likely to succeed. He therefore came up with a new idea. He identified China as the solution. China should twist the arm of its Communist ally North Korea. "If China and South Korea were to cut off North Korea, it could not survive," he observed. But to make China do so, the United States had to twist China's arm. How? By encouraging Japan to build nuclear weapons. For "if our nightmare is a nuclear North Korea,

China's is a nuclear Japan." It irked Krauthammer that the United States alone had to face up to the North Korean threat. Why shouldn't China shoulder some of the burden? He wanted to "share the nightmares." Indeed. He wanted to stop nuclear proliferation with more nuclear proliferation. Here the nuclear age came full circle. The only nation ever to use the bomb was to push the nation on which it dropped it to build the bomb and threaten others.

As a recommendation for policy, Krauthammer's suggestion was Strangelovian, but if it was considered as a prediction it might be sound. Nuclear armament by North Korea really will tempt neighboring nations—not only Japan but South Korea and Taiwan—to acquire nuclear weapons. (Japan has an abundant supply of plutonium and all the other technology necessary, and both South Korea and Taiwan have had nuclear programs but were persuaded by the United States to drop them.) In a little-noticed comment, Japan's foreign minister has already stated that the nuclearization of North Korea would justify a preemptive strike against it by Japan. Thus has the Bush plan to stop proliferation already become a powerful force promoting it. The policy of preemptive war led to preemptive defeat.

The Atomic Archipelago

The administration has thus embarked on a nonproliferation policy that has already proved as self-defeating in its own terms as it is likely to be disastrous for the United States and the world. Nevertheless, it would be a fatal mistake for those opposed to the policy to dismiss the concerns that the administration has raised. By insisting that the world confront the proliferation of weapons of mass destruction, President Bush has raised the right question—or, at any rate, one part of the right question—for our time, even as he has given a misguided answer. Even if it were true—and we won't really know until some equivalent of the Pentagon Papers for our period is released—that the administration used the threat of mass destruction as a cover for an oil grab or some other purpose, the issue of weapons of mass destruction must be placed at the center of *our* concerns. For example, even as we argue that containment of Iraq made more sense than war, we must be clear-eyed in acknowledging that the spread of nuclear weapons would be a disaster—just as we must recognize that the nuclearization of South Asia and of North Korea have already been disasters, greatly increasing the likelihood of nuclear war in the near future. These events, full of peril in themselves, are points on a curve of proliferation that leads to what can only be described as nuclear anarchy.

For a global policy that, unlike the Bush policies, actually will stop—and reverse—proliferation of all weapons of mass destruction is a necessity for a sane, livable twenty-first century. But if we are to tackle the problem wisely, we must step back from the current crisis long enough to carefully analyze the origins and character of the danger. It did not appear on September 11. It appeared, in fact, on July 16, 1945, when the United States detonated the first atomic bomb near Alamogordo, New Mexico.

What, after all, is proliferation? It is the acquisition of nuclear weapons by a country that did not have them before. The first act of proliferation was the Manhattan Project in the United States. (What follows concentrates on nuclear proliferation, but the principles underlying it also underlie the proliferation of chemical and biological weapons.) Perhaps someone might object that the arrival of the first individual of a species is not yet proliferation—a word that suggests the multiplication of an already existing thing. However, in one critical respect, at least, the development of the bomb by the United States still fits the definition.

The record shows that President Franklin Roosevelt decided to build the bomb because he feared that Hitler would get it first, with decisive consequences for the forthcoming war. In October 1939, when the businessman Alexander Sachs brought Roosevelt a letter from Albert Einstein warning that an atomic bomb was possible and that Germany might acquire one, Roosevelt commented, "Alex, what you are after is to see that the Nazis don't blow us up." As we know now, Hitler did have an atomic project, but it never came close to producing a bomb. But as with so many matters in nuclear strategy, appearances were more important than the realities (which were then unknowable to the United States). Before there was the bomb, there was the fear of the bomb. Hitler's phantom arsenal inspired the real American one. And so even before nuclear weapons existed, they were proliferating. This sequence is important because it reveals a basic rule that has driven nuclear proliferation ever since: Nations acquire nuclear arsenals above all because they fear the nuclear arsenals of others.

But fear—soon properly renamed terror in the context of nuclear strategy—is of course also the essence of deterrence, the prime strategic doctrine of the nuclear age. Threats of the destruction of nations have always been the coinage of this realm. From the beginning of the nuclear age, deterrence and proliferation have in fact been inextricable. Just as the United States made the bomb because it feared Hitler would get it, the Soviet Union built the bomb because the United States already had it. Stalin's instructions to his scientists shortly after Hiroshima were, "A single demand of you, comrades: Provide us with atomic weapons in the shortest possible time. You know that Hiroshima has shaken the whole world. The equilibrium has been destroyed. Provide the bomb—it will remove a great danger from us."

England and France, like the United States, were responding to the Soviet threat; China was responding to the threat from all of the above; India was responding to China; Pakistan was responding to India; and North Korea (with Pakistan's help) was responding to the United States. Nations proliferate in order to deter. We can state: Deterrence equals proliferation, for deterrence both causes proliferation and is the fruit of it. This has been the lesson, indeed, that the United States has taught the world in every major statement, tactic, strategy, and action it has taken in the nuclear age. And the world—if it even needed the lesson—has learned well. It is therefore hardly surprising that the call to nonproliferation falls on deaf ears when it is preached by possessors—all of whom were of course proliferators at one time or another.

The sources of nuclear danger, present and future, are perhaps best visualized as a coral reef that is constantly growing in all directions under the sea and then, here and there, breaks the surface to form islands, which we can collectively call the atomic archipelago. The islands of the archipelago may seem to be independent of one another, but anyone who looks below the surface will find that they are closely connected. The atomic archipelago indeed has strong similarities to its namesake, the gulag archipelago. Once established, both feed on themselves, expanding from within by their own energy and momentum. Both are founded upon a capacity to kill millions of people—the one by shooting and starvation, the other by mass incineration. Both act on the world around them by radiating terror.

As an instance of the archipelago's growth, consider India's path to nuclear armament, recounted in George Perkovich's masterful, definitive *India's Nuclear Bomb*. India has maintained a nuclear program almost since its independence, in 1947. Although supposedly built for peaceful uses, the program was actually, if mostly secretly, designed to keep the weapon option open. But it was not until shortly after China tested a bomb in 1964 that India embarked on a concerted nuclear weapons program, which bore fruit in 1974, when India tested a bomb for "peaceful" purposes. Yet India still held back from introducing nuclear weapons into its military forces. Meanwhile, Pakistan, helped by China, was working hard to obtain the bomb. In May of 1998, India conducted five nuclear tests. Pakistan responded with at least five, and both nations promptly declared themselves nuclear powers and soon were engaged in a major nuclear confrontation over the disputed territory of Kashmir.

Indian Foreign Minister Jaswant Singh has explained the reasons for India's decision in an article in *Foreign Affairs*. India looked out upon the world and saw what he calls a "nuclear paradigm" in operation. He liked what he saw. "Why admonish India after the fact for not falling in line behind a new international agenda of discriminatory nonproliferation pursued largely due to the internal agendas or political debates of the nuclear club?" he wrote. "If deterrence works in the West—as it so obviously appears to, since Western nations insist on continuing to possess nuclear weapons—by what reasoning will it not work in India?" To deprive India of these benefits would be "nuclear apartheid"—a continuation of the imperialism that had been overthrown in the titanic anticolonial struggles of the twentieth century. The Nuclear Nonproliferation Treaty (NPT), under which 183 nations have agreed to forgo nuclear arms, and five who have them (the United States, England, France, Russia, and China) have agreed to reduce theirs until they are gone, had many successes. But in India's backyard, where China had nuclear arms and Pakistan was developing them, nuclear danger was instead growing.

Some have charged that the Indian government conducted the 1998 tests for political rather than strategic reasons—that is, out of a desire for pure "prestige," not strategic necessity. But the two explanations are in fact complementary. Prestige is merely the political face of the general consensus, ingrained in strategy, that countries lacking nuclear weapons are helpless—"eunuchs," as one Indian politician said—in a nuclear-armed world.

Curiously, the unlimited extension in 1995 of the NPT, to which India was not a signatory, pushed India to act. From Singh's point of view, the extension confirmed the nuclear double standard. "What India did in May [1998] was to assert that it is impossible to have two standards for national security—one based on nuclear deterrence and the other outside of it."

If the world was to be divided into two classes of countries, India preferred to be in the first class.

The most powerful tie that paradoxically binds proliferator to deterrer in their minuet of genocidal hostility is not mere imitation but the compulsion to respond to the nuclear terror projected by others. The preacher against lust who turns out to take prostitutes to a motel after the sermon sets a bad example yet at least does not *compel* his parishioners to follow suit. The preacher against nuclear weapons in a nation whose silos are packed with them does, however, compel other nations to follow his example, for his nuclear terror reaches and crosses their borders. The United States terrorizes Russia (and vice versa); both terrorize China; China terrorizes India; the United States terrorizes North Korea; North Korea terrorizes Japan; and so forth, forming a web of terror whose further extensions (Israel terrorizes...Iran? Egypt? Syria? Libya?) will be the avenues of future proliferation.

The devotion of nations to their nuclear arsenals has now been strengthened by the hegemonic ambitions of the United States. Hitherto, the nuclear double standard lacked a context—it was a sort of anomaly of the international order, a seeming leftover from the Cold War, perhaps soon to be liquidated. America's hegemonic ambitions give it a context. In a multilateral, democratic vision of international affairs, it is impossible to explain why one small group of nations should be entitled to protect itself with weapons of mass destruction while all others must do without them. But in an imperial order, the reason is perfectly obvious. If the imperium is to pacify the world, it must possess overwhelming force, the currency of imperial power.

II. Solutions

The principal lessons of these episodes from the history of the nuclear age is more than clear. The time is long gone—if it ever existed—when any major element of the danger of weapons of mass destruction, including above all nuclear danger, can be addressed realistically without taking into account the whole dilemma. When we look at the story of proliferation, whether from the point of view of the haves or the have-nots, what emerges is that for practical purposes any distinction that once might have existed (and even then only in appearance, not in reality) between possessors and proliferators has now been erased. A rose is a rose is a rose, anthrax is anthrax is anthrax, a thermonuclear weapon is a thermonuclear weapon is a thermonuclear weapon. The lesson is a moral one but also inescapably practical. The world's prospective nuclear arsenals cannot be headed off without attending to its existing ones. As long as some countries insist on having any of these, others will try to get them. Until this axiom is understood, neither "dialogue" nor war can succeed. In Perkovich's words, after immersing himself in the history of India's bomb, "the grandest illusion of the nuclear age is that a handful of states possessing nuclear weapons can secure themselves and the world indefinitely against the dangers of nuclear proliferation *without* placing a higher priority on simultaneously striving to eliminate their own nuclear weapons."

The days of the double standard are numbered. Neither the United States nor any of the other nuclear powers can preserve it and they should not want to. One way or another, the world is on its way to a single standard. Only two in the long run are available: universal permission to possess weapons of mass destruction or their universal prohibition. The first is a path to global nightmare, the second to safety and a normal existence. Nations that already possess nuclear weapons must recognize that nuclear danger begins with them. The shield of invisibility must be pierced.

If preemptive military force leads to catastrophe and deterrence is at best a stopgap, then what is the answer? In 1945, the great Danish nuclear physicist Niels Bohr said simply, in words whose truth has been confirmed by 58 years of experience of the nuclear age, "We are in a completely new situation that cannot be resolved by war." In a formulation only slightly more complex than Bohr's, Einstein said in 1947, "This basic power of the universe cannot be fitted into the outdated concept of narrow nationalisms. For there is no secret and there is no defense; there is no possibility of control except through the aroused understanding and insistence of the peoples of the world."

Both men, whose work in fundamental physics had perhaps done more than that of any other two scientists to make the bomb possible, favored the abolition of nuclear arms by binding international agreement. That idea, also favored by many of the scientists of the Manhattan Project, bore fruit in a plan for the abolition of nuclear arms and international control of all nuclear technology put forward by President Truman's representative Bernard Baruch in June 1946. But the time was not ripe. The Cold War was already brewing, and the Soviet Union, determined to build its own bomb, said no, then put forward a plan that the United States turned down. In 1949 the Soviet Union conducted its first atomic test, and the nuclear arms race was underway.

The requirements that these dynamics of nuclear danger impose on policy are perhaps not surprising but can be stated succinctly.

In order to deal effectively with proliferation, the existing nuclear powers must, as first order of business, clearly and convincingly make known their readiness to practice what they preach: living without nuclear weapons. At the review conference of the Nuclear Nonproliferation Treaty in 2000, they did make such a vow, announcing an "unequivocal commitment to the speedy and total elimination of their respective nuclear weapons." But they did not mean it. The Bush administration has indeed asked for and obtained funds to work on two new kinds of nuclear weapons—so-called bunker busters, whose mission is to destroy underground facilities—and very low-yield nuclear weapons, which might be used on the battlefield. The United States and Russia have negotiated the Strategic Offensive Reductions, which requires reductions on each side to roughly 2,000 nuclear warheads each, but makes no mention of further negotiations. At the same time, the administration has insisted on maintaining a policy of the first-use of nuclear weapons under certain circumstances, and its Nuclear Posture Review of 2002 names seven nations against whom they might be used. It has also called for studies on reducing the time it might take for the United States to end its moratorium on underground nuclear testing. The message of these steps is clear: the United States plans to rely on nuclear arsenals for the indefinite future.

Each of these steps should be reversed or amended. The United States should:

- Scrap all plans for new nuclear weapons and nuclear testing and sign the Comprehensive Test-ban Treaty.

- Announce that it will never use nuclear weapons first.

- Take the nuclear arsenal off hair-trigger alert.

- Enter into negotiations with Russia to immediately agree upon far lower numbers of nuclear warheads.

- Signal other nuclear powers that when these numbers are reached it will enter into negotiations with them aimed at the complete elimination of the weapons.

Concurrently, it should demand a universally rigorous ban on any further proliferation of nuclear weapons or other weapons of mass destruction, to be backed by the strictest measures of inspection and enforcement, including the use of military force.

A league of great powers that having once built nuclear arsenals, and now has announced a readiness to live without them, will have a clear and irresistible resolve to act in concert to prevent the danger from arising in other parts of the world. The rest of the world will applaud them and assist their efforts.

The task is anything but easy, but the passage of time since the failure in 1946 has also provided us with some advantages. No insuperable ideological division divides the nuclear powers (with the possible exception, now, of North Korea), as the Cold War did. Their substantial unity and agreement in this area can be imagined. Every other non-possessor but one (the eccentric holdout is Cuba) already has agreed, under the terms of the Nuclear Nonproliferation Treaty, to do without nuclear weapons. Biological and chemical weapons have been banned by international conventions (although the conventions are weak, as they lack serious inspection and enforcement provisions).

The inspected and enforced elimination of weapons of mass destruction is a goal that in its very nature must take time, and adequate time—perhaps a decade, or even more—can be allowed. But the decision to embrace the goal should not wait. It should be seen not as a distant dream that may or may not be realized once a host of other unlikely prerequisites have been met but as a powerful instrument to be used immediately to halt all forms of proliferation and inspire arms reductions in the present. There can be no successful nonproliferation policy that is not backed by the concerted will of the international community. As long as the double standard is in effect, that will cannot be created. Today's world, to paraphrase Lincoln, is a house divided, half nuclear-armed, half nuclear-weapons-free. A commitment to the elimination of weapons of mass destruction would heal the world's broken will, and is the only means available for doing so.

Admittedly, such a goal seems a far horizon in today's world. Yet let us try to imagine it: the one human species on its one earth exercising one will to defeat forever a threat to its one collective existence. Could any nation stand against it? Without this commitment, the international community—if I can be allowed this metaphor—is like a nuclear reactor that is shut down. Making the commitment would be to start up the chain reaction. The chain reaction would be the democratic activity of peoples demanding action from the governments to secure their survival. True democracy is indispensable to disarmament, and vice versa. This is the power—not the power of cruise missiles and B-52s—that can release humanity from its peril. The price demanded of us for freedom from the danger of weapons of mass destruction is to relinquish our own.

CHAPTER THREE

A New Global Bargain

ANNE-MARIE SLAUGHTER*

Recommit to a new global bargain whereby the United States agrees to accept genuine constraints on its ability to use force in return for a genuine legal commitment by the nations of the world to do everything possible to combat terrorism, radical (armed) fundamentalism, and the threat of failed states.

I. The Problem

The United States needs to re-forge the global bargain it struck with the world's nations in 1945, when it emerged from the horrific destruction of World War II as the world's unquestioned leading power. In the most basic terms, we agreed to accept genuine restraints on our power, above all our power to decide when and how to use force, in return for a binding agreement by all the other nations of the world, including powers such as the Soviet Union, China, Britain, and France, to accept a set of international rules—political, military, and economic—that served our long-term interests.

The Bush administration has rejected that six decade bargain. More important, it has apparently rejected the idea of any bargain, preferring instead to cast off all international legal rules and restraints in favor of untrammeled freedom of action anywhere in the world. Unfortunately, this freedom of action has not brought us the success we so confidently predicted. It has brought us scorn, hatred, and fear around the world.

This predicament is complicated by our need—indeed a global need—to update and revise the old rules of the international system to meet new threats. U.N. Secretary General Kofi Annan told the assembled members of the United Nations at the 2003 opening of the General Assembly—the first after the Security Council split over Iraq—that they had "come to a fork in the road." He harked back to "a group of far-sighted leaders, led and inspired by President Franklin D. Roosevelt, [who] were

* *ANNE-MARIE SLAUGHTER* is the Dean of the Woodrow Wilson School of Public and International Affairs at Princeton University and President of the American Society of International Law.

determined to make the second half of the twentieth century different from the first half." They created a whole new set of international rules and institutions—the United Nations, the World Bank, the IMF, NATO, the OECD—to serve this purpose. Today, however, the nations of the world must "decide whether it is possible to continue on the basis agreed then, or whether radical changes are needed."

But revising the rules does not mean throwing away the rules. At least it need not. As the world's most powerful nation, and a nation committed to values of international peace, prosperity, and justice, the United States must take the lead in striking a new global bargain. Working with its allies and like-minded nations around the world, it would craft a set of international legal rules adequate to address terrorism, weapons of mass destruction, failed states, sustainable free trade, global warming, and the imperative of fighting AIDS worldwide. In return, it must genuinely recommit itself to multilateralism. Not to the appearance of multilateralism, in which the United States is willing to go to international institutions to get agreement on what it wants to do anyway but with the understanding that it will walk out if it doesn't get its way. But real multilateralism, in which the United States accepts the possibility that it might actually have to compromise its own plans as a condition of getting other nations to follow our lead. In the short term, such compromise will feel like a constraint. In the long term, it is the foundation of our collective security.

The Bush administration has not only rejected the bargain that the United States forged in 1945, but its only apparent alternative is the freedom for all nations to do what they want. The Bush argument is that no nation would actually put its security in the hands of an international body like the Security Council. But that is exactly what the United States and 49 other nations did in 1945. Having seen the destruction wrought by two world wars and having stayed outside the League of Nations, the United States, led by Franklin Roosevelt, decided that a well-functioning Security Council was indeed the world's best hope for maintaining international peace and security. Big powerful nations would agree not to use force in their international relations except in self-defense, but instead to turn all issues concerning the potential use of force over to the Security Council. In return, the big five—the United States, Britain, France, Russia, and China—got permanent membership on the Security Council and the right to exercise a veto.

Note what the United States did not give up. We and every other nation have the right to defend ourselves against armed attack; hence, we did not need authorization from the Security Council to fight a war against al Qaeda and the Taliban in Afghanistan after September 11. Further, when the Security Council is paralyzed through irreconcilable political conflict, as it was for much of the Cold War in the face of a threatened U.S. or Soviet veto on the vast majority of issues that could be brought before it, we can find alternative forums for deliberation over the use of force, such as the Organization of American States (used during the Cuban Missile Crisis) or the Association of Eastern Caribbean States (Grenada). Since 1990, however, the United States had a very good track record of working with the Security Council to authorize the deployment of troops or peacekeepers in civil wars and ethnic conflicts around the world. The benefits were evident: Security Council authorization provides an international badge of legitimacy, making it not only easy but often required for other nations to jump on board. The United States and the European Union typically ended up dividing the costs of a particular military operation with the United States paying for the war and the European Union (with Japan and sometimes the Gulf States) for the peace.

No administration has a perfect track record when it comes to the United Nations. As noted, administrations from Kennedy through Reagan managed to circumvent the Security Council in the defense of what they considered to be important and sometimes vital U.S. interests. Even the Clinton administration broke ranks with the United Nations over Kosovo; when it was clear that the Russians would veto any use of armed force in Kosovo to protect ethnic Albanians from Serbian ethnic cleansing, the United States, Britain, and France went to NATO instead. The intervention in Kosovo was in fact a NATO operation, with target selection, troop deployments, and escalation decisions run through all the NATO capitals. But in that case only three nations in the Security Council were willing to vote to condemn the use of force in Kosovo; after the fact, the entire Security Council effectively legitimized the operation by placing Kosovo under a U.N. mandate.

Every administration, by contrast, has publicly upheld the U.S. commitment to the United Nations. Even when, as during the Clinton administration under pressure from Senator Helms, the United States withheld its dues, it did so to try to force reforms to make the United Nations a more effective and efficient institution. The first President Bush was particularly skillful at building a grand coalition in the United Nations to wage the first Gulf War. He placed the United States at the helm of the international community, demonstrating that in 1991 a nation could not simply invade and occupy its neighbor without a global response. In previous administrations, decisions not to take a problem to the United Nations have been almost always driven by awareness that a fundamental political division would block reasoned deliberation on the merits of the issue at hand.

September 11th and the war on terrorism inevitably affected our relationships with multinational authorities in general, and the United Nations in particular. In the week after the attack, the Bush administration quietly pushed Congress to authorize payment in full of all outstanding U.S. dues to the United Nations. The Security Council quickly passed a resolution condemning the attacks on the United States in the strongest terms and obligating all U.N. members to take sweeping domestic and international measures against terrorism. The United States did not seek authorization for its operations in Afghanistan, but approval was readily forthcoming. A year later President Bush went to the United Nations and challenged it to fulfill the role its founders had envisioned for it as an effective, credible force in world affairs. Two months later, the Security Council passed a unanimous resolution demanding that Saddam Hussein disarm in compliance with a decades-worth of U.N. resolutions.

But then the real trouble started. The Security Council reached an impasse over the actual use of force in Iraq; the United States and Britain concluded in mid-March that they could not get a second resolution directly authorizing the use of force and chose instead to proceed on the basis of the November resolution. Their argument was based on the purportedly imminent threat posed by Iraq's possession and active development of weapons of mass destruction (WMD). In the aftermath of the war, however, with no actual WMD in sight, the administration has not once even suggested that its reading of the available intelligence might have been wrong; that perhaps, just perhaps, those countries that argued for waiting a few more months and giving arms inspections more of a chance might have had a point. Nor, inside the administration, is there any sign of recognizing that occupying and trying to rebuild Iraq might be substantially easier had we been able to create the kind of international coalition that

G.H.W. Bush did in 1991, as opposed to begging countries like Moldova, Nicaragua, and the Dominican Republic to contribute troops.

If anything, attitudes against multilateral institutions seem to be hardening. The view of Bush and company seems to be that we could not actually take the U.N. Charter seriously where our national security is concerned. We will not consult, we will not compromise, we will not cooperate. We will go our own way, maintain our primacy in the world system, welcome states that are willing to go with us, and ignore those who will not.

This is a dangerous, even deadly mistake. And it is based on a fundamental misunderstanding of the purpose of international rules. When challenged on non-compliance with these rules or on U.S. failure to join various international treaties, administration members typically insist that international legal rules are useless anyway, because they are routinely flouted by the nations we would most like to constrain. But according to political scientist John Ikenberry, who has studied post-war settlements and the institutions created by the winning power from 1815 to the present, the dominant power in the international system must contend not only with rival powers, but also with the fears of allies that they will be either dominated or abandoned. In this context, the most important reason for the United States to commit itself to rules is not because they will restrain our enemies, but because they will reassure our friends—and without our friends, we cannot in the end defeat our enemies.

The war in Iraq and its aftermath neatly illustrates the point. The war has severely strained U.S.-EU relations, as well as relations with Canada and Mexico. Even life-long supporters of the United States in these countries are beginning to conclude that we are walking away from the very international system we did so much to create and maintain over the past fifty years—and walking away with no clear destination in sight. No matter how big and powerful we are, we need our allies to tackle a whole host of issues: terrorism, trade barriers, fair labor standards, global pathogens, global warming—to name only a few. These issues require cooperation of *domestic* institutions—police agencies, environmental regulators, intelligence operatives, labor inspectors, health services. No amount of saber-rattling will make any difference. And coalitions of the willing by definition leave out the unwilling—which may be exactly the states we most need to cooperate.

In short, President Bush is making the United States weaker, not stronger. This is isolationist internationalism, characterized by lots of activity and little actual leadership. Our friends do indeed fear domination and abandonment. And our enemies see lots of opportunities to divide and conquer.

II. Solutions

Short-Term Initiatives

We need to revise the global rules governing international peace and security, including the use of force. Underlying this revision must be a new global bargain, whereby the United States agrees to accept genuine constraints on its ability to use force in return for a genuine commitment by the nations of the world to do everything possible to combat terrorism, radical (armed) fundamentalism, and the threat of failed states. We have to acknowledge that not only can we not go it alone but that we may not always know best. We can listen to and even learn from other nations in the process of consultation and collective deliberation.

In 1945 it was clear that one era was ending and another beginning. The nations of the world gathered to determine the rules that they would live by for the coming decades, and formalized it in a treaty. With 191 far more diverse nations in the world today, we will not have that luxury. A new bargain will essentially have to be struck by a new President in 2004 that would change the terms and the tone of many current foreign policy debates quite quickly.

1. Replace primacy with partnership.

The Bush administration's National Security Strategy sets forth a strategy of "primacy": the United States should ensure that we are and remain the biggest kid on the block, so that no one will ever dare attack us. That is the cornerstone of our security. And as long as we are the mightiest power in the world by a substantial margin, we essentially don't need other nations.

The problem with this approach is that terrorist groups don't care about our military capacity; if anything, it is just further incitement to inflict damage on us. And to fight terrorism effectively, we need maximum cooperation from nations around the world, nations that are either frightened or repulsed by our swagger. A far better approach would be to maintain sufficient military strength to ensure that we can both deter and defend against attack, but otherwise to pursue a strategy of partnership with other nations in pursuit of common interests.

The first step would be simply to declare that we no longer seek "primacy" as our principal foreign policy goal. We do not intend to grow weaker, of course. But augmenting our power just for the sake of it makes no sense. We should instead seek to use our power in partnership with other nations or groups of nations to make ourselves and our allies safer.

To take only one example, the Clinton administration adopted elements of a cooperative security strategy, particularly in the area of controlling "loose nukes." Indeed, the Nunn-Lugar Act established a process of cooperative threat reduction with Russia and many former Soviet Republics that has proven quite successful in reducing the economic and the political incentives to sell nuclear and biological weapons components to foreign governments or non-governmental organizations. This approach could be extended to fighting terrorism better by partnering with Pakistan to develop educational alternatives to the *madrassahs* that currently indoctrinate Pakistani youth with the tenets of radical Islam and serve as feeders for terrorist groups. Or by partnering with African nations to reduce small-arms traffic, which fuels so much of seemingly endless civil war in so many African countries. Or by simply asking other nations how they think we could best work together to address common problems and actually listening to the answers.

2. Publicly commit to a rules-based foreign policy and a rules-based international order.

The United States should agree to abide by rules governing the use of force as long as those rules are updated to take account of our and the world's new security needs. Secretary General Kofi Annan has already urged the Security Council to consider new criteria for "early authorization of coercive measures," which is U.N.-speak for preemption. He recognizes that unless the United Nations can act as a body, individual nations will go it alone. That may be a tall order, but it is far more likely to happen if the United States is prepared to live up to its side of the bargain as well.

What would such a commitment mean in practice? The President and the American people would have to accept that we do not go to the

United Nations only as long as other nations are prepared to rubberstamp our proposed plans, but that we might have to change or even shelve those plans in the face of strong and reasonable opposition. Taking the rules seriously would have meant waiting at least another month or even six before using force in Iraq; over the course of that time it might have become clear that Saddam Hussein's degraded conventional weapons did not pose an imminent threat, and that there were no WMD. The international community might still have decided to use force to remove him from office; alternatively, exposing his weakness could well have imperiled his domestic position. In either case, however, the United States would have been able to share the burden of both the war and the peace with all other U.N. members.

Reestablishing a rules-based order will ultimately make the United States stronger and the world safer. What we give up in the short term we gain in the longer term. This is particularly true in any situation involving the use of force. Since we are most likely to be doing the fighting, we are also most likely to need help in rebuilding and consolidating the victory when the war is over.

3. Push U.N. reform.

The U.N. Secretary General has named a panel of Eminent Persons, including many former heads of state, to formulate proposals for important U.N. reforms by the fall of 2004. Such reforms may include tightening the criteria for member states to head up important U.N. committees like the Human Rights Commission or the Disarmament Committee; strengthening the role of the Economic and Social Council as a body charged with addressing critical global issues such as AIDS or development assistance for the poorest countries; and creating a caucus of democratic states within the General Assembly. The United States should support this initiative wholeheartedly, working with members of the panel and interested states and groups worldwide.

Beyond these reforms designed to improve the internal workings of the United Nations, other important collective steps could accomplish a de facto amendment of the U.N. Charter, such as an agreement that all U.N. members have a responsibility to protect their citizens' most basic human rights and a collective responsibility to intervene if one of their number fails in this responsibility. A similar de facto amendment could accept a collective duty to prevent nations without internal checks on their power from acquiring or using WMD. Broad propositions such as these can be adopted as accepted interpretations of the existing Charter through resolutions of the General Assembly or even of the Security Council.

4. Pursue coalitions of the willing as pilot projects within an international or regional framework rather than as an ad-hoc U.S. initiative.

The Bush administration has launched the Proliferation Security Initiative (PSI) with 11 other states to create a collective capacity to interdict the shipment of weapons to terrorists or states supporting terrorism. Many countries would support this initiative and similar innovations if the United States made clear that is trying out various ideas as a precursor to more formal international agreements, rather than as a deliberate rejection of traditional multilateralism. We are alienating many of the countries in the developing world whose cooperation is likely to be most critical to the long-term prosecution of the war on terrorism.

The PSI is a classic instance of Secretary of Defense Rumsfeld's oft-quoted assertion: "The mission determines the coalition...the coalition must not be permitted to determine the mission." In fact, it makes sense to move ahead with some initiatives with a small group of nations rather than trying to gear up the formal international decision-making machinery. But the PSI could have been a NATO initiative. Or it might have been authorized by the Security Council itself as a kind of pilot project to plug the holes in the existing nonproliferation regime. Or the administration could even take the more unusual step of convening the defense ministers of the G-20 countries, the group that has met regularly as a network of finance ministers in the wake of the East Asian financial crisis.

Long-Term Proposals

Looking back to the beginning of the Cold War, it may appear as if the guiding principles of U.S. national security strategy emerged quickly and certainly in a few short years, aided by thinkers like George Kennan and statesmen like George Marshall. This is myth, of course. The concepts of containment, strong support for Europe through the Marshall Plan, NATO, and the European Coal and Steel Community (the first baby steps toward European integration), mutual assured deterrence, and indeed the very idea of a National Security Council to advise the President emerged over the course of a decade, roughly from 1945 to 1955.

If the principal threats we face in the wake of the Cold War and 9/11 are terrorism, extremism, global disease, poverty, and environmental destruction, years could pass as we work out the foundations of a new national security strategy that is intellectually grounded and practically tested. If, as proposed here, that strategy includes a new global bargain, then a new administration should be thinking about longer term steps to assure other nations that we are serious about accepting restraints on our own freedom of action in return for a resumed position of leadership in devising collective solutions to collective problems. Those longer term steps must include actual proposals for new rules as well as a new commitment to live up to them.

1. Negotiate a New Atlantic Charter with the European Union.

U.S.-EU relations are at their lowest point in a quarter-century, just at a time when our common values and common interests in fighting for a world free from fear should be most evident. We should seize the moment of the passage of a new EU constitution to come together as two great powers on either side of the Atlantic and negotiate a New Atlantic Charter. This Charter would hark back to the Atlantic Charter of 1943, when the Alllies came together to "make known certain common principles...on which they base their hopes for a better future for the world."

The old Atlantic Charter helped forge an enduring alliance between the United States and Western Europe against totalitarianism, the principal scourge of the twentieth century. A New Atlantic Charter should affirm a common U.S.-EU commitment to fight terrorism, tyranny, and the grinding toil of illness and want in the twenty-first century. It should establish principles of mutual consultation on all important issues of common concern and provide for informal transatlantic institutions to put these principles into practice.

2. Regain leadership of global efforts to stop global warming.

A new administration should treat the Kyoto Protocol the way Ronald Reagan handled the Law of the Sea treaty: announce that the United States will abide by most of the Protocol's provisions as a matter of customary international law, even though we have not signed it. The next step must be to propose a new and more effective agreement to combat global warming, stimulating the development and use of as many non-carbon-based technologies as possible in both developed and developing countries.

Further, the United States should lead the world not only in seeking effective approaches to reduce the causes of global warming, but also to find new technologies to blunt its effects. Many current schemes for creating shields from the sun's rays or otherwise reducing the Earth's temperature may sound harebrained, but current predictions about the extent of warming even if all nations drastically reduced their carbon emissions today make it virtually certain that we will need mitigating as well as preventative strategies. The United States could jumpstart a collective initiative to increase the gain from accepting the pain. (See Chapter 10 by Carl Pope.)

3. Join the International Criminal Court.

No single step would do more to assure other nations that the United States is willing to play by the same rules as everyone else as long as those rules also serve U.S. interests than joining the International Criminal Court (ICC). The U.S. vote against the ICC treaty (in the company of only seven other nations such as Libya, China, and Yemen) has become a powerful symbol of U.S. arrogance and exceptionalism elsewhere in the world. Fair or not, the interpretation abroad is that the United States wanted a set of rules that would subject the soldiers of every other nation in the world (including Great Britain, France, Russia, Australia, and others who regularly send troops into the field) to potential liability for genocide, war crimes, and crimes against humanity, except our own. Today, whenever the United States proclaims that it stands for the rule of law, we are vulnerable to charges of hypocrisy from even our closest allies.

Far from threatening our troops, the ICC can be an instrument to help keep them home where they belong. Instead of only attacking countries, inevitably including civilians, we should be indicting individual leaders guilty of horrific crimes against their own citizens and often those of neighboring countries. Imagine if Saddam Hussein had been indicted by an international prosecutor for genocide and crimes against humanity after he gassed Kurdish Iraqis in 1988, or for grave war crimes for his use of chemical weapons in his war against Iran? In the days before he had eradicated any hint of domestic opposition, an international indictment and a warrant for his arrest, perhaps coupled with a reward for bringing him to justice, would have at the very least created a new set of policy options in dealing with Iraq. At best, it could have avoided two wars led by the United States in Iraq and a decade of military and economic sanctions.

Joining the ICC would not subject our soldiers to the prospect of trial in The Hague. It would only mean that the ICC would be able to scrutinize our normal military justice system and assure itself that in a suspected case of grave war crimes, genocide, or crimes against humanity we were willing and able to investigate the case and try the defendant if warranted on the evidence. We should be proud enough of our soldiers' record to accept that scrutiny, confident that we would be gaining far more in terms of holding other countries' soldiers and leaders to account than we could conceivably lose. And indeed, if a U.S. soldier were taken prisoner in a country like Iraq or Liberia or Bosnia, to name a few places where our troops have recently seen action, we would vastly prefer that such a soldier be sent to The Hague, there to be returned to us, than to be tried for war crimes or crimes against humanity or genocide on site.

The consensus in 1945 was that the United States could lead through law; that we gained more from accepting constraints on our behavior in return for generally agreed rules and principles that we could apply against other nations than we did than from short-term freedom of action. The Bush administration, by contrast, often seems to equate U.S. leadership with defiance of international law, an attitude of "damn the international community, full speed ahead." We are alienating our allies and losing both influence and integrity in world affairs. It is time once again to lead the world not only by imposing the law of force but also the force of law.

CHAPTER FOUR

National Security in the Age of Terrorism

GARY HART★

In response to the transformation of war, restructure America's military forces and intelligence services away from unilateralism and preemptive invasion and toward more human intelligence and swifter troop deployments.

I. The Problem

In one of history's many ironies, the last decade of the twentieth century made the United States more vulnerable even as it solidified its unique position as the only super-power in the world. This paradox was made possible by the changing nature of conflict and the revolution in warfare.

Following the Peace of Westfalia in 1648, nation-states became the principal political building blocks of the world order. Like their predecessor city-states, nation-states were the products of bargains between the people (the nation) and the government (the state) whereby the state provided security and a degree of economic stability to the people in exchange for their loyalty.

To ensure security for their people, state governments developed a monopoly on violence. Already ritualized, warfare was permitted only between nation-states and its rules became codified in international law and custom. Under the surface of the Cold War stalemate, however, guerilla warfare, largely in the guise of anti-colonial "wars of national liberation," seriously eroded the formal systems of warfare as well as the state's monopoly on violence. Civilian targets were attacked. Prisoners were rarely taken, except now as hostages for ransom. Those that were taken were often tortured. As traditional warfare between and among nation-states developed mass casualty barbarities, so the relatively new forms of small unit engagements became noted for their newer forms of barbarity.

★ **GARY HART**, *a U.S. Senator from Colorado (1975–1987), is a former member of the U.S. Senate Armed Services Committee. He is co-founder of the Congressional Military Reform Caucus, co-author of* America Can Win: The Case for Military Reform, *and co-chair of the U.S. Commission on National Security for the 21st Century.*

With the virtual overnight collapse of the Cold War, the world—and conflict—began to rearrange itself. Nation-states, such as Yugoslavia, began to disintegrate. Tribalism, such as in Rwanda and Somalia, began to re-emerge in murderous fashion. Gangsters and dope dealers became rulers in Panama and Colombia. Mafias, including newly formed ones in such places as post–Soviet Russia, sprang up in new venues. Even the long-lost art of piracy surfaced in the waters off Southeast Asia. Whatever order the era of the nation-state had to offer rapidly began to disintegrate.

Just months before the collapse of the Soviet Union and the birth of a post–Cold War era yet to be named, the United States led a real "coalition of the willing" to drive Iraq out of Kuwait. In the process the United States billeted combat troops in Saudi Arabia, the site of Islam's holy places. Ten years later, in the caves of Afghanistan, al Qaeda documents were found identifying this decision as the beginning of the *fatwa* against the perceived godless American empire. In the interim, the World Trade Center in New York was bombed, the U.S. Army barracks in Saudi Arabia was blown up at the cost of 200 American lives, U.S. embassies in Kenya and Tanzania were truck bombed, and the U.S.S. *Cole* was blown open while at anchor in the Arabian Sea.

Then came the twenty-first century's own "day of infamy," September 11, 2001, a decade almost to the day after the end of the Cold War. Three thousand Americans were killed and a new era, a new century, and a new millennium of conflict were born. The United States was confronted with a new form of fanatical warfare for which it was totally unprepared.

But it had been forewarned. On September 15, 1999, the U.S. Commission on National Security/21st Century issued its first report, entitled *New World Coming*, in which it stated: "America will be attacked by terrorists using weapons of mass destruction, and Americans will die on American soil, possibly in large numbers." Completing its work on January 31, 2001, the Commission urged the new president, George W. Bush, to create a national homeland security agency to coordinate existing federal government assets to repel and, if necessary, respond to these predicted terrorist attacks.

Needless to say, that and most of the other 49 specific Commission recommendations were not heeded by the Bush administration. Indeed, after the 9/11 attacks, the president appointed an "Office of Homeland Security" in the White House, apparently to avoid the charge that he was

being guilty of "expanding the size of government." Of course, the proposed new federal department was not "new government" but government
reorganization in the nation's national security interest. Eventually, the failure of the powerless "Office of Homeland Security," predicted by many,
finally propelled the President into real action and he endorsed the idea of
a national homeland security department but only a year and a half after it
had been recommended to him by a bipartisan panel of experienced
Americans.

All this, of course, brings us near to the present day, a day less of threats
from other nations and a day much more of threats from "non-state
actors," terrorist organizations whose political agendas are basically limited
to killing Americans. There are, of course, other threats in the new world
of the twenty-first century, threats from failing states, threats from uncon-
trolled south-north migration, threats from epidemics, threats from environmental poisoning, the threat of the proliferation of weapons—especially into the hands of tribes, clans, and gangs—and threats from nations that
possess weapons of mass destruction and that wish us ill.

With the possible exception of the last, what characterizes most of
these new threats are two things: they do not respond to traditional military solutions; and they require multinational or international cooperative
response. What this fact suggests is the need for a much more sophisticated and layered national security structure than we presently have for the
new world of the twenty-first century, and much greater, not lesser,
reliance on proactive international security arrangements.

Through much of the twentieth century's three great wars, two world
wars and the Cold War, general bipartisan support for America's military
role prevailed. One significant exception was the Vietnam War, which,
though undertaken by Democratic presidents Kennedy and Johnson, came
in its later years to be opposed by large elements of the Democratic party.
This fact ironically underscores the canard recurring throughout the century that the Democratic Party was the "war party." Indeed, as late as 1976,
the national election featured the Republican candidate for vice-president,
Robert Dole, charging that Democratic presidents, Wilson, Roosevelt,
Truman, Kennedy, and Johnson, had all "gotten us into war." The conclusion was—If you want to stay out of war, vote Republican. Somewhere
thereafter, the Republicans became the hawkish party and the Democrats
resistant to the use of force, at least as a first resort.

Both parties must understand twenty-first century threats more clearly and prepare to anticipate them. The greatest threat is further terrorist attacks on the United States. This is followed by the threat of attack on U.S. citizens and diplomatic and military facilities worldwide. Then there is the continuing threat to world oil supplies. There is a serious threat of the proliferation of weapons of mass destruction to nations such as North Korea and the potential for a major theater war on the Korean peninsula. Next is the threat of the destabilization of moderate regional governments such as Pakistan, Russia, and Indonesia. There is a continuing threat of ethnic conflicts, such as Bosnia and Kosovo, with the potential for regional conflagration. Finally, but not exhaustively, the twenty-first century will see a continuing danger from failed states.

Each of these threats requires a different diplomatic and military response and capability and almost all of them require international, not unilateral, U.S. response. Anticipation of danger through highly focused intelligence capability remains the best defense. The entire U.S. intelligence network must be reorganized around this array of post–Cold War threats. Our intelligence priorities must be fundamentally altered to make technology serve humans rather than the reverse. The most important intelligence source in the new century will be the human not the satellite.

All of which makes the statement of a progressive national security strategy for the twenty-first century doubly important. The elements of such a strategy may be summarized as follows: First, threats must be prioritized and their nature understood; second, our intelligence networks and systems must be reorganized; third, homeland security must be made more urgent; fourth, intervention and expeditionary forces must be made lighter, faster, more mobile, and more lethal; fifth, a new paramilitary intervention force must be created; sixth, a new constabulary, peacekeeping force must be created; seventh, an international peacemaking force must be established to suppress local conflicts; eighth, counter-terrorist efforts must be consolidated; ninth, the Western coalition must be broadened to include Russia and China.

II. Solutions

Short-Term Initiatives
As the Council on Foreign Relations reported in October 2002, the

sense of urgency brought by the Bush administration to war in Afghanistan and Iraq is almost totally missing where homeland security is concerned. If we truly are at war against terrorism, the National Guard must be trained and equipped for the homeland security mission, our emergency health response must be dramatically expanded, local police, fire, and emergency response units must be better trained and equipped, their communications systems upgraded and coordinated and their access to data bases improved and seaport protection must become a centerpiece. Perhaps due to its original inattention, the Bush administration is awkward at best and disinterested at worst in homeland security. It is our greatest vulnerability.

The military component necessarily remains at the center of national security. Few doubt that legitimate requirements for the use of force in our defense will continue to arise despite our best efforts to replace misery and hopelessness with opportunity and democracy. But the military of the twenty-first century must look and perform much differently from that of the twentieth. We will need at least five separate kinds of military capabilities: nuclear capabilities to deter enemies from strategic attack; homeland security capabilities; conventional capabilities sufficient to win major wars; rapidly deployable expeditionary and intervention capabilities; and humanitarian relief and constabulary capabilities. Paradoxically, our military establishment will become more technological but it will also be more human. Technologically, our military will expand into space. But that component must be defensive not offensive. Because other major nations won't allow us to unilaterally win a "space race," it would be a mistake of immense proportion to encourage or even permit introduction of weapons into space, let alone take the lead in doing so.

United States military forces of the twenty-first century will look different, literally, but they will also be organized differently. Increasingly, brigade and regiment sized units will replace the traditional large divisions in importance and in deployment. Their characteristics and values will be speed, precision, and intelligence. The various services will conduct more joint and combined training, and their command, control, communications, and intelligence systems will be more integrated across traditional service boundaries. There will be greater importance given to anticipation of crises before they occur, and cooperative security arrangements will provide basing, equipment pre-positioning, and overflight rights before, not after, conflict arises.

Perhaps most importantly, special forces such as Delta, Rangers, and Seals will train and operate more jointly. Consideration should be given to the joint special forces combining to become a formal fifth service branch.

In terms of equipment, both the Navy and Air Force require more strategic lift, air, and sea transport to move troops and equipment rapidly and then resupply them. The Army and Marines require less heavy armor for traditional battlefield engagements and more light, quick, and flexible armor for urban warfare, and both can replace helicopters vulnerable to shoulder-fired surface-to-air missiles with unmanned aircraft.

In addition to increased sea-lift, the Navy must convert some ballistic missile submarines to cruise missile launchers. As fixed land bases become more difficult to maintain in the trouble-spots where an American military presence may be legitimately required, greater weight and importance will be given to the off-shore basing represented by carrier-led task forces. Mobility, flexibility, and sustainability will become even more important naval attributes over time. Large-scale, land-based, forward-deployed forces are in decline and small-scale forces are limited in capability, and therefore vulnerable, yet are often maintained to demonstrate political support. Naval fleets can quickly depart, it is argued, but so can small enclaves.

Further, the twenty-first century military will also involve more precision guided munitions. In the first Persian Gulf war in 1991, 10 percent of munitions were precision guided, and even those were not as consistently accurate as we were led to believe. In the Afghan war in 2002, 90 percent of our munitions were precision guided. But even that dramatic increase in precision guidance did not prevent us from occasionally bombing the wrong targets. Precision is an asset only if the human factor, accurate intelligence, controls.

We are indeed in a "revolution of military affairs" largely driven by technology but dependent on intelligence collected and analyzed by humans. Our fighting forces are increasingly directed by and through a complex web of information, command, control, and communications networks all interwoven and interrelated. The first Persian Gulf war was directed from a makeshift headquarters in Saudi Arabia. A decade later the Afghan war continues to be directed from Central Command in Florida. We are relying on UAVs (unmanned air vehicles) and UCAVs (unmanned combat air vehicles) as fast as we can produce them. The commander-in-chief now can monitor in the White House real-time pictures from these vehicles in the combat zone.

But high technology can be both extremely vulnerable to and dependent on the human actor. Exotic Pentagon communications networks are vulnerable to "21-year-old hackers." And precision-guided munitions on board B-52s flying from Diego Garcia or fighter-bombers launched from aircraft carriers in the Indian Ocean were guided by Delta Force personnel wearing civilian clothes and riding mules across the hills of Afghanistan. Even then, wedding parties were wiped out because of the failure of human intelligence.

Paradoxically, once again, the most technologically superior superpower in human history is now more than ever dependent on human ingenuity. If intelligence fails, as it did with terrorist attacks on the World Trade Center and the Pentagon, all the technology in the world cannot save us. To know when, where, and how terrorists intend to strike, and what they intend to use to do so, is almost entirely dependent upon human intelligence collection. Electronic surveillance methods, overhead intelligence satellites, telecom intercepts, and wiretaps/bugging all together cannot replace the human agent.

In the age of terrorism and "crime/war," we will continue to need expeditionary forces when major conflicts arise. But these must be lighter and swifter than the heavily armored, often cumbersome ground forces of the past. Getting to the conflict fast is now often more important than getting there in massive size. Ultra-sophisticated, post–Cold War conventional weapons platforms—ships, planes, and tanks—will have to be different. Despite our enormous wealth, we can no longer afford to integrate technology so closely to platforms that the platform must be replaced when technology changes—as it does with lightening speed. We cannot afford ships, planes, and tanks that are outdated the year they come into service, if not before. Platforms must be built for durability and long-life. The weapons and sensors we place on them must be "plugged in," that is, readily removable when new technologies become available.

The two illustrations are, of course, the venerable B-52 bomber and the aircraft carrier. The B-52, now in its sixth decade of life, is still performing—even though it is older than the *fathers* of the pilots who fly it. We also keep aircraft carriers in service for over half a century. These platforms rarely change. But the technological sensors and weapons change almost yearly. Even so, human ingenuity will continue to trump technology. In Afghanistan, Delta Force used a 3000-year-old transportation system, the mule, to direct twenty-first century technology.

The roots of the Defense Department's belated and uneven attempts to transition from twentieth-century weapons and warfare to preparation for what some have called the "fourth generation of warfare" of the twenty-first century trace to the military reform movement of the late 1970s. Even then, reformers were advocating unit cohesion and officer initiative, maneuver doctrine and lighter, faster, more replicable weapons. Without attention to new and innovative strategy, cancellation of weapons such as the Crusader artillery piece will by themselves not transform the military sufficiently for a new kind of conflict.

The support of the American people is crucial to any military engagement, and the longer the engagement may be the more crucial popular support becomes. Consequently the people must know, as accurately as possible, the estimated costs of our commitments. They must know which significant members of the international community openly support us, including those who will provide military resources. They must be given, most of all, the most candid casualty estimates available for both sides. In Iraq we were told none of these things. It cost us 57,000 American lives in Vietnam to learn the lesson that the American people must not be misled, lied to, or treated as incompetent on military engagements.

Any national security strategy must acknowledge that the U.S. military does not belong to the President; under our Constitution the military belongs to the American people who elect a president to command them. Public support for commitment of our military to combat is crucial for its success. That support cannot be granted in the dark and without a candid statement by the commander-in-chief regarding the probable costs in human lives and national treasure of its commitment.

Sound strategy requires that military engagements be undertaken only after the nation is prepared for their consequences. Such was not done in the war on Iraq. The United States was not prepared for what the Secretary of Defense, among others, believed would be virtually inevitable retaliatory terrorist attacks on the United States for our invasion of an Islamic country. Some Democrats (I among them) argued that war in Iraq should not be preemptively undertaken unless the standard for preemption under international law was met, namely that the threat to the United States was "immediate and unavoidable." This standard was not met. Further, it was argued that the president was required to inform the American people exactly what allies would support us militarily, what casualty estimates might be, how long a post-war occupation would be, and how much the total cost of the operations might be. None of these questions was answered, that is until our occupation actually began and it became clear that we would be in Iraq for years at the cost of hundreds of billions of dollars and continuing loss of American lives.

Further, a Council on Foreign Relations task force reported that we were woefully unprepared for, and are still at risk from, future terrorist attacks. It is imprudent in the extreme to preemptively attack a nation in a region seething with religious enmity and suicidal forces when we are still vulnerable to their retaliation. This experience should give the nation an historic opportunity to redefine the nature of genuine military strength and how our power should, and should not, be exercised.

Long-Term Proposals

From this discussion emerges the outlines of a national security structure and a set of strategies, tactics, and doctrines necessary to protect us in an age of multiple revolutions. First, we must understand the changing nature of conflict and the concurrently changing nature of security. Second, we must appreciate the nature of threats and respond to the causes of those threats not only with military means but also with economic and diplomatic imagination to reduce the despair that fuels terrorism. Third, the military means we use when necessary will look dramatically different from the recent Cold War age. Our military assets should capitalize on our technological superiority but recognize its increasing dependence on skillful human direction. And fourth, homeland security must achieve a balance between security and liberty by constant recognition of our peculiar constitutional heritage and the mandate that heritage provides to rely on citizens and citizen-soldiers devoted to civic virtue and civic duty.

The ideas presented here are but a framework for consideration of a twenty-first century, post-Cold War national security policy available to the traditional internationalist party, the Democrats. They neither are nor have been the "war party." Nor are Democrats the isolationist party unwilling and afraid to use military force when it is required to defend ourselves and our legitimate interests. But a new revolutionary age—an age of globalization, information, redefined sovereignty, and the changing nature of conflict—requires us to think anew. Strength in the new century will no longer be defined as simply voting for every weapons system, however useless, or sending in the Marines, however questionable. Strength will be defined by being smarter than our adversaries and by enlisting the wider world in the search for our collective security.

ECONOMY:

TOWARD A MORE PROSPEROUS AMERICA

An Economy, Not an Empire:
A Program for Growth and Jobs
After the Election

JAMES K. GALBRAITH*

Stop investing in an empire abroad and start publicly investing in our economy at home by such new approaches as a Federal Infrastructure Bank, Office of Capital Investment, and Revenue Sharing so states don't cut services just when they're needed—all funded by repealing tax cuts on the wealthiest Americans.

I. The Problem

The basic standard for economic achievement in America ought to be quite simple. Decent jobs for all who want them. Decent pay for all who work. Opportunity for those who can grasp it. Decent care for those who cannot. A rising standard of life, widely shared and enduring. Security at home in a difficult and unstable world.

Despite the surge of favorable economic news in the fall of 2003, we remain far from that standard. As of early 2004, over eight million are still unemployed. Millions more are underemployed and, most of all, underpaid. Forty-four million lack health insurance. Our schools, colleges, universities, roads, water systems, power lines are in decay—and the funds required to repair and expand them are being cut. Not least, we are at war with no end in sight. *That* is our economic problem.

George Bush did not entirely create this problem. The late 1990s were a moment of genuine prosperity and that rarest of economic achievements, full employment. But they were based on dreams, illusions, and mortgages. The bubble in high technology, the rise in inequality, the debt buildup of American households, the squeeze on public investment, al Qaeda—these existed before we got George Bush. They set the stage for a slump which began in early 2001 and for the massive job losses from which we have not recovered.

---

* *JAMES K. GALBRAITH is Lloyd M. Bentsen Jr. Chair in Government/Business Relations at the Lyndon B. Johnson School of Public Affairs, University of Texas at Austin, and Senior Scholar of the Levy Economics Institute.*

The essential effect of George Bush has been to make our problem harder to fix in the long run. Parts of the 2001 and 2003 tax cuts helped support consumer spending, and are responsible for the growth of spending and output observed in the run-up to the election. But the bulk of the Bush tax cuts in the long term flow to the very wealthy, whose spending is much less affected by extra income. Hence, the future tax cuts will be much less effective at sustaining growth than the present ones have been at starting it. Other Bush bills, affecting agriculture, energy, military procurement, and Medicare, also systematically place public money in the hands of affluent and powerful private interests. Meanwhile middle-class and working Americans are squeezed. They face property and sales tax increases at the state and local level. They face drastic cuts in education and health services, particularly those provided at the state and local level. And Bush is bent on eroding pay and working conditions, as in the assault on fair labor standards affecting overtime and on the public sector unions. As for the minimum wage?

Forget about it.

For its first 30 months, the administration repeatedly forecast a recovery that did not occur; instead, we lost nearly three million jobs, and over half a million in the year following the 2002 election. The strong growth rate of late 2003 was the first piece of seriously good news. Moreover, with tax refunds surging early in 2004, good growth news will presumably continue, though perhaps with spurts and remissions, at least into the fall of the election year.

But will it continue after that? The important issue is not whether Bush and company can start a recovery. It is whether they can go the distance with the policies they have put in place. It is not whether the airplane can take off, but whether it will fly. To borrow a metaphor from Iraq, the issue is not whether our soldiers can triumph in the invasion but whether they can make a success out of occupation and nation-building in the long haul, in the face of obstacles that may not be apparent at first.

The year 2003 proved two simple Keynesian truths. The first is that a big increase in government spending, mainly on the military, is a fast and efficient way to pump up the economic growth rate. The second is that when you give strapped households more money (mainly through increased child care credits and mortgage refinancing), they will spend it. But the pace of military spending is an unstable way to generate an enduring economic expansion, and business investment remains a doubtful reed on which to rest hopes for strong and sustained recovery. Also, it remains uncertain that the American household sector will provide the foundation for sustained increases in demand over the long haul.

There is also a political reality that should be taken into account. The men in charge will take every political benefit from the perception that a recovery has started. But in the deeper analysis, economic stagnation is to their taste. Does Team Bush really want full employment prosperity, strong labor unions, and rising wages? One is entitled to doubt it. The oil, mining, defense, media, and drug firms who form their constituency rely on monopoly power, patents, public contracts, and the control of public resources for their profits. They are threatened by strong labor and do not depend, very much, on strong demand. For this segment of American business, unified in remarkable fashion around this administration, full employment is not an unmixed blessing. Indeed, it is not a blessing at all but rather principally a risk and a cost.

Stagnation, moreover, helps to justify even more tax cuts. If the demand for stimulus is never quite satisfied, then it can be met again and again by tax measures that really serve another purpose entirely. The administration's core tax policy objective is the simple distributive goal that financial wealth should, eventually, be freed of tax. In 2001, estate and income taxes were cut. In 2003, it was capital gains, dividends, and again the top tax rate, and then, in the closing days of Congress, medical savings accounts. In 2004 the sunset provisions in various measures will be removed. As things are going, quite soon federal taxes will fall mainly on payrolls and current consumption. Such taxes are paid mostly by the middle class, by the working class and by the poor. The result will be a system in which the burden of providing public social benefits will fall most heavily on Americans who are already struggling to make their private ends meet.

For the moment, the concept of fiscal discipline has been forgotten, and rightly so. The nation needs large federal budget deficits now, to get the growth rate up. But the architecture of huge projected budget deficits in the future, combined with the emancipation of the wealthy from taxes, will set up a climate of relentless erosion of public programs—especially Social Security—in future years. When the fiscal train wreck is again placed at the top of the agenda, after the election, one can be very certain that privatization will again be proposed. That is what the administration wants, and it is what—if they remain in power—they are exceedingly likely to get.

The news is also bad for all those services, especially education, health care, public safety, and public transportation, now provided heavily at the state and local level. As financial wealth escapes tax, neither states, nor cities, nor the federal government can provide these services, except by taxing consumption, sales, and property at rates that will provoke tax rebellions, especially when middle-class incomes are not rising. Every public service will fall between the hammer of tax cuts and the anvil of deficits in state, local, and federal budgets. The streets will be dirtier, as also the air and the water. Emergency rooms will back up even more than they have; more doctors will refuse public patients. More fire houses and swimming pools and libraries will be closed. Public universities will cost more; the public schools will lose the middle class.

Meanwhile excess capacity and depressed expectations continue to affect the future of business investment. By conventional measures, capacity utilization by American business remains exceptionally low. This problem will not last indefinitely; in due course the overbuilding of the late 1990s will cease to matter. There are now signs that the ordinary course of obsolescence and aging, particularly of computers and electronic equipment, have begun to be reflected in higher business equipment orders. But in other sectors, such as telecommunications, the problems are longer-lasting. For this reason it would not be prudent to expect a return to full employment driven by technology investment in the near future.

There is also the fact that the reputation of American financial markets has been damaged by fraud and abuse—by what can be accurately called a corporate crime wave. Many believe that law enforcement in this area by the Justice Department and Securities and Exchange Commission (SEC) have been compromised by a political fact—namely, the prevalence of criminal practices among companies with close ties to Mr. Bush and this administration. Enron, whose CEO was Mr. Bush's largest contributor, is only the most notable example. This perception will impede the enduring recovery of asset values, though no one can say to what extent. It could also affect the valuation of the dollar, which has depended on the United States appearing as a safe haven for international capital holdings.

Can monetary policy keep a recovery on track? The Federal Reserve

Chairman, Alan Greenspan, has done his best to keep the housing bubble blown up, through low and stable interest rates. He has had much more success with this, so far, than skeptical economists would have believed likely. But the fact remains that not even Mr. Greenspan can forever prevent bubbles from popping, and if the housing phenomenon is a bubble, as many believe, then it will eventually deflate. There were signs by late 2003 that home-buyers were in a rush to take advantage of low interest rates before the long period of cheap mortgages ended. Whether this will mark the end of the housing boom, or another phase of it, can't be known.

A final reason to be skeptical that we now have a solid foundation for return to full employment lies in the core fact that American households are in financial trouble. In the late 1990s American households embarked on a period of sustained overspending in relation to incomes, financed by borrowing that was supported first and foremost by the rising value of housing, and secondarily by the stock bubble. Debt levels reached all-time highs. In the short term, this unprecedented phenomenon was masked by rising asset prices, so that household balance sheets appeared to be very strong. But household assets values vary, while debts tend to be fixed. The collapse of the stock bubble in 2000 undermined household balance sheets, and prompted an adjustment toward past norms—toward a realignment of spending within the general limits of income. That slowed the economy substantially in 2001 and 2002. A slowdown in the housing market, if and when it comes, would be the next shoe in this process—one that has so far not yet dropped.

The effects of low interest rates, tax rebates and credits, and increased military spending have been to keep the household adjustment process from slowing down total consumer spending. Mortgages have continued to be refinanced, and debt has continued to grow. The ultimate barrier to household debt acquisition is the ability to pay interest, and so far—at present interest rates—this has not reached the crisis point.

But now, for household spending actually to lead a recovery, household debt would have to resume its rise *in relation to* household income. Such a turn of events would be normal at some stage in most recoveries, when initial debt ratios are lower. But under current conditions it is less likely, and if it does occur for a time, it is still less likely to endure. The boom of the 1990s created financial conditions that were highly *abnormal*. Therefore the path of recovery is more likely than not to be abnormal as well—

abnormally weak and abnormally fragile—once the strong impetus of rapidly rising short-term government spending and middle-class tax cuts has
faded. The potential therefore remains for a substantial deceleration in
household spending still to come. And a consumer deceleration would be
much aggravated by increasing interest rates—a risk to which very little
attention has been paid.

The other big problem going forward is our very weak position in foreign trade. We have a propensity, now deeply entrenched, to run very large
foreign deficits at full employment. This is the product of a witches' brew
of international economic factors: the high dollar (mainly in relation to
trading partners in Asia and Latin America), the decline of the financial system supporting international economic development, and the erosion of
parts of our own manufacturing base. Given this structural weakness, an
increasing share of extra purchasing power leaks abroad and it is all the
more difficult to reach full employment at home.

So long as households, businesses, and also state and local governments
are limited in the degree to which they are willing to take on new debts
and expand activity, an expansion sufficient to generate return to full
employment would require one of two events. *Either* federal budget deficits
must rise by a large amount, over and above what has already happened,
and stay high for a sustained period. This is a development sure to meet
political resistance, after the election.

Or, in the alternative, the United States must find a way to increase
exports and reduce imports relative to Gross Domestic Product, thus making it possible for a smaller budget deficit to do the job on domestic
employment. But how to achieve this goal is very far from being clear.

Can the falling dollar square the circle, giving us lower foreign deficits
and so reducing the need for fiscal expansion? It appears unlikely. On one
side, the price elasticity of American exports is low, suggesting that a lower
dollar will not increase foreign demand by leaps and bounds. On the other
side, U.S. consumer goods imports come substantially from countries such
as Mexico and China against whose currencies the dollar has not declined,
and who are prepared to suffer considerable hardship to prevent such a
decline in order to maintain their market access. Therefore these imports
are not becoming more expensive and the demand for them is unlikely to
be choked off by considerations of cost. Things could change on their own:
American households might tire of cheap clothing, athletic shoes, and elec-

tronic toys. But given how much these items contribute to the modest comforts of working-class life, this also seems unlikely.

Immediately, the decline of the dollar against the euro has a positive effect on reported corporate earnings (because major American companies with operations in Europe can report earning more dollars) and so possibly on the stock market. But one may doubt the willingness of the Treasury and Federal Reserve to tolerate a declining dollar—even one that is falling only against the euro—for an indefinite period. At some point, a demand to preserve the dollar's role as international reserve currency will be made. A dollar defense, effected by raising interest rates, would of course only make the domestic position much worse.

The baseline outlook then, is not one where a return to full employment prosperity is likely to be achieved on the current course, nor by small policy changes. Pushing a few well-chosen buttons in the tax code will not do it, however desirable pushing such buttons may be on other grounds. And the Federal Reserve seems to have largely run out of new magic tricks, however much its officials may hint otherwise. The baseline outlook is for an economy functioning well below full employment because of hidden obstacles to growth. And this—following on the good growth rate news in the period before the election—is just as the current administration anyhow prefers. Conversely, a new administration, committed to a better economic result, will have to be prepared with strong measures, with a new vision for the economic future.

To round out the current economic picture, we need to consider the world outside, and particularly the economic dimensions of the evolving role of the United States in the world. For the inevitable fact is, as we pursue a policy of attack and control overseas, we are acquiring an empire, in fact if not in name. The difficulty of empire is that it is expensive in material and moral terms, as we are learning in Iraq. There, for a very brief period, the Bush administration could pretend that a vast country could be governed from the outside by a skeleton crew, consisting mainly of young soldiers, trained well for combat but poorly for civil administration. The men in charge did not want to pay for more than that. They had no serious interest in providing security, infrastructure or civil administration. Instead, the administration started out by proposing a version of "shock therapy" modeled on the market Bolshevism of the collapsing Soviet Union back in 1991.

Such an approach cannot work—and the early blueprints for a free market approach to Iraqi reconstruction have been sidelined by the preoccupations of security and guerrilla war. In this contest, the local adversary has advantages, including considerable cover among the local population and access to cheap and effective means of resistance, including explosives, mines, automatic rifles, and rocket-propelled grenades. And so the burdens of empire are growing palpably as time passes. Sooner or later, we may have to choose between leaving our conquered territories or putting in the full force required to control and to run them. One way we lose control, while the other can only add to the miseries of our balance of payments, as well as forcing the mobilization of hundreds of thousands of young Americans into military and occupation service and exposing them to a high level of violence.

How can the cost be met, especially, if the coin of our realm, the U.S. dollar, is at the same time vulnerable? It may not be impossible, but it won't be easy. The problem of empires, historically, is not military defeat. It is bankruptcy: moral, political, and also economic. Empires do not tend to business at home, and they tend to lose out to rivals who do. Investments made in distant places are sunk; once the empire ends they bring no more benefit to the country that bore the cost. By contrast, investments made at home accumulate and yield a return for centuries into the future. Although Europe faces formidable problems of economic governance, it is not too difficult to foresee a day when this difference in current behavior will give Europe an economic advantage over the United States.

To the Bush administration, the world outside is mainly a supplier and the object of complex financial relations. It is not, mainly, what it ought to be: a market. Cheap labor and secure oil supplies are the mainstays of the administration's external economic policy. Development and mutual gain are no longer high on the external agenda. And this means that many export markets in which U.S. firms have a strong advantage (e.g. electronics, telecommunications, and aerospace) are not flourishing. This represents a failure of vision and strategy on the international economic front, and one which leaves the American position in the world dangerously dependent on our role as financial center and military power.

This is vulnerability. And there is irony here for America's wealthy. It is true that a group of great wealth holds the levers of power in the country today. But this group, in large measure a coalition of big contractors and corporate welfare cheats, does not have interests in common with the full range of wealthy individuals in this wealthy land. There are many others— exporters, retailers, the residents of large cities, the creative sector, providers of services to the broad population, and many passive investors—whose interests align with those of working Americans and who would prosper even more under an economy investing vigorously at home. They are not well served by a program of stagnation and empire, even partially compensated by tax cuts on capital income. For, ultimately, an economy that fails for working Americans cannot work for the wealthy, either. The core vision of the Bush administration appears to be that the interests of its core constituencies can be met without attending to the long-term interests of the middle class. This is an illusion that may work for a time. But there is no example of sustained prosperity built on such a foundation, anywhere in the world.

II. Solutions

Short-Term Initiatives

All Americans hope that our position in Iraq will improve. Especially, we hope that local security and Iraqi self-government will begin to take hold. If they do, a decent and honorable reconstruction may yet be achieved. But should the present pace of bombing and sabotage not abate, the next administration will face an extremely difficult choice. One route would be to commit much larger forces—and to accept a much higher level of violence, as well as economic dislocation here at home. Or, in the alternative, the next administration may choose to work toward a withdrawal from the Iraqi quagmire. In that event, major power will be ceded to the surviving organized forces, which are mostly religious at this moment and whose loyalty to the American agenda in Iraq is, at best, a matter of expedience.

This is the very ugly reality. We eliminated a brutal dictator but one who was no friend to al Qaeda and whose threat to regional security—let alone that of the United States—had been essentially eliminated by the United Nations. We now face a situation of much greater risks, and it will take very deft diplomacy to extricate ourselves without leaving terror in charge. However, with success or without it, an indefinite commitment to the occupation of Iraq is neither realistic, nor sustainable, nor in our national interest. And therefore it is prudent to make economic plans on the assumption that Iraq's problems will not continue to command our presence there indefinitely.

As we come home from Iraq, the human and financial resources and the intellectual and creative energies currently being devoted to foreign military operations will need to be put to work here. In some ways, it will be the ideal moment for such initiatives. Our private enterprises will, indeed, resume their leadership role in due course. But they won't do it immediately. For a full and complete recovery, private enterprise will need a sense of direction and a sense of security, which it is up to public policy to set. And at this moment, the failure of the Bush security strategy—of the grand illusions that some maintained for the effect of military power on the Middle East—creates priorities for major change in the way the American economy functions, which it is no longer possible to ignore.

As John Maynard Keynes said, there will be work to do. There will be people to do it. Let us bring them together. Public activity should grow, not contract, when people and resources remain unemployed as they are now and will likely continue to be. The virtue of public activity in these conditions is three-fold. First, it does not rest on the profit motive, and so can be launched in hard times when private business investment is lethargic. Second, it can be designed to meet pressing needs, which private firms may be unwilling to meet at acceptable cost. Third, it generally leaks less to imports than policies that merely boost private incomes; hence a smaller public initiative has a larger net effect on employment.

While a long-term economic security initiative will be outlined below, in the immediate future we should build on the solid foundations of education, health, safety, and the environment, repairing the damage and neglect of the Bush years. If interest rates are low, why shouldn't states and localities borrow—with a federal guarantee—and do the work that needs to be done? Why not establish a capital asset accounting mechanism in the federal budget, that would make it possible for states and localities to invest and build steadily through periods of slow economic growth?

Let us invest in our science and technology. We need utilities like water, power and communications under effective public regulation or in public hands. Why not establish a Federal Infrastructure Bank to provide a revolving fund of low-cost public capital to support the initiatives of state and local governments in these areas?

Social Security and Medicare are the pillars of life in this country for the elderly. These programs must be defended and protected for as long as it takes. The elderly are not going to go away; the only real question is whether we provide and care for them properly or not. Let us firmly resolve not to privatize or otherwise undermine these two vital programs. We can repair the damage done by the 2003 Medicare bill, in particular by reducing subsidies to private competitors to Medicare, by allowing Medicare to negotiate drug prices on behalf of elderly patients and by extending the new drug benefit so that it provides meaningful assistance to seniors with high drug costs.

Moving forward, we must finally design a decent system of health care for all, with costs under adequate control. We must raise the minimum wage and support collective bargaining and restore a legal climate within which unions can work. We can fight poverty by expanding the Earned Income Tax Credit, by strengthening the Community Reinvestment Act, and by investing in public education rather than simply declaring it to be a failure. To protect those in deepest trouble, let's keep personal bankruptcy safe and legal.

To meet the immediate state and local fiscal crisis with a concrete proposal, let us return to what was once a Republican idea. Revenue Sharing can prevent the worst cuts in schools and firehouses and basic health services over the next few years. We should make this a flagship program, on a scale large enough—say fifty billion dollars a year for three years—to make a serious difference. As a matter of economic principle, states and localities should not be cutting services simply because the overall economy is weak. Instead, they should be supporting activity, while the private economy takes the time it requires to recover. And only federal help can prevent what is socially and economically destructive.

To pay for this, not immediately but over the years ahead, the long-term Bush tax cuts for America's wealthiest should be repealed. To our friends among the wealthy of this country, let us say plainly: You are better off being prosperous and paying tax, than going down in the first-class cabins of a sinking ship. The estate and gift tax has been an important force in the social architecture of the country, strongly motivating charitable bequests. It should be maintained at a reasonable level affecting the largest estates. Special treatment of corporate dividends should be repealed. However, it's reasonable to consider reduction of the corporate profits tax rate, offset or if necessary more than offset by a return of capital gains rates to equal those applied to ordinary income, and a new higher bracket on very large incomes. Users of public lands and resources should pay the full economic cost, including the environmental costs, of their usage.

Finally, the next administration should establish, in the Executive Office of the President, an Office of Capital Investment charged with the coordination and financing of the rebuilding of America on substantial and sustainable grounds. That new office should be independent of the Office of Management and Budget, and hence not subject to near-term limits on the scale of activity. With this measure, the United States Government would in effect bring its budget accounting into line with accepted practices in the private sector and at the state and local level. It would seek balance at full employment in current operations, but run capital investments on the scale required to reach and maintain full employment. Obviously that scale would be greater at first, when urgent national objectives must be met, and would be reduced later as private enterprise returns to its leadership role.

Long-Term Proposals

Our task is not merely to boost the economy for a year or two, but especially to prepare for a different and better world by 2010. For that, we need to be serious about what we think, what we say, and what we propose. The times call a new spirit of public action where the United States plays a far more constructive leadership role. They will require that we redefine and restate what we stand for in the country. They will require that we reaffirm what our country ought to stand for in the world.

Because of the damage already done, sustaining a full and effective economic recovery all the way to full employment from 2005 forward will be hard. It will not be merely a matter of spending more, of "stimulus"—an ugly metaphor that falsely depicts full recovery as a one-shot affair and reminds most people of a hypodermic stick. It will not be a mere matter of finding the right taxes to cut—or to increase. It will certainly not be a simple matter of balancing the budget. While the Clinton years were prosperous, they did not reveal a single best economic policy for all time. Conditions have changed, the past however agreeable cannot be rerun.

This is therefore not a moment for "me-too" politics. If one accepts the Bush administration's agenda on taxes or on empire, then game is up;

there is no escape from the rest. The positions that wealth must not be taxed and that security requires unilateral preemptive wars together imply everything else. This is a moment for serious alternatives or none at all.

We may usefully begin on the international front, as this is where the departures of the Bush administration are most radical. Let us reject the vision of America as the New Rome. It is an illusion—the Bush illusion—that the United States can control the world through the unilateral projection of military force and also survive as the world's leading economy. Ending this illusion is the indispensable first step toward facing the larger task of living safely in a world characterized by real limits to power. Just as we must build a security framework based upon friends and allies, we must work toward a world economic system that is governed more effectively in the common interest.

Backing off from the unrealistic exercise of power will not be easy. Today, our economic stability depends far too much on our oil supplies. The geophysical reality is that while we can usefully and prudently begin to diversify our energy economy and conserve scarce resources, we cannot escape reliance on overseas oil easily or soon. Worse still, the Middle East will hold an increasing share of a decreasing world oil reserve as time goes on, as oilfields elsewhere go into secondary and tertiary production and ultimately into eclipse.

From this point of view, the Bush administration's bid to control Iraq and its oil had a primitive economic logic. It was ostensibly a way to guarantee control over oil prices, the profits and therefore the stability of oil production elsewhere, and the continuity of existing U.S. patterns of transportation and energy use. But this goal could have been achieved only if it were possible to install an effective successor regime in Iraq, and then to reduce the U.S. military presence before it became the object of a general insurrection. If the present drift toward failure in this regard deepens in the year ahead, we could face the prospect of an indefinite war for an objective that won't be achieved. This would have the makings of a true national disaster.

At that point, serious choices will have to be faced. If we leave Iraq—or the parts of it that we cannot control—what then? Of course, we will still be present in the Gulf: with military forces in Kuwait and the emirates, and with friendly authorities in power in Iraqi Kurdistan and, for now, in Saudi Arabia, and perhaps tolerable relations with the Shi'a authorities in oil-rich Southern Iraq. Oil will still be available, even in the worst case. But the problems of homeland security, energy security, the environment and the economy will become intertwined in a way that will require action on a large scale, more integrated and more comprehensive than has been contemplated up until now.

Certainly also, the war on terror will go on. But there is a critical distinction between putting our military to use where they can succeed, and setting them up to fail. Ultimately, we need a deeper security strategy, which begins with building up our friends and neighbors. *Collective security*—the United Nations, NATO, and the balance of power with the Soviet Union and China—made possible the modern world and only collective security can maintain it, as other chapters discuss in more detail.

Real security also rests on an appropriate path of economic development here at home. We can reduce our vulnerability to a situation we cannot fully control. And we should do so, urgently, in three areas that need to be seen as clear components of true homeland security: energy security, the environment, and the economy.

Energy security can be pursued by a range of measures that diversify our energy sources, conserve on use, and provide both alternative means of transportation and alternatives to excessive energy use. Diversifying sources will mean an emphasis on renewables, and particularly in the area of electric power, where the production and transmission networks need major upgrading as part of a coherent national plan. The objectives of that plan should include a revival of electric-powered transport, both for commuting (light rail, subways) and inter-city travel (high-speed trains). It should include a corresponding reduction in greenhouse gas emissions, along the lines of the Kyoto Protocol—whose urgency is now increasingly evident. It should include a long-term strategy to reduce automobile use in urban areas, to increase fuel efficiency, to weatherize, to combat energy-inefficient suburban sprawl. Any full-fledged alternative energy strategy must also consider measures to stabilize oil prices in the home market, consistent with long-term resource and security costs.

Rebuilding America in this way will require a serious program of investment in our industrial base. Why are we granting huge public subsidies to ranchers, corporate farms, mining, and timber on public lands—and allowing our steel industry to collapse? This policy makes no sense except as a perverse and reactionary political choice. In the next administration, we should save steel, and if we have to sacrifice citrus and sugar to do it, then let them go. Steel can be saved, incidentally, without protectionism: a buy-America strategy for energy security could do most of the job.

At home, therefore, let us pursue the old goal of full employment—now using our public capacities as needed, in cooperation with the private sector. Let us do so for the clear public purpose of protecting our economy and our prosperity into the future. This is the only alternative available to the untenable strategy of dominating the entire Middle East by military force.

It's also time to begin to explore how to build a new foundation for worldwide financial stabilization, including management of capital flows to developing regions. Such measures will be difficult. They will require reining in the renegade multinational corporation, represented by predators like Enron. It will mean adjusting the present world role of the international banks. But the current system of unfettered capital flow is both unfair and unstable, and our North-South trading patterns are coming to be dominated (apart from Mexico) by China, which has succeeded by following a strong national development program. The system is doing very little for the development prospects of most other countries, including in Africa and Latin America, where crushing debts impinge on every social initiative. The failure of development strategies in much of the world cannot be the basis for an enduring reduction of war, violence, and terror. The international financial system we now have is unlikely to survive in the long term, and the job of repairing it should begin before forces we cannot control start to break it apart.

In conclusion, one might well wish that the challenges facing the United States and the world economy were less dire, less complex, and less demanding than they are. But the current complex of critical issues, the ugly nexus of oil and war in international relations, is the *cause* of the present administration's policies. To change the cause, and prevent a deepening of the calamities into which are we being pressed, will require time, effort, discipline, and imagination. It is past time to get started.

CHAPTER SIX

A Broken Federal Fiscal Policy...
and How to Fix It

ROBERT GREENSTEIN AND PETER ORSZAG[*]

*Avoid saddling future generations with unsustainable budget deficits—and threat-
ening the ability of the government to function effectively—by increasing revenue,
reforming the entitlement programs for the elderly, and enacting new "pay-as-you-
go" budget rules.*

When George W. Bush took office a little over three years ago, the
nation enjoyed the prospect of budget surpluses for several decades. No
longer. Not only do we face large deficits in the years immediately ahead,
but over time the combination of substantial tax cuts, the aging of the
population, rising health care costs, and significantly increased defense and
anti-terrorism expenditures threaten to produce deficits of alarming pro-
portions. These developments will have direct economic consequences and
also have profound implications for the ability of the federal government
to continue functioning effectively in the future, outside of a limited number of areas.

Major changes in fiscal policy are imperative. The first step is for the
nation's leaders to stop "digging the hole deeper" and passing legislation
each year that makes the nation's long-term fiscal problems markedly
worse. The second step is the enactment, possibly in increments, of a major
program of fiscal reform that covers taxes, entitlements, and the rules under
which the federal budget is crafted.

I. The Problem

The deficit is currently projected to be about $450 billion in fiscal year
2004, or some 4 percent of Gross Domestic Product (GDP), the basic
measure of the size of the U.S. economy. If this large deficit were only a

---

[*] **ROBERT GREENSTEIN** *is Executive Director of the Center on Budget and Policy
Priorities.* **PETER ORSZAG** *is Joseph A. Pechman Senior Fellow at the Brookings
Institution and co-director of the Urban Institute-Brookings Tax Policy Center. Much of this
chapter draws on joint work with Richard Kogan, William Gale, Isaac Shapiro, David
Kamin, and Henry Aaron, but the views expressed here represent those of the authors alone.*

temporary phenomenon, it would not arouse concern. However, a forecast issued jointly by the Center on Budget and Policy Priorities, the Concord Coalition, and the Committee for Economic Development in September 2003—as well as separate forecasts from Brookings economists, Goldman Sachs, and other analysts—project cumulative budget deficits totaling approximately $5 trillion over the next ten years, even assuming a full economic recovery.

How large are these projected deficits? Sufficiently large that if policymakers decided to balance the budget by 2013, their options would include: raising income taxes by 27 percent, cutting Social Security benefits by 60 percent, terminating Medicare entirely, eliminating three-fourths of defense expenditures, or cutting everything other than Social Security, Medicare, defense, and homeland security by 40 percent. Such actions are politically unimaginable. Yet this barely begins to convey the magnitude of the budgetary crisis that lies ahead. For after 2013, these fiscal problems grow much more severe.

In subsequent decades, the Bush tax cuts (assuming they are extended) will reach their full dimensions, while Social Security, Medicare, and Medicaid costs will swell with the retirement of increasing numbers of baby boomers and continued rapid increases in health care costs. Currently, federal expenditures for Social Security, Medicare, and Medicaid equal about 8 percent of the GDP. Twenty-five years from now, if we remain on our current course, these costs will equal 14 percent of GDP.

One might expect that with the demographic changes and increases in health care costs that lie ahead, policymakers would be laying the groundwork for a gradual *increase* in revenues to help defray at least part of the inevitable increase in expenditures. Instead, we have been pursuing the opposite course, instituting major changes in the tax system that are causing revenues to *decline* as a share of the economy.

In 2003, total federal tax revenues, measured as a share of the economy, were at their lowest level since 1959, and revenues just from the income tax were at their lowest level since 1942. This is a remarkable development given that, in 1959, there were no Medicare or Medicaid programs to finance and various other major programs did not yet exist. To be sure, revenues are projected to rise above 1959 levels as the economy fully recovers, but they will remain quite low by historical standards. If the Bush tax cuts are extended, the average level of revenues over the next decade will remain lower, as a share of the economy, than the average levels in the 1960s, 1970s, 1980s, or 1990s.

We thus are heading toward historically high levels of federal expenditures due to the aging of the population and rising health costs, coupled with historically low levels of revenue due to the Bush tax cuts. This toxic combination will generate spiraling and unsustainable budget deficits that impose significant costs on the economy and inequitable burdens on our children and grandchildren. Although the precise magnitudes of these deficits are uncertain, the existence of a dangerously large long-term fiscal gap is not.

Persistent large deficits harm economic growth because they reduce national saving. National saving is the sum of private saving and public (or government) saving. (Budget surpluses represent public saving; a budget deficit results in negative saving because a portion of private savings must be used to cover the deficit.) Since public saving declines when the budget deficit increases, higher budget deficits reduce national saving, all else being equal. A reduction in national saving means Americans do not accumulate as much capital to invest in new plants, equipment, and other enterprises, which deprives future generations of the income that would have been earned on those investments and produces a smaller economy—and lower wages and salaries for U.S. workers—than would otherwise have been the case.

To get a sense of the magnitudes involved, consider the projected deficits of approximately $5 trillion over the next ten years. Under reasonable assumptions, these projected deficits will reduce income in the United States by more than $200 billion in 2014, or an average of about $1,500 per household. Moreover, the problem is expected to worsen substantially in subsequent decades. Under current policies, deficits are projected to swell from 3 to 4 percent of the GDP ten years from now to 12 percent of GDP by 2030 and more than 20 percent of GDP by 2040, leading to an explosion of the national debt. Over time, the economic cost of the deficits the nation faces will increase markedly, leaving future generations with a smaller economy and considerably less income than they otherwise would have.

In addition, because large deficits cause the debt to grow rapidly, an increasing share of the federal budget will have to be devoted to paying interest on the debt rather than financing necessary or worthwhile programs, such as investments in education, children's health, and infrastructure that could improve long-term growth. Interest payments for the ten years from 2002 to 2011 are now expected to be nearly $2 trillion higher than was projected in early 2001. If we continue on the current policy course, interest payments will be about $450 billion a year by 2013 and continue rising after that.

The projected deficits are now so large that they ultimately could result in what former Treasury Secretary Robert Rubin has called "fiscal disarray." As investors become increasingly concerned that the government could resort to high inflation (to reduce the value of the debt it owes) or that a fiscal deadlock with unpredictable consequences could arise, investor confidence may weaken substantially, interest rates could rise markedly, and the role of the dollar as the primary currency of international transactions could be threatened. Such developments would have consequences even more serious than those already described.

It is unthinkable that the nation would endlessly pursue fiscal policies that ultimately do such substantial damage to the economy. Sooner or later, something will have to give. And that is what some conservative activists are counting on. They seek to use tax cuts and the specter of massive deficits to "starve the beast"—that is, to force radical shrinkage in the federal government.

This should not be regarded as an idle threat. If we remain on our current tax-cutting course but also seek to prevent deficits from becoming unsustainably large, there will be no alternative to curtailing federal activity sharply in a wide range of areas. We'd have to abandon initiatives to reduce the ranks of the uninsured, combat child poverty, or adequately rebuild the nation's aging schools, roads, and rail lines. In fact, if we proceed down this course, major parts of the Great Society and the New Deal are likely to be dismantled over time. By mid-century, the federal government may be a pale shadow of its current self, with consequent adverse effects on poverty, education, health care, the environment, and other areas of national life.

How did we get to this fiscal precipice? In early 2001, the nonpartisan Congressional Budget Office projected cumulative budget surpluses of about $5 trillion over the next ten years (2002–2011). Today, the projection is for *deficits* of about $4 trillion over the same ten-year period. On a comparable basis, the negative swing in the federal government's fiscal position amounts to about $9 trillion.

About three-fourths of the swing is due to reduced revenues rather than higher expenditures. The drop-off in revenues stems from both the tax cuts and changes in budget estimates; the level of revenues assumed in 2001 was unrealistically high even without the tax cuts. On the spending side, the increases in projected expenditures have stemmed primarily from defense and homeland security, followed by the costs of the Medicare prescription drug bill. Other increases in domestic spending have generally played only bit roles in the fiscal deterioration.

The tax cuts merit particular attention. When fully in effect, their annual cost will equal four times what the federal government spends on education. Indeed, their annual cost will exceed everything the federal government spends on veterans' programs, transportation, housing and urban development, agriculture, food assistance, national parks, environmental protection, the Department of Homeland Security, and Department of State *combined*.

Moreover, if the tax cuts are made permanent, their cost over the next 75 years will be *triple* the Social Security shortfall. Their cost also will be more than the shortfall in Social Security and Medicare Hospital Insurance combined. In other words, if all the revenue from the tax cuts were instead devoted to Social Security and the Medicare Hospital Insurance program, the entire 75-year deficits in those programs could be eliminated. (We would not recommend such a course; it would go too easy on the large retirement programs while leaving highly insufficient revenues for other priorities.)

Advocates of the tax cuts argue, however, that these tax reductions will increase long-term growth and boost the economy. To be sure, reduced marginal tax rates may, by themselves, have a positive economic effect by increasing incentives for work, investment, and risk-taking, although the available evidence suggests such effects are generally modest. But tax cuts also increase budget deficits and thereby reduce national saving and future national income, an effect typically glossed over by tax-cut proponents.

The net effect of tax cuts on long-term economic growth reflects the combination of any positive effects on economic incentives *and* the negative effects from larger budget deficits. Given the structure of the 2001 and 2003 tax cuts, independent analysts have generally concluded that the positive effects on growth from reduced marginal tax rates will be cancelled out—and, in fact, are likely to be outweighed—by the negative effects from much larger deficits. When Congress's own Joint Committee on Taxation (whose head was appointed by the Congressional Republican leadership) evaluated the 2003 tax legislation, it concluded that "eventually the effects of the increasing deficit will outweigh the positive effects of the tax policy." An array of other economists at institutions such as the Federal Revenue Board and the Brookings Institution have reached much the same conclusion about the 2001 tax cut. Rhetorical claims that the tax cuts will come close to paying for themselves are not supported by any credible evidence. The evidence suggests that, if anything, the net effect of the recent tax cuts will be a reduction in long-term growth, in which case the tax cuts will cost even more than official estimates indicate.

A second justification advanced for the tax cuts is that they have helped the economy in the short run. Almost any tax cut or spending increase, however, can temporarily boost a weak economy. The challenge for policymakers facing a weak economy is to secure the maximum economic stimulus per dollar of cost to the federal Treasury. But the tax cuts enacted in recent years will remain in effect and grow larger after the economy has recovered and stimulus is no longer needed, and will lead to lower national income in the future because of the large, ongoing deficits they generate. Furthermore, the tax cuts are concentrated primarily on higher-income individuals, a group that is more likely to save rather than spend its tax cuts than people who live paycheck to paycheck; this makes the tax cuts less effective as immediate economic stimulus. We could have achieved greater short-term stimulus at much lower long-term cost by focusing on temporary fiscal relief to the states, temporary expansions in unemployment insurance benefits, and temporary tax cuts for low- and middle-income families, who are more likely to spend their tax-cut benefits quickly.

II. The Bush Response

The Bush administration and Congress continue to pursue a course that will make these problems more severe. In the first half of 2003, Congress passed and the President signed a new package of large tax cuts, the cost of which is reflected in the budget figures cited above. In the second half of 2003, Medicare drug legislation was enacted that, according to Congressional Budget Office estimates, will cost approximately $1.3 trillion in the second decade it is in effect and continue rising in cost after that. The design of the Medicare legislation imposes costs substantially greater than is necessary to pay for the modest, rather patchy drug benefit it provides.

In the first half of 2004, the Bush administration has proposed yet another round of tax cuts that would have large costs over time: the creation of Lifetime Saving Accounts (LSAs) and Retirement Saving Accounts (RSAs). The LSAs and RSAs would exacerbate the misguided thrust of recent pension changes, which have substantially expanded opportunities for high-income households to shelter more saving and investment income from taxation. The administration's new proposal would go further and ultimately lead to a very large share of investment income escaping taxation. The proposal would engender mounting revenue losses but generate little new private saving, since high-income households could shift other assets into the tax-subsidized savings and investment accounts that would be created instead of having to undertake new saving to make use of the tax breaks. And the proposal would result in mushrooming revenue losses over time. Over the next 75 years, the revenue loss would amount to more than one-third of the entire Social Security deficit. In the face of massive projected budget deficits in future decades, forgoing such large amounts of revenue to create major new tax shelters which will subsidize saving that most high-income households would have undertaken anyway seems perverse.

What of the administration argument that provoking a fiscal crisis will force policymakers to address long-term "entitlement reform?"

If successful, such a strategy likely would result in larger reductions in Social Security and Medicare benefits for most beneficiaries than would otherwise be needed in exchange for lower taxes primarily for high-income households. Alternatively, the strategy could fail. Although crises do tend to force action, a transparently self-imposed crisis is different from a crisis imposed by external forces, just as an arsonist is different from someone whose house burns down due to lightning.

More than two decades ago, Ronald Reagan's budget director David Stockman declared that in seeking to shrink or eliminate large budget deficits, policymakers should go after "weak claims, not weak clients." The current policy course threatens to stand this sentiment on its head. Powerful clients with weak claims—from the pharmaceutical industry to health insurance companies to HMOs, oil and gas companies, the financial securities industry, large agribusiness firms, and the nation's wealthiest individuals and families—are reaping substantial rewards from legislation enacted in recent years. Meanwhile, weaker clients—especially those with low incomes—are increasingly at risk. Current administration proposals would begin to erect a structure under which resources for some of the key programs for poor households would likely fail to keep pace with need. This would enable the federal government to save increasing amounts over time but could cause many of the nation's poorest citizens to face growing hardship.

As one example, the Bush White House has proposed beginning to convert the Medicaid program into a block grant. Medicaid is now an entitlement; all low-income children, parents, elderly people, and people with disabilities who apply and meet their state's eligibility criteria (which are set within federal parameters) are enrolled, and the federal government pays an average of 57 percent of Medicaid health care costs. Under a block grant, the federal government would pay a fixed amount to state Medicaid programs each year. If the costs of providing health care to the low-income population rose more rapidly than federal block grant funding—because, for example, an increase in job losses has caused more people to lose their health insurance, or as a result of a flu or infectious disease epidemic—the federal government would *not* contribute to covering the higher expenditures, which would fall exclusively on state budgets. The likely result would be that over time, states would feel compelled to scale back health care coverage for low-income households.

The administration also has proposed to convert the nation's largest low-income housing program to a block grant, as well as to freeze funding for a number of years to come, with no adjustment for inflation, for the welfare "reform" block grant. This, despite the fact that funding shortages already have led more than half of the states to cut welfare-to-work programs, child care assistance, or similar forms of job-related assistance that were supposed to be the centerpiece of welfare reform.

Taken together, such proposals suggest the Bush administration may be seeking to convert a growing number of entitlement assistance programs for low-income families and individuals into block grants as part of a slowly emerging "spending control" strategy. To help secure enactment of such proposals, the proposals may be designed to provide adequate funding in the initial years the block grants would be in place. After that, funding for such block grants is likely to fall steadily further behind need. In addition, when full-blown federal budget crises begin to hit at some point in the future, the block-grant funding structure would provide a ready mechanism to ratchet funding for these programs down further.

This fiscal policy course also is likely to result in a further widening of income disparities already at, or close to, their widest levels in decades. The most reliable data on this matter come from the Congressional Budget Office, which combines Census Bureau data with Internal Revenue Service data drawn from federal income tax returns. These data show that between 1979 and 2000 (the most recent year for which the data are available), income inequality grew sharply, as income gains at the top of the income spectrum far outpaced gains in the middle and at the bottom. Average after-tax income increased by 9 percent over this period among the bottom fifth of the population (after adjusting for inflation) and by 15 percent for the middle fifth. But average after-tax income rose 68 percent for the top fifth. And for the top 1 percent, average after-tax income registered a stunning 201 percent increase. Disparities in after-tax income appear to have been wider in 2000 than at any time since 1936, and possibly at any time since 1929. The recent tax cuts will only worsen these trends by raising after-tax incomes by much larger percentages for high-income households than for those in other parts of the income spectrum.

A continuation of the current policy course poses considerable risks to state and local governments, as well. Federal policy has begun to batter state and local finances through such measures as federal tax cuts that engender *state* revenue losses, due to linkages between federal and state tax codes. (Most state income tax codes use the federal definition of taxable income; shielding more income from the federal income tax consequently causes the same result at the state level, unless states can enact legislation delinking their tax codes from the federal tax changes, which can be difficult politically.) As the federal budget crunch takes increasing hold in coming years and decades, state and local governments also may face declines in federal grants-in-aid, as well as a shift of more responsibilities from the federal government to state and local levels without commensurate federal resources to cover the costs of those responsibilities.

Due in substantial part to the coming retirement of the baby boomers and continued increases in health care costs, long-term fiscal prospects are deeply troubled in many states. Federal policy threatens to exacerbate these problems.

III. Solutions

As this discussion suggests, changing course on fiscal policy and budget priorities is one of the most crucial tasks the nation faces. Indeed, if we do not change course, the resulting fiscal failure is likely to foreclose consideration of many of the other recommendations made in this volume.

Stop Digging the Hole Deeper

The first step is to "stop digging the hole deeper." The key mechanism to achieve this goal is well known: to reestablish the "pay-as-you-go" rules that served the nation well through most of the 1990s. Under these rules, all tax cuts and entitlement increases would have to be offset by tax increases or entitlement reductions of equal magnitude. The experience of the 1990s demonstrates such a regimen can work effectively and result in substantial budget restraint.

The pay-as-you-go rules should be applied to all future tax cuts and entitlement expansions, except for emergency measures that are strictly temporary in nature (such as temporary tax cuts or unemployment insurance increases during a recession). These rules should apply, for example, to legislation to extend the recent tax cuts, including tax-cut provisions that have broad appeal. If tax cuts are meritorious, their extension should be paid for through offsetting tax or entitlement measures. These rules should similarly apply to efforts to fill gaps in the new Medicare drug benefit.

In reinstating the pay-as-you-go rule, policymakers also should close a loophole in the rule. Because budget costs typically are measured over a period of five or ten years, policymakers have become adept in using gimmicks to design tax cuts and other measures so that their costs remain moderate in the first five or ten years, only to explode thereafter. A reinstated pay-as-you-go rule should direct the official cost-estimating agencies to estimate the revenue losses from a tax cut or an entitlement expansion over a longer period and require that other budget changes offset the budgetary costs over the extended period.

A "Grand Agreement"

The second step is the most difficult, especially in the current political environment—to craft a "grand agreement" that marries reform in Social Security and several other entitlement programs with revenue-raising measures. A combination of entitlement-restraining and revenue-increasing measures was the hallmark of the 1990 and 1993 deficit reduction packages, which played an important role in erasing deficits in the 1990s. A new package also could establish reasonable limits on discretionary spending, as the 1990 and 1993 packages did. In addition, as in 1990 and 1993, a new package could devote the majority of the savings it generates to getting the budget picture under control but use some of its savings to address critical unmet national needs. The following are among the elements of such a "grand agreement."

1. Social Security

One of America's most successful and revered government programs, Social Security faces a long-term deficit. Addressing the long-term Social Security deficit would put both the program and the federal budget on a sounder footing. Lawmakers do not, however, have to destroy Social Security in order to save it.

In a new book—*Saving Social Security: A Balanced Approach*—Peter Diamond and Peter Orszag present a proposal that would restore long-term balance to Social Security while preserving the program's basic structure and strengthening its social insurance functions. Their plan would make Social Security solvent for the next 75 years and beyond without drawing on general revenues and further squeezing the rest of the budget. Instead, it combines revenue and benefit changes, reflecting the type of balanced approach adopted in the 1983 Social Security reforms.

The plan addresses the various factors that underlie Social Security's long-term deficit. One factor, for example, is increasing life expectancy. As life expectancy grows, beneficiaries collect Social Security benefits for more years, on average, and that raises program costs. The Diamond-Orszag plan contains modest benefit reductions and payroll tax increases that, between them, finance the increased Social Security costs that the growth in life expectancy will generate.

Similarly, the plan includes measures to counter the adverse effects on Social Security financing of the growing disparities in earnings in the United States. Because of these growing disparities, an increasing share of earnings escapes the payroll tax, which does not apply to earnings above $87,900 in 2004. On a related front, life expectancy is increasing more rapidly among affluent individuals than among those at lower income levels; this tends to increase the total amount of Social Security benefits paid over the course of an individual's retirement more substantially among those on the higher rungs of the income ladder, making Social Security less progressive over time. To address these matters, the Diamond-Orszag plan gradually increases the ceiling on the amount of earnings subject to the payroll tax and also includes a benefit reduction targeted on people with high lifetime earnings. These elements of the plan help restore Social Security solvency in a progressive manner. The plan includes several other adjustments, as well.

Workers who are 55 or older in 2004 would, under the plan, experience no change in benefits from those promised under current law. A worker age 45 today who earns average wages over his or her career would experience a benefit reduction of less than 1 percent. An individual who is 25 today and earns average wages would face a benefit reduction of less than 9 percent. (The benefit reductions are larger for those who are younger today because the reductions phase in gradually.) The payroll tax increases also would be modest. Today's 25-year-old average wage-earner would face a payroll tax increase equal to less than 0.3 percent of his or her lifetime wages.

In addition to these benefit reductions and payroll tax increases, the plan contains a series of improvements in Social Security's financial protections for particularly vulnerable beneficiaries, such as workers with low lifetime earnings, widows and widowers, disabled workers, and young survivors of deceased workers. The Diamond-Orszag plan demonstrates that it is not necessary to replace part of Social Security with individual accounts—which would bring a new and serious set of problems—to restore long-term, sustainable solvency to this valuable program.

2. Superlative Consumer Price Index

Many government benefit programs (including Social Security) and various provisions of the tax code (including the personal exemption, standard deduction, and the marginal tax bracket ranges) are indexed each year to inflation. Research has shown that the index used to adjust these amounts each year, the Consumer Price Index (CPI), slightly overstates inflation. The consequence is that revenues are lower and benefit payments higher than they would be if a more accurate index were used.

The Bureau of Labor Statistics has now developed a "superlative" CPI that measures inflation more accurately than the traditional CPI does.

Using the improved index in the future would reduce measured inflation by an estimated two-tenths of 1 percent per year. Applying the more accurate index to both benefit programs and the tax code would reduce the deficit by tens of billions of dollars a year. Over time, the positive effects on deficit reduction would become very substantial.

3. The Rate of Growth in Health Care Costs

Among changes in Medicare should be the elimination of excessive subsidies to private health plans such as HMOs. Under the recently enacted prescription drug legislation, HMOs will be paid approximately 25 percent more to serve Medicare beneficiaries than it costs the regular Medicare program to provide equivalent services. Unwarranted subsidies of this nature essentially constitute an unacceptable form of corporate welfare. Subsidies that Medicare provides to teaching hospitals also have been found to be larger than is necessary and can be reduced. In addition, Medicare should use its purchasing power to lower the amounts it pays for prescription drugs and certain other items such as durable medical equipment. Finally, given the gravity of our long-term fiscal problems, Medicare premiums may need to be raised. Lower-income beneficiaries and state governments should be shielded from such premium increases.

Medicare and Medicaid costs will rise rapidly, however, even with changes such as these. Making further progress in moderating expenditure growth entails moderating health care cost growth *systemwide*—that is, in the public and private sectors alike. To reduce cost growth substantially in Medicare and Medicaid without similarly restraining expenditure growth in the private health care sector would entail requiring poor, old, and disabled people to pay excessive amounts to use covered health care services, denying them coverage altogether for some important services, making significant categories of poor, old, and disabled people ineligible for these programs and thereby increasing the ranks of the uninsured, or instituting cost-control measures that lower the costs of public-sector programs primarily by shifting costs to the private sector.

The United States spends considerably more on health care than other industrialized nations, without corresponding increases in health care quality and coverage. Achieving change in the structure of the U.S. health care system is a daunting task. It may prove critical, however, to efforts to maintain a federal government that provides adequate levels of service in other areas. (See also Chapter 9, by Ron Pollack.)

4. Defense, Agriculture, and Other Budget Savings

Savings also can be sought in some other areas. Work by various defense analysts, including Lawrence Korb—a leading defense analyst who served as a former assistant secretary in the Pentagon during the Reagan administration—suggests that significant savings can be achieved in the Defense Department without reducing national security. Farm price supports and related agricultural subsidies are another target for savings, as are certain business subsidies sometimes referred to as "corporate welfare" that can distort economic activity and do not benefit the overall economy.

5. Tax Reforms

Restoring fiscal discipline will require raising substantial revenue. Closing the projected budget deficit largely or entirely through program cuts is implausible; the public will not stand for cuts in basic benefits and services of the depth that would be required. Relying largely or entirely on budget cuts also would be undesirable, as the steep cuts that would result could lead to outcomes such as increased poverty, more Americans without health insurance, further deterioration of the nation's physical infrastructure, and weaker environmental and health and safety protections.

Revenue-raising measures can help reduce the budget deficit and thereby increase national saving. As a result, carefully designed revenue increases can have a beneficial long-term effect on the economy. Just as deficit-financed tax cuts can *reduce* long-term growth, so can well-designed revenue increases that shrink deficits *enhance* long-term growth.

This raises several questions. If a pay-as-you-go-rule is instituted under which the cost of extending the recent tax cuts must be offset—as we recommend—which tax cuts should be extended and which jettisoned? And how can we raise additional revenue as part of a long-term deficit reduction plan? Here are some guidelines for revenue measures that warrant consideration.

- *Reform rather than repeal the estate tax.* The 2001 tax-cut legislation eliminates the estate tax in 2010. A sound way to retain tens of billions of dollars of badly needed revenue would be to preserve the estate tax but only for estates with assets above $3 million or so ($6 million for a couple). Such an estate tax would apply only to the estates of about five decedents of every 1,000—or approximately 10,000 estates out of the more than two million people who die each year. (Another option is to replace the estate tax with an inheritance tax, which would contain exemptions for inheritances up to some level, such as $1 million per heir.)

- *Cancel the income tax cuts not yet in effect, which overwhelmingly benefit high-income households.* In addition, once the economy has recovered, either discontinue certain income-tax cuts already in effect or allow them to expire, particularly tax cuts that are costly and provide benefits disproportionately to affluent households (such as upper-bracket rate cuts and the reductions in tax rates for dividends and capital gains).

- *Close corporate loopholes and broaden the tax base.* Broadening the tax base would generate additional revenue without increasing tax rates. It also could improve economic efficiency by lessening the degree to which investment and other economic decisions are distorted by differential tax treatments for otherwise similar types of activities. For example, the corporate tax code provides subsidies, through special depreciation schedules and other measures, to the mining, timber, and oil and gas industries. Many of the tax-subsidized activities are environmentally detrimental. Removing unwarranted subsidies such as these could both raise revenue and protect the environment. Corporations also are able to reduce their tax liabilities through "corporate inversions," under which they move their official headquarters to foreign tax havens. While policymakers have adopted some restrictions on corporate inversions, more stringent rules are needed to prevent such tax avoidance.

- *Ensure that the temporary business tax cuts enacted as part of the 2002 stimulus legislation are not extended.* These provisions were intended to spur business investment during the recession, not to serve as a permanent subsidy. They should expire when the economy recovers, just as the temporary program of federal unemployment benefits has.

- *Reform the Alternative Minimum Tax (AMT) in a deficit-neutral manner.* The AMT was originally designed to collect taxes on higher-income filers who aggressively sheltered much of their income but is on course to extend to an ever-growing number of taxpayers over time. Without changes, more than 30 million filers will have to pay the AMT by 2010, up sharply from the three million taxpayers who are subject to the AMT today. The AMT could be redesigned in a deficit-neutral manner so it accomplishes its original goal without burdening ever-growing numbers of middle-income filers. This could be done by freeing most middle-income filers from the AMT, while making it more robust and effective with regard to very-high-income filers, who largely escape the AMT today.

- *Improve IRS enforcement.* The IRS lacks sufficient resources to enforce tax obligations effectively, and many taxpayers do not pay the taxes they owe. Providing the IRS with the resources it needs to collect taxes that people owe would cost approximately $2 billion a year and could boost revenues by roughly $30 billion a year.

- *Increase "sin" taxes.* The excise tax on cigarettes raises the price of cigarettes and discourages smoking; an increase in this tax would help cut smoking, particularly among teenagers, who are more sensitive to the price of cigarettes. Similarly, taxes that raise the price of alcohol discourage drinking, even among heavy drinkers. Raising the excise taxes on alcohol and tobacco products could promote better health but would be regressive. To offset the regressivity, such tax increases could be coupled with progressive tax reductions, such as improvements in the Earned Income Tax Credit or the low-income component of the Child Tax Credit.

- *Reinstitute a luxury tax.* At times in the past, the United States has levied a luxury tax on the purchase of such items as yachts, private airplanes, and items such as very expensive automobiles and jewelry. Reinstitution of such a levy could be considered.

- *Another possibility is to introduce a value-added tax (VAT) in the United States to help reduce long-term budget deficits.* Most developed nations and all members of the European Union impose a VAT. A broad-based VAT (one that excludes only small businesses, education, religion, and health care) would generate revenue equal to about one-half of 1 percent of GDP for each 1 percentage point of the tax. By itself, a VAT would be regressive, so it would need to be accompanied by other tax-code changes to maintain the overall progressivity of the code.

6. Addressing Priority Needs

A portion of the savings from the measures just outlined should be devoted to meeting critical needs. The list of competing demands (and competing interest groups) far exceeds what can be afforded, however, so only high-priority initiatives would be able to be funded. Many desirable proposals and program initiatives will not "make the cut."

Determining the highest priorities for new resources lies beyond the scope of this chapter, but the following are among the areas that represent strong candidates for priority designation.

- *Increase international assistance.* Roughly three billion people across the globe live on $2 a day or less. More than one billion people live on $1 a day or less. Targeted investments—for example, in fighting AIDS, malaria, tuberculosis, and other global health problems and in adequately funding the Millenium Challenge Account initiative that targets aid to low-income countries—could reap large rewards. Yet the United States spends only about 0.6 percent of the federal budget on international development and humanitarian assistance, well below its historical average and much smaller as a share of the economy than other industrialized nations.

- *Reduce substantially the ranks of the uninsured.* It's untenable that 44 million people in the United States lack health insurance and that, in the typical (or median) state, the income cut-off for working-poor parents to qualify for public health insurance through Medicaid is only 71 percent of the poverty line, or $10,840 a year for a family of three (in 2003). Expanding Medicaid and the State Children's Health Insurance Program, and establishing a counter-cyclical matching formula for Medicaid so the federal share of

Medicaid costs increases during recessions, would be a good first step.

- *Boost child care assistance for low- and moderate-income working families.* Only about one in seven children in low- and moderate-income families that meet the federal eligibility criteria for child care assistance received such assistance in 2000. Inadequate assistance can limit participation in the work force. It also can lead to young children being placed in low-quality care that can hinder their educational development. In this vein, expansions and improvements in early childhood education, Head Start, and Early Head Start would represent sound investments.

- *Reduce child poverty and related problems of hunger and homelessness.* Child poverty—affecting one in every six children—remains substantially higher in the United States than in Canada or Western Europe. In addition, the number of households seeking emergency food assistance continues to rise, and nearly five million low-income households face what HUD terms "worst case housing needs." These households pay more than 50 percent of their income for housing, live in severely substandard housing, or both. The need for these households to pay such large percentages of their small incomes for housing can leave them with insufficient funds for other necessities such as food and can push some families into homelessness.

- *Enhance retirement security.* Many households are not accumulating sufficient assets to finance a dignified retirement and pay for the long-term care they may need. Instead of continuing to increase the amounts that high-income households can save in tax-subsidized accounts, policymakers should expand an existing tax credit that can help modest-income families save for retirement and make the credit (known as the Saver's Credit) refundable—that is, make it available to workers who earn too little to owe federal income tax. Policymakers also should encourage the spread of pension plans in which workers are automatically enrolled (unless they object) and should seek to enhance financial literacy.

- *Improve higher education.* In recent years as state budgets have come under increasing pressure, funding for state colleges and universities has been scaled back. Tuition has risen, often sharply. There also has been a slow deterioration in the quality of public higher education. With roughly three-quarters of college students enrolled at public institutions, the implications are serious for both students and the economy. Significant additional resources, including increased resources for financial aid to low-income students, are necessary. The federal government also should simplify the process of applying for financial aid to make the process less intimidating for low-income households.

The United States has lost its fiscal bearings. The tax cuts enacted under the current administration will reduce long-term growth, exacerbate income inequality, and impose an unfair burden on our children and grandchildren. Rather than continuing to provoke a fiscal crisis, policymakers should seek a "grand bargain" in which pay-as-you-go budget rules are reinstated, revenue increases instituted, and the large entitlements for older Americans reformed.

Chapter Seven

Corporate Accountability:
Bolster the SEC and Litigation

Joel Seligman*

Promote corporate accountability by creating SEC self-funding and strengthening private litigation to deter fraud and excessive executive compensation.

I. The Problem

Rarely is corporate accountability a topic of national political concern. In 1932, after the stock market crash of 1929, reform of stock exchange practices clearly was. In 2004, after the slow motion burst of the 1990s stock market bubble, corporate governance reform again is likely to stay on the national political agenda.

Superficially there are parallels between the crash of 1929 and the millennium bubble burst. Both were preceded by long, accelerating bull markets (the "Roaring Twenties"; the 13-fold increase in the Dow Jones Industrial Average from 875 at year end 1981 to 11,497 at year end 1999). Late in both bull markets, there were self-confident assertions that the old rules no longer applied to the "New Economy" of the 1920s or the dot-com boom of the 1990s.

Both bull markets collapsed brutally with subsequent investigations depicting a broad canvass of fraud. Between September 1, 1929, and July 1, 1932, the value of all stocks listed on the New York Stock Exchange (NYSE) shrank from a total of nearly $90 billion to just under $16 billion—a loss of 83 percent. Later congressional investigations revealed stock market pools, fraudulent foreign bond sales, "preferred" stockholder lists of insiders, bribed journalists who "touted" securities, and stock market manipulation.

By late summer 2002 it seemed as if securities regulation had swung full circle to where it had been at the conclusion of the 1920s. Multi-billion

---

* *JOEL SELIGMAN is the Dean and Ethan A. H. Shepley University Professor at Washington University School of Law. He is the author or co-author of numerous books on legal issues related to securities and corporations, including the 11-volume treatise co-authored with the late Louis Loss,* Securities Regulation.

dollar financial scandals involving Enron and WorldCom bracketed the period between November 2001 and July 2002. On July 23, 2002, the Dow Jones Industrial Average closed at 7,702, after a seemingly unending series of major audit failures involving companies also including Global Crossing, Tyco and Adelphia. Between 1997 and 2001 the number of earnings restatements grew each year from 116 in 1997, to 158 in 1998, 234 in 1999, 258 in 2000, and 305 in 2001.

In March 2002 Arthur Andersen was criminally indicted for shredding documents related to Enron, the first indictment of a Big Five accounting firm. After Andersen was convicted of obstruction of justice in June 2002, the firm ceased practicing before the Securities and Exchange Commission (SEC).

In April 2002 New York Attorney General Eliot Spitzer reached a tentative settlement with Merrill Lynch, after earlier that month obtaining a court order requiring Merrill Lynch to make disclosures to investors regarding its relationships with investment banks. Spitzer had alleged that Merrill's investment analysts were not independent and in some instances engaged in fraud. By December 2002 ten brokerage firms had agreed to pay $1.4 billion to resolve charges related to their research analysts filed by the New York Attorney General, the SEC, the New York Stock Exchange, and the National Association of Securities Dealers.

Shortly later the New York Stock Exchange Corporate Accountability and Listing Standards Committee, "in the aftermath of the 'meltdown' of significant companies due to failures of diligence, ethics, and controls," recommended a broad set of corporate governance reforms to the NYSE Board of Directors, which generally adopted the recommendations and proposed them to the SEC for approval.

In all, between March 2000 and July 2002, the Wilshire Total Market Index declined over $7 trillion (or 42 percent), from $17.25 trillion on March 24, 2000, to $10.03 trillion on July 18, 2002.

Subsequently, in 2003, former SEC Chairmen Richard Breeden and Arthur Levitt would bemoan a widespread "ethical erosion" in mutual fund sales to 95 million U.S. investors by which

- Investors are misled into buying funds based on past performance, even where that record actually may be very poor.

- Investors are left in the dark about the level of most fees, and about the effect that fees, expenses, sales loads and trading costs have on their actual investment returns.

- Most shockingly, fund management in many instances offered pricing and trading prerogatives to hedge funds and other large investors, with some sponsors indirectly sharing in the profits from improper trading practices. Apparently, $80 billion in annual fees is enough to induce a bad case of ethical myopia.

But there was supposed to have been a crucial difference between corporate governance in the 1920s and the 1990s. Between 1933 and 1940 Congress enacted six federal securities laws and created the SEC. During and immediately after the New Deal period, the SEC earned the reputation as one of the most ably administered federal independent regulatory agencies, principally because of the competence of the Commission's staff, the agency role in restoring confidence in the safety of securities investment in the 1935-1937 period, its 1937–1938 reorganization of the NYSE's governance, and enforcement of the geographic integration and corporate simplification provisions of the Public Utility Holding Company Act.

Why did the SEC seemingly perform so poorly in the late 1990s? Four pivotal factors converged.

First, the Commission was woefully underfunded. During the first Bush administration, 1989–1993, the Commission budget grew from $142.6 million to $253.2 million, an average of 19 percent per year; its staff grew from 2,604 positions to 3,083 or an average of 4.6 percent per year. Growth during Arthur Levitt's 1993–2001 chairmanship was considerably slower. Between 1993 and 2000 the SEC budget grew from $253.2 million to $382.4 million or an average of 6 percent per year. Staff positions grew from 2,940 to 3,235 or an average of 1.4 percent per year. During the 1990s bull market, virtually every significant measure of securities activity grew far faster. Between 1993 and 2000, for example, the dollar value of securities filed for registration swelled from $868 billion to $2.3 trillion, an average increase of 24 percent per year; the number of underwritten securities more than doubled in the shorter period of 1993 to 1999 (increasing from 6,443 to 13,923).

After the 1994 congressional elections turned control of Congress to the Republicans, budget appropriations for the Commission became particularly difficult. Between 1995 and 1998, not one new staff position was added to the SEC.

Only in the 1999 budget did Congress add 62 positions and $36 million to the SEC appropriation. In retrospect it is clear that the 1999 increase was too little, too late. As early as 1998, the *Wall Street Journal* was publishing articles with headlines such as "SEC Turnover Rate Leaves Agency Scrambling in Fight against Fraud." Or as a May 1998 *Smart Money* magazine article put it: "Ten Things the SEC Won't Tell You: Number 1: 'We're Overwhelmed.'" That year, in a move unprecedented at the Commission, a growing number of the staff began to explore unionization as a response to increased uncompensated extra hours, known as "donated time," and low pay. By a greater than two to one vote, unionization was approved in 2000 for 1,800 non-management SEC lawyers, accountants, and support workers. This symbolized a low point in staff morale, largely a response to the inadequate budgets approved by Congress and the inability of the Clinton administration to effectively address a growing problem that persisted year after year.

Perhaps most significant about the growing imbalance in staff relative to its workload was that it tended to undermine such core functions of the Commission as review of corporate issuer annual reports by the Division of Corporation Finance more severely than it reduced the effectiveness of the Commission to pursue new initiatives. An October 2002 staff report of the Senate Governmental Affairs Committee found that in 2001 the Division of Corporation Finance was able to complete a full review of only 2,280 of 14,600 Form 10-K annual reports filed by public companies, roughly 16 percent, far short of the Division's stated goal to review every company's annual report at least once every three years. "Of more than 17,300 public companies [including a separate list of mutual funds and investment companies], approximately 9200, or 53 percent, have not had their Forms 10-K reviewed in the past three years." Enron, then the most notorious example of staff neglect, had last received a partial review of its Form 10-K annual report in 1997 and had been last subject to a full review in 1991.

Second, the 1990s witnessed a diminution in the effectiveness of private federal securities litigation as a deterrent to fraud. The class action is the key to private securities litigation. Beginning with a $5.3 million settlement in 1963 in a Securities Act case, the device had grown dramatically in frequency of use and size of settlement or award, reaching an apogee late in the 1980s.

In 1994 the Supreme Court implicitly sided with those who sought to limit the federal securities class action in its 5-4 decision in *Central Bank of Denver, N.A. v. First Interstate Bank of Denver, N.A.* The narrow majority ruled that a private plaintiff could not maintain an "aiding and abetting" lawsuit under Rule 10b-5 against parties who knowingly provided substantial assistance to a securities fraud such as an accountant or an attorney. Aiding and abetting liability had an equivocal reputation in private securities litigation. On the one hand, many lawsuits were only brought because of the resources or "deep pockets" of accountants or attorneys alleged to have substantially assisted the primary law violator; from the perspective of accountants and attorneys, the motivation of this litigation was often their wealth rather than the misconduct of a corporation that engaged in fraud. On the other hand, precisely because accountants and attorneys risked legal liability, they had a powerful motivation to work to prevent corporations from engaging in fraud. Given this long-accepted deterrent aspect—and the virtual unanimity of lower court precedent since 1966 implying a private cause of action for aiding and abetting in §10(b) and Rule 10b-5 claims—the *Central Bank* decision came as a shock. In a dissent joined by three other Justices, Justice Stevens wrote, "[I]n *hundreds* of judicial and administrative proceedings in every circuit in the federal system, the courts and the SEC have concluded that aiders and abettors are subject to liability under §10(b) and Rule 10b-5."

After the Republican congressional takeover in 1994, a movement to curb private securities litigation took on a heightened fervor. Following a tortuous enactment process, including President Clinton's first unsuccessful veto, the Private Securities Litigation Reform Act (PSLRA) was adopted late in 1995. The Act included amendments to the Securities Act of 1933 and to the Securities Exchange Act of 1934 that required, among many other provisions:

- In general, all discovery and other proceedings under the Act were stayed during the pendency of any motion to dismiss "unless the court finds ... that particularized discovery is necessary to preserve evidence or to prevent undue prejudice to any party."

- Under the Securities Exchange Act, Congress adopted new and potentially far-reaching pleading requirements.

Inspired, in part, by this Act, the federal circuits have dismissed a significant proportion of federal securities class actions on the basis of the complaint filed (usually before discovery of documents or deposition of witnesses). An empirical study of motions to dismiss under the PSLRA between 1996 and 2001 found that the Ninth Circuit (which includes California) granted motions to dismiss 61 percent of the time; the Second Circuit (which includes New York), 37 percent of the time.

Third, state corporate law, which operates concurrently with the SEC, establishes fiduciary duties to preclude corporate director and officer negligence, impermissible conflicts of interest, and excessive corporate payments. State corporate law, however, has been erratic in preventing extravagant corporate compensation payments. In 2000, the Delaware Supreme Court declined to allow a particularly important complaint to proceed to trial. Michael Ovitz, president of Walt Disney Company, was paid approximately $140 million at the conclusion of an unsuccessful 14-month period with board of director processes described by the Delaware Supreme Court as "casual, if not sloppy and perfunctory." Only in 2003, after Enron and an amended complaint, did the Delaware Chancery Court revive the possibility of a trial on the merits of what was then labeled the *Walt Disney* case. These decisions have occurred simultaneous with a dramatic increase in the ratio of the compensation of the corporate CEO to that of the average corporate blue collar employee. In 1980 this ratio was 42 to 1; by 1990 it had grown to at least 120 to 1; by 2000 it was estimated to be at least 475 to 1.

Fourth, the integrity of corporate financial statements also deteriorated during the 1990s. The Financial Accounting Standards Board (FASB), for example, was forced under congressional pressure to back down from a proposal to recognize the expensing of stock options. Auditing of corporate financial statements simultaneously went from the core of what public accounting firms did to being a loss leader for more profitable management consulting services. In 1981 only 13 percent of the Big Five accounting firms' total revenues had been generated by management consulting. By 1999 management consulting has grown to 51 percent with audit service revenue down to 30 percent. This created a stark conflict of interest for accounting firms. The SEC, fearful that auditors' objectivity in performing audits would be diminished if they were competing for consulting income, proposed tougher conflict of interest standards to reduce the ability of auditors from receiving income for providing information technology and for providing internal audit activities. After the presidential election of 2000, the SEC temporized on both issues, permitting an outside auditor to conduct up to 40 percent of internal audits while auditing the firm (equivalent to a batter calling balls and strikes) and to frequently design financial information systems for audit clients.

Within one year these cumulative bases of the deterioration of corporate accountability standards abruptly caught up with the White House, Congress, and the SEC with a year of scandals, beginning with Enron's billion dollar earnings restatement in November 2001. In July 2002, after WorldCom announced a multi-billion dollar restatement of its financial reports, Congress, by a 99-0 vote in the Senate and a 423-3 vote in the House, enacted the Sarbanes-Oxley Act.

The most consequential provisions of the Sarbanes-Oxley Act addressed auditing. Title 1 created a new Public Company Accounting Oversight Board, soon reduced to the acronym, PCAOB.

A battle that SEC Chair Arthur Levitt had partially lost in November 2000 to ban certain audit firm conflicts of interest was largely won in §201(g) of Sarbanes-Oxley, which prohibits nine specified types of non-audit services. Separately the Sarbanes-Oxley Act also addressed audit committees, providing in §301 that the audit committee is required to be comprised entirely of independent directors and be authorized to engage independent counsel and other advisors.

Finally, in what was among the most unexpected consequences of the final frenzied Sarbanes-Oxley Act enactment process, §804 of the Act generally lengthened the statute of limitations for private lawsuits to two years after discovery of the facts constituting a securities law violation and five years after the violation from the earlier one- and three-year limitations.

II. Solutions

Short-Term Initiatives

The Sarbanes-Oxley Act represents the most important federal securities law since the New Deal. Potentially it may make a significant improvement in the quality of corporate financial statements. Nonetheless, the Act leaves unaddressed several key issues of corporate accountability that a sympathetic Congress could solve in the near term.

The Act does not address a fundamental cause of the late 1990s breakdown in the corporate review function of the SEC—namely, an agency substantially underfinanced by Congress with a staff inadequate to fully perform its core functions. After periods of crisis, such as the one leading up to enactment of Sarbanes-Oxley, Congress and the President have been willing to make dramatic adjustments to the SEC's budget. A better approach to boom–bust budgeting for the SEC (and perhaps other independent regulatory agencies) is agency self-funding such as that which has long operated at the most effective independent agency, the Federal Reserve Board.

Section 109 of the Sarbanes-Oxley Act establishes a form of self-funding for the newly established PCAOB as well as the earlier established FASB. Both, it bears stressing, are not independent regulatory agencies but private organizations. The PCAOB is expressly subject to SEC oversight for rulemaking and PCAOB board members are appointed by the Commission. Under §109(b), the PCAOB prepares an annual budget that is approved by the Commission. The income to pay for the PCAOB and the FASB is largely derived from annual accounting fees that are to be equitably allocated among issuers.

The SEC already has in place an effective fee collection mechanism which in 2000 and 2001 generated over $2 billion each year. In 2002, the agency collected more than $1 billion. Each of these year's collections exceeded the most ambitious SEC budget proposals for 2003 and 2004. If they did not, fee levels could be adjusted. So a movement to self-funding does not raise questions of feasibility.

There are persuasive arguments why this new approach is preferable. SEC budgeting in the post–World War II period has, in at least two very significant periods, been overwhelmed by market surges. During the early 1950s bull market, the Commission declined from its New Deal high of 1,678 employees in 1941 to 667 employees in 1955. In the 1990s, the decline of staff effectiveness occurred coincident with booming stock market prices. In both periods this was followed by a serious increase in fraud and subsequently by large staff increases.

SEC self-funding would likely reduce the extremes that have been evident in the applicable OMB–congressional process and to some extent depoliticize budgeting.

A difficult question is neither feasibility nor need, but accountability. Who would watch the guardians? For the Federal Reserve Board, Congress has two accountability mechanisms. First, there is an annual independent audit of the financial statement of the Board (as well as each Federal Reserve bank). Second, Congress retains its general oversight and legislative powers with respect to the Board.

The Federal Reserve Board's self-funding has been the key to its historic high level of performance, its professionalism and its ability to withstand political pressures. The alternative approach would require the Fed to seek annual budget approval from Congress, a step that most observers believe would severely compromise its vaunted independence.

As with the Fed, the SEC should be empowered to specify assessment levels on an annual or semiannual basis. Fees should solely be intended to achieve cost recovery, including, however, a contingent reserve to even out assessment volatility. The SEC should be required to file an annual audited financial statement with Congress, which could be the basis of oversight hearings. Congress, in any event, would retain its general oversight powers and ability to amend, add to, or rescind federal securities legislation.

A significant practical advantage of the Fed approach to SEC budgeting would be to avoid the periodic atrophy of SEC staff during boom economies. Just as it has historically been regarded as essential to insulate the Federal Reserve Board from political pressures to protect its independent judgment on questions of monetary policy, it is also wise to insulate the SEC from staff size declines during market surges. The need for budgetary independence is similar, but not identical. History has taught us that a fundamental threat to support for an independent SEC is a surging stock market. Both Congress and the president are most likely to be supportive during periods when investor protection and fraud enforcement are more emphasized. An independent budgetary process would be more effective in adjusting the size of the SEC staff to the agency's regulatory needs during the good times, which ironically are when the SEC is more vulnerable to lack of budgetary support.

Private securities litigation should simultaneously be strengthened as a means to reduce securities fraud. There are significant risks that a private litigation system that is ineffective in deterring fraud will lead to more fraud (such as we saw in the late 1990s), encourage less effective audits, and reduce investor confidence in securities markets. These risks, though real, should not be exaggerated. The SEC, the Department of Justice, and state securities administrators also play significant roles in fraud deterrence.

At the least a new approach must more effectively address both the need for and cost of pretrial discovery. No matter how desirable the objective of investor protection, the time and length of pretrial discovery in pre-1995 securities class actions was among its least attractive features. There are a number of different approaches that various federal courts have taken here. These include mandatory mediation or arbitration and limiting the number of depositions in various types of litigation. The challenge in federal securities litigation is that effective discovery often requires the review of a substantial number of documents. It is very difficult to predict in advance how many documents will be involved.

The approach of the 1995 Act to the challenges of pretrial discovery was akin to a sledgehammer. Rather than attempt to limit the number of documents or to make more efficient depositions by such means as video conferencing, the Act simply cuts off most discovery. It would be far preferable to allow Federal District Court judges greater discretion to establish the amount of permissible discovery rather than continue the post-1995 Act system in which cases appear to be too frequently dismissed on a pretrial motion. Giving judges greater discretion would increase the likelihood that meritorious cases would be tried before a jury. In other fields this would appear to be the predictable result of litigation. In securities law today, it would be a heroic achievement. Virtually no post-1995 private class action has actually been decided at trial. Almost every case has been settled or dismissed before trial.

Could greater judicial discretion coexist with the Private Securities Litigation Reform Act of 1995? It could, but only if the Private Securities Litigation Reform Act was significantly amended. Congress should take steps to amend the 1995 Act's automatic discovery stay and pleading requirements in favor of a return to the pre-1995 standards and greater discretion for the federal judiciary.

Congress also should address fundamental substantive weaknesses in corporate litigation. The theoretical approach of the initial Securities Act of 1933 was to emphasize the joint responsibility of specified corporate officers and directors, securities underwriters, and "experts" such as accountants as the key technique to discourage fraud. Each can be held liable for securities fraud in a registration statement when a corporation issues a security. The courts extended this concept of joint responsibility to all other types of securities fraud by implying aiding and abetting liability under Rule 10b-5 of the Securities Exchange Act of 1934. When accountants, attorneys, or brokers who provided substantial assistance to a primary violation of law could be held liable, they had a powerful incentive to discourage fraud before it occurred. The Supreme Court's 1994 *Central Bank* decision significantly weakened this system. The single most important substantive step Congress could take today to vitalize corporate accountability would be to restore aiding and abetting liability in private securities litigation. This would revitalize a crucial balance that was lost in the system after the *Central Bank* case.

Long-Term Proposals

As a broader approach to corporate accountability, Congress should enact a new federal cause of action under the Securities Exchange Act to provide a remedy for excessive executive compensation. State law in theory provides such a remedy in its waste doctrine, but as the *Walt Disney* case illustrates, state judicial results have been erratic. During the 1960s when Congress was troubled by the application of the state law waste doctrine to mutual fund advisory fees, Congress added §36(b) to the federal Investment Company Act to provide a federal remedy for excessive fees. A similar approach should be taken to executive compensation. This would not be a wholesale preemption of state law but rather a new federal standard in an area where state law has not consistently been effective. This is why the federal securities laws selectively preempted state corporate law in the 1930s. It would be the most effective means to address the excesses in stock option grants and executive compensation generally.

This proposal—and earlier ones—focus on litigation that deters misconduct rather than on corporate governance mechanisms such as the duties of the board of directors. Proposals to address the board, including proposals currently before the SEC to allow direct outside shareholder nomination of directors under specified circumstances, potentially also can strengthen corporate accountability but they are likely to be secondary in significance. Few investigative reports of recent corporate dysfunction were more sobering than that prepared by Richard Breeden, a former SEC

Chair acting as Corporate Monitor, in his review of MCI, the successor to
WorldCom. A poster child for 1990s dysfunction with overall investor losses of $200 billion, Worldcom in many respects had a board that followed
corporate base practices, with at least 80 percent of its members, for example, being independent of corporate management. It nonetheless was a case
study in board ineffectuality. Only when boards consistently believe they
have something to lose from quiescence are they likely to be an effective
check on self-interested or non-law compliant senior management.

A key lesson of the recent past is that laws or reform mean little in the
realm of corporate governance unless there is a general belief that they will
be enforced.

DOMESTIC AFFAIRS:

TOWARD A FAIRER AMERICA

Out of the Quagmire: A Human Investment Strategy for Federal Education Policy

RICHARD F. ELMORE*

Redraft the failed No Child Left Behind Act to increase access of all students—particularly low-income, minority students—to high-level academic work, and invest in the human capital infrastructure for teachers and schools that will promote this access.

I. The Problem

In the next five years, the U.S. education system will face a number of challenges unlike any the country has faced before. The demographics of the youth population have changed dramatically. An increasing proportion of the school-age population will be children of color, children for whom English is not their home language, or children coming from low-income families. These children and their families are no longer staying in the inner cities but they are increasingly moving into suburban and outlying communities that have previously been homogeneously white and middle class. The problems and opportunities that accompany diversity of all kinds—race, class, culture, and ethnicity—will become increasingly visible in schools across a broader range of communities.

Education is the primary route into economic self-sufficiency in the United States. The strongest predictor of a person's income is the number of years of schooling that person has accumulated—the best predictor of the number of years of schooling a young person will acquire is presently that person's race and income. There is a steep earnings penalty for failing to complete high school, and those who fail to complete high school are a group of disproportionately poor children and children of color. The structure of the U.S. labor market is becoming increasingly bi-modal:

* **RICHARD F. ELMORE** *is the Gregory Anrig Professor of Educational Leadership at the Graduate School of Education, Harvard University. His research and teaching focus on accountability issues in education and on the improvement of teaching and learning in public schools.*

Low-skill service jobs are increasing; traditional, well-paid blue collar jobs are declining; jobs that require repetitive, routine work are declining; jobs that require non-repetitive, non-routine problem-solving skills are increasing. Other things being equal, as the youth population becomes poorer, more minority, and less English-speaking, the gap in income and quality of life between those for whom schooling is taken for granted as an accoutrement of class and those for whom it is a hard-won accomplishment will increase. But as inequality of access and attainment in education increases, the capacity of the economy to produce jobs that are competitive in a global economy declines, and the total wealth available to society declines.

Most industrialized countries figured out this powerful relationship between access to education and the wealth of society immediately after World War II, and set about creating national education systems that were comprehensive in their reach—expanding access to schooling as broadly as possible—and that set relatively high expectations for the level of academic content students would be expected to master at the so-called basic level, namely the level at which mandatory attendance ceased and students were given increased choice over what to do. As a consequence, most industrialized countries have better educated workforces, less inequality of access to learning, and less inequality of income than the United States.

America chose a different path. The resilient practice of racial discrimination in access to schooling made it at first impossible and later extremely difficult to have any sort of "national" policy toward education in the United States following World War II. When the federal government finally did enter the field in the late 1950s through the mid-1960s, it did so with heavy deference to the states' "traditional" role as primary providers of elementary and secondary education. In reality, states were never the primary providers of elementary and secondary education, despite their formal constitutional authority; localities were. The federal government chose to treat state and local educational agencies as franchisees for national policy—funneling money through a complex system of grants-in-aid to state and local agencies and charging them with fidelity to federal regulation. National policy toward education in the United States has become synonymous with what might be called "regulatory federalism."

Not surprisingly, this system has had mixed results. States and localities have grown dependent on federal funding, even though it constitutes less than 10 percent of their expenditures, and are therefore unlikely to challenge federal policies, even when they are manifestly ineffective and mis-guided. The federal government, on the other hand, has become com-pletely dependent on states and localities for the implementation of national priorities, even when the interests of states and localities are man-ifestly at odds with national goals.

In this regime of regulatory federalism, "national" policy is synony-mous with "federal" grants and regulation directed at state and local agen-cies. But this is not a necessary conclusion. The federal government does not blink at setting national priorities for research and development in education through its research funding agencies in the Department of Education and the National Science Foundation. One might argue with the priorities set by these agencies, but they are relatively clear and they are distinct from—and one hopes complementary with—the research priori-ties of private philanthropies and other governmental agencies. Public and private institutions compete for research funds and produce results with minimal federal regulation. Likewise, the federal government has long had explicitly national policies toward student financial aid in higher educa-tion, first through the GI bill and later through grant and loan programs designed to increase access. One might argue with the adequacy and dis-tribution of these funds, but they are distributed in a way that reflects national priorities with a minimum federal regulation. So it is not a fore-gone conclusion that "national" policy and priorities in education can only be expressed through regulatory federalism.

The rationale offered for regulatory federalism as a national education strategy is that the federal government can only reach children in schools by regulating the behavior of state and local agencies, which is the educa-tional equivalent of Willy Sutton's famous response to the question of why he robbed banks. So why does the federal government intervene in educa-tion by regulating schools? "Because that's where the kids are." Further, advocates argue, the federal government has a special interest in the welfare of poor children and children of color, given the history of racial discrimi-nation in the country and in our schools. Regulatory federalism is seen by its advocates as an expression of the federal government's unique role in guaranteeing, or as least encouraging, equal opportunity for children whose interests are likely to be overlooked by state and local agencies.

This view of the federal role in education sounds plausible, even enlightened, as long as one stays at the level of political rhetoric...but not when you descend to the level of the institutional realities of how education policy actually gets made. For the past decade and a half, the major locus of education reform has been the states, not the federal government. The federal government has, in fact, been struggling, not very successfully, to position itself in some productive relationship to education reform through the past several national administrations. But given the massive increase in state activity around educational reform directed at equalizing access to high-quality teaching and learning, it's far from clear that the federal government any longer has a real comparative advantage in serving or protecting the interests of poor and minority children. Nor is it clear that the federal government has any comparative advantage in the design and implementation of accountability systems for schools, which is the centerpiece of education reform.

Indeed, the accountability movement started in the states. The major innovations in policy around accountability, and the substantial problems those innovations raised for schools, were being addressed primarily in relations between states and localities. Largely without the aid of the federal government, states found ways to collaborate in sharing experience in the design and implementation of accountability systems through voluntary, collaborative institutions. In other words, there were substantial institutional advantages to keeping education reform and accountability a primarily state matter, leaving the federal government to struggle with its own identity crisis.

But it is politics, not rational design, that determines public policy and intergovernmental relations. The Bush administration saw an opportunity to position itself politically by—of all things—dramatically increasing the regulatory role of the federal government in state and local decisions about the design and implementation of accountability systems. Congressional Democrats, who were looking for a way to position themselves on the issue, agreed to cooperate—a decision they later lived to regret. On one level it is cosmically ironic that a nominally conservative administration, ideologically allergic to federal governmental intervention, would sponsor the single greatest intrusion of the federal government into state and local education policymaking in the history of the country. On the level of *real politique*, however, the rationale for the Bush administration's move is much clearer. Politics, like nature, abhors a vacuum. The federal government was largely disengaged from the major educational reform movement afoot in the country. It was only a matter of time before some clever politician running for federal office would figure out how to capitalize on the movement and hijack it for political ends. In the face of political opportunity, ideology is expendable. There is a kind of breathtaking audacity to this kind of expediency. Breathtaking, that is, if you don't have to live with the consequences. The Bush administration's education reform agenda probably spells the end of regulatory federalism in national education policy.

The Quagmire of No Child Left Behind

No Child Left Behind (NCLB) is the Bush administration's revision of the long-standing Title I program of the Elementary and Secondary Education Act. The process by which the law was passed was unique in the history of federal education policy. The law was assembled by a small group of insiders in White House and Congress with minimum consultation with experts or educational interest groups. There was no shortage of prior research and expert advice available on the issues raised by the law, most of it raising serious questions about the law's fundamental premises; neither the White House nor the Congress chose to ask for or use this advice.

NCLB essentially federalizes accountability policy in education. For the prior 15 years, the states had been engaged in a steady, massive movement toward a new approach to educational accountability—a focus on the student performance—which was initiated in the late-1980s by the National Governors' Association under the leadership of then-governor of Arkansas, Bill Clinton. States would set standards for the level of learning expected of students at various grade-levels in various content areas and develop measures of student performance consistent with those standards. Schools and school systems would be charged with developing the curricula and teaching strategies consistent with those standards and outcome measures. State and local agencies would oversee school performance and devise various kinds of sanctions and supports that would lead schools to improve their performance.

The idea was initially not much more sophisticated than this. Yet in a relatively short period of time—less than ten years—almost all states had developed some version of this model of performance-based accountability. The variation among states was considerable. Some states set very high standards and chose very high-level tests—Vermont and Maryland, for example—but set relatively low stakes for schools and students, on the theory that everyone would learn over time how to move schools in the direction of high-level work. Other states—Texas and Florida, for example—set relatively low standards and used relatively low-level tests, on the theory that as schools became accustomed to operating under perform-ance-based accountability, the standards and tests could be adjusted upward. Some states—Kentucky and Vermont, for example—focused pri-marily on schools as the unit of accountability, putting less focus on stu-dents. Other states—New York and Massachusetts, for example—set rela-tively challenging high school graduation standards, putting high stakes on students, with relatively less emphasis on schools. As more and more states adopted performance-based accountability systems, they began to discover the assets and liabilities of various approaches and to make adjustments in their policies based on their impact on schools and students. The consid-erable variation among states in the design of accountability systems, it is important to note, was an accurate reflection of the lack of fundamental knowledge about how to improve schools. States were involved in a com-plex learning process about how to manage their role in accountability.

NCLB has curtailed this learning process. It essentially collapses the wide diversity of designs in state accountability policies into a single model. States receiving Title I funding (no state has yet declined the money, although some have considered it) are required to construct accountability systems that meet a specific set of parameters. They must test all students annually. They are required to set standards for each grade level and to create indices of annual yearly progress (AYP) by which the per-formance of schools and certain demographic groups of students will be judged. States retain some discretion around where to set the standards and how to judge AYP, but the U.S. Department of Education must approve these decisions. An individual school's AYP is determined both by its aver-age performance and by the performance of specific groups of students (poor students, African American students, Latino students, limited English proficient students, special education students, etc.) and schools can fail to meet the AYP requirement if they fail to meet the performance improve-ment for any single group of students. States are required to set AYP improvement targets for schools. States and local school systems are required to administer increasing levels of sanctions to schools that fail to meet these targets, and to provide parents in those schools with the option of moving their children to other schools.

While the basic accountability structure of NCLB is tighter than any previous federal education policy, the Bush administration argues that it is "flexible" in making adaptations to the general requirements of the law for specific states. The overall effect of the law, however, is to narrow the range of permissible accountability policies at the state level, and, therefore, to narrow the range of possible learning about the potential benefits and adverse effects of performance-based accountability systems. Because the Bush administration has staked considerable political capital on that position, it is, not surprisingly, quite uninquisitive about the possible short-comings of the law.

The fundamental strategic error embodied in NCLB is the belief that federal policymakers can understand enough about how to improve schools to prescribe what is essentially a single accountability model for all states and localities. The logic here is political, and has little or nothing to do with knowledge about the actual process by which schools improve. NCLB does not exist because there is font of knowledge in Washington about how to improve schools. In fact, Washington is the *very last* place one would go for an answer to this question. NCLB exists because the President and his policy advisers saw an opportunity to hijack a powerful reform movement and federalize it for their own political benefit. Congressional Democrats were either too dim, or too compliant, to figure what was happening. In any event, the logic of regulatory federalism has a certain lava-like inevitability about it. If you create regulatory authority at one level of government over another, other things being equal, politicians will look for opportunities to expand that regulatory authority for their own political benefit. This opportunity was simply too juicy for the Bush administration to pass up.

There are a number of fundamental flaws in NCLB that stem directly from the hubris of regulatory federalism. First, there is a tendency for per-formance-based accountability policies to drift into over-reliance on tests as the most important measure of student learning and to attribute false precision to test results. For testing is accountability on the cheap. Tests are both relatively inexpensive to administer compared with other school improvement mechanisms and also have an air of authority, whether they are accurate or not. So policymakers who prescribe testing on a large scale look to their constituents like they are "doing something" about the prob-lems of schools.

In fact, the evidence is that tests, as they are currently constructed, are not very reliable measures of either individual student performance or of school performance. Empirical studies indicate a widespread misclassification of schools in accountability systems based solely on the unreliability of the tests. The fact that tests are less-than-perfect measures of performance is *not* an argument against using tests to make judgments about student and school performance. It *is* an argument for being careful and deliberate about using test scores as a single measure of performance and using them as the only basis for making judgments on an annual basis. The annual testing requirement in NCLB has pushed many states and localities toward less useful tests focused on lower-level knowledge and skills, merely because these tests are cheaper and easier to administer and score. Tests of higher-level knowledge and skill are more expensive to develop, administer, and score. States that used higher-level tests prior to NCLB did not administer them annually because they chose deliberately to get better information about higher-level learning. This choice is now not available to states and localities under NCLB.

The second major flaw of the law revolves around a basic problem of regulatory theory that drafters overlooked. An effective regulatory system is one that identifies an optimal number of "cases" for enforcement based on the objective of the regulatory agency, the degree of difficulty of compliance, and, most importantly, the resources available to the regulatory agency for enforcement. In order to be credible, a regulatory agency has to focus on a discrete number of cases that fall within this zone of optimal enforcement. Because of the specificity of the AYP requirements under NCLB, school systems are classifying, conservatively speaking, anywhere from 30 percent to 70 percent of their schools as underperforming and therefore subject to corrective action under the law. State and local administrators are candid in their admission that they have no idea how respond to this level of demand for corrective action. Even more absurdly, parents in schools under corrective action have the option under the law to choose to move their children to other, higher-performing schools. When the number of schools under corrective action reaches a certain proportion, the available places in other schools become increasingly scarce, creating a logistical nightmare for schools and districts. The U.S. Department of Education, which essentially has no capacity to respond to anything at the state and local level, insists, with the indifference that can only come from ignorance, that the law is binding.

So NCLB has essentially created a regulatory nightmare that no one can figure out how to solve. Conspiracy theorists in the educational community allege that the Bush administration has hatched this plot intentionally, as an effort to discredit public schooling in general, leading ultimately to the privatization of public education. A more likely explanation is that federal officials simply don't know what they are doing. States and localities, however, have chosen, out of fear of losing Title I money, to pretend that the Feds actually do know what they are doing and to grumble to each other about the absurdity of the policy. Meanwhile, since no one who is actually responsible for running schools is confronting the Feds with the absurdity of the situation, they are behaving as if nothing is wrong. This situation reminds me of a saying often heard in the period immediately before the collapse of the former Soviet Union, "We pretend to work. They pretend to pay us."

What is remarkable about this situation is that NCLB has actually made it *more difficult* for local school systems to create strategies for the improvement for low-performing schools. The demanding work of school improvement requires levels of knowledge and an intensity of focus that are not widely distributed in school systems. When a policy results in the identification of more schools for corrective action than a district can reasonably handle, it encourages districts to engage in superficial compliance with the law rather than thoughtful, strategic improvement. This is the situation most urban school systems find themselves in at the moment.

A third major flaw with NCLB, and the most serious by far, is its deliberate under-investment in the knowledge and skill of teachers and school administrators. Stripped to its bare elements, NCLB is essentially a compliance-based policy. The underlying theory in compliance-based policies that the people in the organizations you are trying to influence with policy basically know what to do to comply with the policy, but for some reason they aren't doing it. There are some problems—teaching reading to early elementary students, for example—about which we do know a great deal, and the essential problem is getting the knowledge into the heads and hands of teachers in classrooms. So the problem here ultimately isn't that we don't know what to do, but rather how to get teachers involved in the

development of their own skill and knowledge in ways that improve reading on a large scale. This requires improving the administrative and organizational capacity of school leaders, as well as the knowledge and skill of
teachers. So the idea that you can "improve" schools by banging harder on
the people who work in them is, on its face, absurd.

Accountability and improvement in schools is essentially a process of
developing, mobilizing, and focusing the skill and knowledge of teachers
and administrators on problems that are worth solving. Low-performing
schools exist, not because people in schools know what to do and are
deliberately choosing not to use their knowledge, but because they don't
know what to do; they are trying to solve extremely difficult and complex
problems of teaching and learning when they themselves need support in
learning what to do.

NCLB largely punts on the question of how to improve the knowledge and skill of practitioners who are charged with school improvement.
It sets in place a requirement that all teachers will be "qualified" by a certain date, but doesn't acknowledge the organizational and economic conditions that determine the adequacy of supply of teachers. Nor does the
law speak directly to the fact that most learning related to school improvement has to occur inside schools, after "qualified" teachers are hired. The
level of problems that schools are being asked to address are beyond the
level of knowledge possessed by even the most "highly qualified" teachers.
So the requirement for qualified teachers is another example of an idea
that seems plausible in Washington because no one there actually has to
solve the problem, and no one in Washington actually knows how to solve
the problem. The job of NCLB is to create problems for other people to
solve, regardless of whether the knowledge exists to solve them.

NCLB has become a quagmire. The basic design flaws in the law are
evident in its implementation. The logic behind the law is essentially political, not substantive. The driving purpose behind the law is to position the
President as an activist on education reform, not to address the underlying
problems of school improvement and accountability at the base of education reform. As states and localities try to respond to the requirements of
the law, its essential logic becomes more evident.

But NCLB has become a quagmire for another, more troubling, reason. Regulatory federalism in education policy is an attractive nuisance.
Under any circumstances, in any political administration, regulatory feder-

alism creates very strong incentives for political decision makers to get involved in issues in which they have no comparative advantage, no special expertise, and no effective governmental capacity to influence outcomes. At this writing, the U.S. Department of Education is trying to find its way out of an regulatory morass created by NCLB's requirement that immigrant children be tested in English during their first year in school, whether they have any prior familiarity with English or not. What's interesting about this issue is not so much what the "right" answer is to the real problem of when to include non-English-speaking children in assessments for accountability purposes. What's more interesting about the issue, in this context, is that federal bureaucrats and policymakers, including the U.S. Secretary of Education, have to pretend that they do know something about how to solve this problem into order to preserve their position in the regulatory hierarchy. The political imperatives of regulatory federalism require the U.S. Department of Education to intervene in issues of practice and policy at the state and local level, regardless of whether it has any comparative advantage, expertise, or capacity in those issues. If the department doesn't intervene, it forfeits its authority to regulate. If it does intervene, it is creating another set of problems that stem from its own incapacity to manage outcomes at other levels of government.

That we should be discovering the limits of regulatory federalism in a nominally conservative Republican administration has a comic, juicy irony to it. But the lesson of this quagmire should not escape visionaries in any future progressive administration. The lava-like logic of regulatory federalism is not a partisan phenomenon; it is the product of powerful political and institutional incentives that are deeply embedded in the American political system and much more powerful than partisan, ideological politics. Governmental agencies will, unless checked by countervailing political forces, always move to maximize their interests and positions relative to other institutions; politicians will always abet this tendency of governmental institutions to maximize their interests when doing so enhances their electoral success.

II. Solutions

The federal government has gotten drawn into No Child Left Behind largely by inertia. Title I set the basic ground rules for federal involvement in elementary and secondary education in 1965: The federal government would work out its national priorities through grants-in-aid and regulations directed at state and local educational agencies. This confounding of "national" priorities with "federal" grants and regulations imposed on states and localities leads inevitably to the quagmire of NCLB. While the federal government is using its relatively modest financial leverage to coerce states and localities into complying with a badly designed law, states and localities cannot muster the collective will to assert political counter-pressure—and there is no plausible alternative to existing policy that opponents of NCLB can use as an alternative rallying point.

The federal government has over-extended its reach in NCLB by adopting a theory of intergovernmental relations that it cannot possibly adhere to over the long run. There is no way that the federal government can oversee and regulate the accountability systems of 50 states and more than 16,000 local jurisdictions without reducing them to a caricature of what they were originally designed to do. Least of all can the federal government perform this task in a period of general downsizing of government. The whole project of federal control embedded in NCLB is absurd and should be gracefully abandoned.

Since Title I has become the equivalent of the federal rivers and harbors act for schools—a major source of political credit to federal officials and pork for states and localities—it is unlikely that the Congress or any new president would chose to abandon it. The most graceful retreat would be to retreat to a more sophisticated version of where federal policy was before NCLB. The law ought to be amended to remove requirements for annual testing, disaggregation of test results by subgroup except for descriptive purposes, and the current annual yearly progress requirements. The teacher quality requirements should be eliminated in favor of a national initiative for the improvement of teaching. The federal government should then focus its accountability policies in Title I in a few select areas that clearly express its comparative advantage: It should help establish and partially fund a national, non-federal organization that conducts and publishes annual reviews of state accountability systems, both their design and their results. Over time, this organization should, with the full cooperation of states, develop standards against which states can evaluate the adequacy of their accountability systems. Those states that receive the highest ratings under this system should receive a premium under Title I. Those states that receive the lowest ratings should receive a penalty. In keeping with the underlying theory of performance-based accountability, the federal government should focus on *the results* achieved by state accountability systems, and not be drawn, as it currently is, into regulating the content and design of those systems.

Then the federal government should shift its attention to developing a national policy on the improvement of human skill and knowledge in the education sector. What the federal government does have a comparative advantage in is (a) the development and dissemination of knowledge and skill focused on the deeply rooted problems of school improvement and (b) issues of access for all students to high-quality academic work.

It is clear that localities are under-investing in professional development for teachers and administrators and in the development of new pedagogical and administrative practices associated with school improvement. Why? Local school systems have to run schools. Their focus is primarily on getting new knowledge into classrooms, not on the development of new knowledge, the benefits of which accrue to everyone, not just to themselves. States are generally weak players in accountability and improvement because they are removed from the immediate demands of making schools work. Their comparative advantage is to sustain and develop knowledge about how accountability systems can be made to serve the purposes of school improvement. The political discipline required to keep policymakers focused on sustaining continuous improvement in accountability systems is more than enough for states to focus on. At the national level, as most industrialized countries discovered after World War II, the compelling interest is keeping the country focused on the development of human talent. Since the benefits of large-scale investments in human talent accrue powerfully to society as a whole, and are not necessarily visible to individual parents, students, and local or state officials, it is important for the national government to keep policy focused on this level of aggregation.

A human investment strategy for education would have an explicit strategic focus: to increase access of all students, particularly low-income, minority students, to high-level academic work, and to invest in the human capital infrastructure for schools that will promote this access. While the determination of specific projects should be political, in the best sense of that term—with Washington seeking advice from experts and citizens before spending scarce dollars—it is possible to provide some examples of the kind of issues that represent a particularly national focus.

1. *A national system of indicators of access, performance, and quality in education.* From its origins, the comparative advantage of federal agencies in education has been the collection, analysis, and dissemination of data on schooling in America. This tradition role can be made to serve powerful national, strategic purposes, much as the current system of employment and economic indicators focuses attention on pressing economic issues. This system would develop national indicators of course-taking, attainment, and access patterns among the school-aged population, with special attention to populations at risk of failure. The system would develop state-by-state samples, in addition to a national sample, so that the federal government could report on the progress of individual states in increasing access and quality through their accountability policy. The system would be designed, like the national Bureau of Labor Statistics (BLS), to be insulated from direct political pressure, and it would be required, like BLS, to report on leading indicators of access, quality, and performance on a prescribed, periodic basis.

2. *A national initiative on teacher quality.* The Congress should charge the U.S. Department of Education with the responsibility for mounting a ten-year initiative to improve the quality of teaching in American schools. The initiative could involve: (a) competitive grants to states and localities that are willing to develop strategies for recruitment, training, career development, and retention of teachers; (b) research and development projects designed to test the longitudinal effects on student learning of teachers prepared in different types of programs; (c) research and development at the state and local level focused on the relationship between various strategies of professional development for teachers in their workplaces and student performance; (d) research and development projects, conducted jointly with states and localities, on alternative career structures for teachers designed to increase retention and reward increased skill and knowledge.

3. *Early literacy and English language learners.* It is apparent now in most school systems with large numbers of children whose first language is not English that our best-development reading and writing programs are often ineffective with children who come to

school not literate in their home language. These children don't get access to our best reading and program programs because they haven't developed literacy skills in any language. The consequence is they lag their peers in development and often don't catch up. Many schools and school systems are struggling with this issue; few have access to the knowledge and practice necessary to address it.

4. *Secondary literacy.* We have relatively powerful models of literacy instruction for children in the early grades. But the number and sophistication of models decreases as students rise in grade structure. When students arrive in the ninth or tenth grade reading at the fifth grade level or below, how can we hold their new teachers and schools accountable for their academic performance? On the other hand, we want schools to take responsibility for the learning of these students, and not to assign responsibility completely to other grade levels. Hence, secondary schools need literacy models that are of equivalent power and range to those available to elementary schools. These models should address not only the cognitive processes of learning to read and write, but also the motivational issues that arise when students have experienced repeated failures through successive grade levels.

5. *High-level content for all students.* A central problem of schooling in America, which doesn't exist to the same degree in other industrialized countries, is that access to high-level, challenging content in schools is determined by parents and educators based on ill-defined ideas about "talent" or "aptitude." Most industrialized countries design and organize academic content on the assumption that all students should have access to the highest levels of content at the "basic" level (typically up to eighth or ninth grade), and then students should be able to specialize above that level. In America, the idea that all students should have access to a demanding curriculum is considered to be controversial. The persistence of the ideas of talent and aptitude essentially relieves teachers of the responsibility for adapting their pedagogy to a broader array of students. Accountability systems increase stress on academic achievement for all students, pressing schools to develop and use curriculum and pedagogy that is more challenging than most stu-

dents are accustomed to. Right now the development of these curricula is largely in the hands of commercial textbook publishers,
who operate in markets that are, by definition, not designed to
challenge prevailing assumptions about what students can do.
There is a compelling case for national efforts to develop and test
a diverse range of curriculum materials and teaching strategies that
speak to the issue of access to high levels of content for all students.

6. *Internationalizing the curriculum.* American students are the least literate students in world about other languages and cultures. For the
most part, local curriculum decisions are driven by local preferences, and therefore are often not geared to preparation of students
for participation in a global society and economy. In most industrialized countries, all students leave the "basic" education level
with a working knowledge of at least one foreign language, often
more than one, and with a familiarity with the culture associated
with that language. Schools create learning experiences for students that involve travel to those countries as a way of illustrating
the importance of being able to operate in a culture other than
one's own. American schools, however, are largely disconnected
from global society. The incentives to focus on this dimension of
schooling are largely at the national level, not at the state or local
level.

7. *Recruitment and introduction to high-demand careers.* A common complaint of critics of the U.S. education system is that knowledge of
high-demand careers in the economy often doesn't get translated
into education and experience for students at the pre-collegiate
level, so students have no idea why it is important for them to do
well in school or how school connects to their later life chances.
Most career familiarization courses in schools are undemanding
academically and directed at students who are not on the college-
bound track. There are few incentives for states and localities to
address these issues because, if they are conscious of their connections to the world of work at all, their focus is typically regional
and local, rather than national and international. There is a powerful rationale for sophisticated work involving the analysis of actu-

al practices of people in high-demand careers and the conversion
of that knowledge into curriculum and teaching strategies in
schools.

These seven illustrative examples characterize a more explicitly
"national" education policy directed at increasing access to high levels of
learning for all students and developing the human skill and knowledge
necessary to make good on that promise. To make these ideas work would
require a different kind of institutional structure at the federal level, involving much less traditional bureaucratic organization and much more use of
partnerships with private organizations and state and local agencies. It
would also require a different view of the role of elected and appointed
officials in educational policymaking. The role of elected officials would be
to exercise influence over that direction of longer-term development projects connected to high-priority national needs, rather than focusing on the
details of regulatory policy and funding cycles. The analogy would be that
congressional and executive officials would operate more as they currently do in the national intelligence, medical research and development, and
science policy areas, than as they do in public works and environmental
policy areas.

The key strategic issue is to move as quickly as possible out of the
quagmire of regulatory federalism into a more flexible, agile, and influential role of leading the national debate on access, quality, and performance
in schools.

CHAPTER NINE

Making Health Care Affordable and Accessible

RON POLLACK[*]

Base public health coverage on need rather than family status (covering one-half of currently uninsured people), provide for reinsurance support so small businesses can cover their employees, and give states federal support to experiment with expanded health coverage—three steps that would move us much closer to affordable health coverage for all.

I. The Problem

Major changes in America's health care system are creating turmoil and causing profound problems for a growing portion of the American public. These changes are making health care increasingly unaffordable and inaccessible for working and middle-income families—and, of course, for those with lower incomes. As a result, concerns about our nation's health care system—which, years ago, were largely altruistic worries about a relatively small and disadvantaged segment of the population—have become a matter of self-interest for most Americans.

Evidence of these problems abounds. In September 2003, for example, the U.S. Census Bureau released its annual survey of the number of people who were without health coverage in the previous year. According to the Census Bureau, 2.4 million people were added to the ranks of the uninsured between 2001 and 2002—the largest increase in a decade. In total, 43.6 million Americans, *more than the cumulative population of 24 states and the District of Columbia*, were uninsured in 2002.

As large as this figure is, however, it significantly understates the number of Americans who have been affected by a lack of health care coverage. This is because the Census Bureau's annual survey is designed to calculate the number of people who were uninsured throughout the entire year; it is not designed to indicate how many were without health cover-

---

[*] **RON POLLACK** *is the Executive Director of Families USA, the national organization for health care consumers.*

age during portions of the year. The number of people uninsured during all *or part* of the year is considerably larger.

To assess that larger impact, Families USA, on behalf of a prestigious group of ideologically diverse organizations, prepared a report, based on Census Bureau data, which calculated how many Americans were without health coverage *for all or a portion of* 2001–2002. The report, released by the Robert Wood Johnson Foundation, found that 74.7 million people under 65 years of age—almost one-third of the non-elderly population—were uninsured at some point during the past two years. The vast majority were uninsured for lengthy periods of time: almost two-thirds were without health coverage for at least six months; over half were uninsured for at least nine months; and almost one-quarter had no health coverage throughout the entire two-year period. Four out of five of those who experienced a lack of coverage were in working families.

This large and growing number of people without health coverage is the result of what has aptly been called "a perfect storm." It is caused by the confluence of four factors:

1. Health care costs are rising annually at double-digit rates, making health coverage increasingly unaffordable for individuals, business- es, and government agencies. A combination of skyrocketing pre- scription drug costs, consolidation of hospital systems, the increased availability of expensive technology, increased profits by insurance companies, and the relaxation of managed care approval systems for the receipt of care are all contributing to increasing health care costs. These cost increases are projected to continue over the next several years, if not longer.

2. With the labor market softened because of our nation's weak and job-losing economy, employers are increasingly passing on health costs to their workers. Workers are paying larger amounts in pre- miums, deductibles, and copayments. Health coverage in employ- er-provided health packages is shrinking. And health coverage for the dependents of workers, and especially for retirees, is diminish- ing. As these cost shifts continue, more and more employees are finding health care unaffordable.

3. Unemployment rates are high, as are the numbers of discouraged job-seekers who have temporarily left the workforce. Since most

people receive health coverage through their jobs, the loss of employment means increases in the number of uninsured. Although the vast majority of these laid-off workers are eligible for COBRA coverage through their previous employer, the costs of such coverage are unrealistically high. Under current law, laid-off workers seeking COBRA coverage must pay all of the costs— costs that now average over $3,400 for individual coverage and $9,000 for family coverage, amounts that are simply unaffordable for the vast majority of workers subsisting on modest unemployment insurance checks. As a result, four out of five people eligible for COBRA coverage do not receive it.

4. Virtually all of the states, experiencing fiscal crises, are making significant cutbacks in state-administered public health programs, such as Medicaid and the State Children's Health Insurance Program (SCHIP). Inasmuch as Medicaid is the largest single program expenditure in most states, the vast majority of states are either cutting income eligibility standards for coverage, reducing benefits, and/or increasing low-income beneficiaries' out-of-pocket costs. These changes are undermining the program's counter-cyclical function, which, by design, provides increased assistance in times of greater need.

These four troublesome trends are likely to continue for the foreseeable future, thereby increasing the high numbers of people without health coverage.

Going without health insurance not only causes family insecurity, it also can have irreparable consequences for those affected. The Institute of Medicine estimates that 18,000 people a year die because they were uninsured and did not receive the treatments and care they needed. Uninsured people are less likely to have a usual source of care outside the emergency room; often go without screenings and preventive care; frequently delay or forgo needed medical care; are usually sicker and die earlier than those who have insurance; are likely to become bankrupt if they need significant health care; and are charged much more for health care services than people who have insurance.

But insecurity about America's health care system is not confined to the large and growing number of people who have experienced a lack of health coverage. As health care costs rise, and as businesses pass more of those costs to their workers, more families are becoming *under*-insured. Although estimates of the number of *under*-insured vary widely, ranging up to more than 30 million, it is clear that the resulting economic burdens on family budgets are substantial. As these cost shifts increase and heighten anxiety and insecurity among our nation's families, health benefits are becoming the most contentious aspect of labor-management relations across the country.

Senior citizens are also increasingly insecure about the affordability of health care, even though Medicare has made them the least likely to be uninsured. Although Medicare has been enormously effective in improving the health and longevity of seniors, huge gaps in coverage remain. Among the most important benefits not covered by Medicare are prescription drugs and long-term care. At any given time, approximately one-third of America's seniors have no drug coverage and, over the course of a year, almost one-half have no drug coverage for at least part of the year. Fewer than one out of ten seniors has coverage for long-term care. Yet, prescription medicines and long-term care are extremely expensive.

Today, seniors spend, on average, $2,322 for prescription drugs each year. Approximately 11 percent spend over $5,000 per year. And these costs keep on growing. From January 2002 to January 2003, the average price of the top-50 drugs prescribed for seniors rose by almost three-and-one-half times the rate of inflation. These costs are increasingly unaffordable to the vast majority of seniors who live on fixed incomes that rise, at best, commensurate with inflation. Last year's price increases follow a pattern that has been documented throughout the past decade.

Long-term care is even more expensive. The average annual cost of nursing home care today is almost $60,000. Home care and other long-term care services in the community are less costly but, over time, can easily lead to bankruptcy. Premiums for private long-term care insurance are very high. As long-term care costs mount and if insurance companies continue to have limited success in marketing such coverage to younger and less risky populations, those premiums will keep escalating.

II. Recent Developments

Upon the demise of the health reform initiative in 1993–1994, policymakers and health system stakeholders embarked on two different paths.

The first path—taken mainly by progressive and moderate policymakers and organizations—seeks bipartisan support for incremental improvements that would make health coverage more accessible and affordable. It is based on the premise that comprehensive reform of America's health care system—especially in a single piece of legislation—will be difficult to achieve and, in the foreseeable future, may be a political impossibility.

This bipartisan, incremental path has greater credence today. With increased acrimony and partisanship, big budget deficits, and huge divisions in America's political landscape, let alone the recent ascendancy of conservative leadership in the White House and the Congress, comprehensive health reform appears to be politically unfeasible. Those who chose this incrementalist path have developed a host of proposals, as described more fully below.

The second path—pursued vigorously by special interest groups (especially the insurance and pharmaceutical lobbies), conservative institutions, and the Bush administration—is designed to privatize and undermine public health programs (such as Medicare and Medicaid) and, under the beguiling banner of "choice," to segment private health coverage to the potential detriment of sicker, older, disabled, and moderate income persons. It has led to pending proposals that would convert Medicaid to a block grant, induce seniors to leave Medicare for private health plans, establish tax credits for people purchasing *individual* (rather than group) health plans, and promote medical savings accounts.

Incremental Proposals

The most prominent incremental proposal of the past decade, successfully enacted in President Clinton's second term, has been the expansion of health coverage to millions of children in low-wage working families. Other incremental efforts—including subsidization of health coverage for recently laid-off workers who cannot afford COBRA coverage, improvements in the Medicaid program, and prescription drug coverage for seniors and people with disabilities—remain policy battlegrounds today.

Expanding Children's Health Coverage

In 1997, as part of the Balanced Budget Act, Congress adopted the State Children's Health Insurance Program (SCHIP). The legislation, championed by Senators Orrin Hatch (R-UT) and Edward Kennedy (D-

MA), provided funds to the states so that health coverage could be extended to children in low-wage working families with incomes marginally above the Medicaid program's eligibility standards. As a result of this legislation, the vast majority of states now allows children to receive public health coverage if their family incomes are below 200 percent of the federal poverty level ($31,340 in annual income for a family of three, $37,700 for a family of four).

Children's participation in SCHIP has grown rather steadily since the program's inception, and more than 5 million children participated during the course of the last reporting year. However, according to the most recent Census Bureau report, there still are approximately 8.5 million uninsured children in the United States—and most of them are in families with annual incomes below 200 percent of the federal poverty level. (In 2001–2002, approximately 20.2 million children were uninsured for some portion of that two-year period.) The failure to reach these lower-income children with SCHIP coverage results from several limitations: inadequate federal and state funding commitments to the program; inconsistent outreach and program enrollment systems; and cumbersome, annual re-certification requirements that make it difficult for working families to keep their children enrolled.

Health Coverage for Laid-Off Workers

As more and more workers lost their jobs during the economic downturn and the jobless recovery, concerns about laid-off workers' health coverage grew. Most laid-off workers are eligible for so-called COBRA coverage under either federal or state laws—laws that enable these laid-off workers to continue receiving coverage through their previous employer's health plan. However, to obtain such coverage, unemployed workers are required to pay 102 percent of their past employer's insurance costs for their coverage. As noted, these costs are mostly unaffordable for a worker subsisting on unemployment insurance payments.

The chairman and ranking minority member of the Senate Finance Committee, Senators Chuck Grassley (R-IO) and Max Baucus (D-MT), respectively, have introduced legislation that would subsidize 65 percent of COBRA costs through tax credits for laid-off workers receiving unemployment insurance. It is estimated that this legislation would enable approximately 1.4 million laid-off workers to receive COBRA coverage.

This legislation has not yet been enacted, and a previous attempt by congressional Democrats to secure direct subsidies for 75 percent of COBRA costs was defeated due to opposition from President Bush and congressional Republicans.

Prescription Drug Coverage for Seniors and People with Disabilities

In December 2003, with great fanfare, President Bush signed legislation that constitutes the largest changes in Medicare since that program's inception in 1965. Most notably, the legislation provides prescription drug coverage. It also makes structural changes to the program that are intended to push seniors away from traditional Medicare and into private managed health care plans. Survey data indicate that, as seniors learn more about this legislation, they are increasingly displeased about it—with good reason.

The new prescription drug benefit is both bizarre and meager. When the benefit is implemented in 2006, seniors and people with disabilities wishing to obtain prescription drug coverage under the standard plan will need to pay $35 per month ($420 per year) in a new premium. After an annual $250 deductible (which they will have to pay out-of-pocket), enrollees will receive coverage for their annual pharmaceutical purchases between $250 and $2,250 per year: Enrollees will pay 25 percent of those costs and the new benefit will cover the remaining 75 percent. At this point, the benefit becomes truly strange.

Once an individual's annual drug costs reach $2,250, there is no coverage whatsoever until costs reach $5,100. In Washington-speak, this is euphemistically called a "doughnut hole." Seniors and people with disabilities will be required to pay 100 percent of drug costs in this $2,850 gap—or refrain from obtaining the medicines they need. It is only after an enrollee has paid $4,020 out-of-pocket (the $420 premium, the $250 deductible, $500 in copayments, and $2,850 in the "doughnut hole") that meaningful "catastrophic coverage" kicks in.

The inadequacy of this new drug benefit will grow over time. The legislation requires enrollees to pay larger amounts in premiums, deductibles, and "doughnut hole" gaps each year as the costs of drugs increase. The Congressional Budget Office now projects that, by 2013, the prescription drug premium will have grown from $420 to $696; the annual deductible will have increased from $250 to $445; and the "doughnut hole," initially a $2,850 coverage gap, will have reached $5,066.

The main beneficiaries of this legislation will be the pharmaceutical and insurance industries. The pharmaceutical industry is the biggest winner: Not only will it experience increased drug sales, it will do so without the need to moderate prices. Indeed, the new legislation, at the behest of the pharmaceutical lobby, actually prohibits the Medicare program from bargaining with drug companies to secure lower prices. Moreover, seniors will continue to be prohibited from purchasing cheaper drugs in Canada unless the Secretary of Health and Human Services certifies that such purchases are cheaper and safe—a certification that the Secretary says he will refuse to issue.

Private insurance companies will also receive a huge windfall under the legislation. The insurance companies that serve Medicare beneficiaries—mainly HMOs and other managed care companies—"cherry pick" when they enroll seniors: they seek to enroll the youngest and healthiest seniors, leaving the older, sicker beneficiaries for the traditional Medicare program. Despite the much-lower costs associated with serving a younger, healthier population, those insurance companies will receive a huge windfall of increased federal payments ideologically designed to lure seniors away from traditional Medicare into a much more privatized health coverage system.

Because the new Medicare legislation does much for the pharmaceutical and insurance industries and precious little for America's seniors, there is likely to be a hue and cry to significantly amend this legislation in the near future.

Harmful Proposals Promoted by the Bush Administration and Special Interest Groups

The proposals promoted by the Bush administration, often in concert with key special interest groups (especially the insurance and pharmaceutical industries), would exacerbate the insecurity already felt about America's health care system. Among the key proposals are: converting Medicaid to a block grant program with considerably lower public funds; privatizing Medicare by pushing seniors and people with disabilities out of the traditional Medicare program and into private managed care plans; and supporting a potpourri of proposals that would undermine group health coverage and would segment poorer, older, and sicker people into insurance pools separate from richer, younger, and healthier populations to the detriment of those who need health care the most.

Medicaid Block Grant Proposal

In January 2003, the Bush administration announced a proposal that would significantly alter Medicaid, most notably by (1) eliminating the guarantee that all people eligible and applying for program coverage are entitled to receive it, and (2) converting Medicaid to a block grant. The proposal would have capped federal funding with fewer resources over time, and the inflexible block grant would have made it increasingly difficult for states to serve low-income and uninsured populations during economic downturns.

The proposal offered three enticements to the states to induce their governors to support it:

- *First*, the proposal would have advanced approximately $13 billion in additional Medicaid funds during the first three years, but would have subsequently required the states to repay that amount. More significantly, in later years, the federal "allotments" to the states would have been considerably smaller than the amounts they are projected to receive under current law. The proposal was cynically crafted this way because sitting governors would no doubt have welcomed the upfront money—especially since the repayment of those funds, and the considerably diminished funding thereafter, would have occurred after they left office.

- *Second*, it would have provided new flexibility to the states by eliminating key federal rules affecting Medicaid eligibility, benefit coverage, and limitations in beneficiary cost-sharing. This new flexibility would have cut state spending but would have done so by reducing the number of people enrolled in Medicaid, diminishing health benefits low-income families receive, and increasing low-income beneficiaries' out-of-pocket costs.

- *Third*, and perhaps most enticing to the states, the proposal would have explicitly and significantly reduced the amount of money that states needed to commit to Medicaid. This reduction in state funding, coupled with later-year cuts in federal expenditures, would have cut annual support for Medicaid—in comparison with current law—by 16 percent within the next decade. As a result, millions of low-income families would have lost essential health coverage.

Although this block grant proposal would have caused considerable harm to low-income families, it is clear that states need help sustaining their Medicaid programs. States are experiencing their worst fiscal crisis in history. Since Medicaid constitutes the single largest program expenditure in most state budgets, and since state Medicaid costs, on average, comprise approximately 15 percent of total state spending, it is not surprising that virtually all states are implementing program cuts.

To forestall the need for more program cutbacks, a bipartisan group of moderate senators introduced—and tried to incorporate into the huge tax-cut bill of 2003—legislation that would temporarily increase the federal fund matching rate in Medicaid. The Bush administration opposed this effort, both because it might undermine its block grant proposal and because it would reduce the amount of money available for tax cuts. The temporary increase in the federal matching rate for Medicaid, however, ultimately passed when a number of key senators conditioned their support for the tax package on the inclusion of such fiscal relief to the states. This short-term improvement in federal Medicaid funding expires in June 2004. The administration remains opposed to its extension and is committed to reviving its destructive block grant proposal instead.

Privatizing Medicare

Even though eight out of nine seniors and people with disabilities have enrolled in the traditional Medicare program rather than private health plans, the Bush administration is intent on privatizing Medicare. At the outset of the Medicare debate in 2003, the President proposed to limit prescription drug coverage to those who left traditional Medicare for private health plans, such as HMOs and other managed care organizations. Although this proposal was rejected by congressional leaders in both houses of Congress and both political parties, other proposals toward the same end have been enacted.

Private plans have a very poor record in comparison to the traditional Medicare program. They refuse to serve seniors in rural communities, and a significant number of plans decided to abandon communities deemed inadequately profitable, disrupting care for millions. Although conservatives promote private plans as a means of providing "choices" to Medicare beneficiaries, most private plans, unlike traditional Medicare, establish limitations on the doctors and hospitals seniors can go to without incurring substantial additional costs. Also, unlike the traditional program, private plans "cherry pick"—they seek to enroll only the youngest and healthiest seniors, those who are least likely to need health care services. And, as recent studies make clear, private plans are considerably more cost-ly—and have increased more rapidly in cost—than the traditional Medicare program.

Despite these failures, the most recent Medicare legislation provides substantially new subsidies to private plans so they can lure seniors out of the traditional Medicare program. The additional funding is intended to underwrite enhanced benefit coverage in private plans so those plans can compete with traditional Medicare on an unleveled playing field. Moreover, through a series of experimental programs scheduled for implementation in 2010, the unleveled playing field would be even more tilted in a way that would result in seniors being priced out of traditional Medicare. Over time, these measures will increasingly, and unwisely, convert Medicare to a privatized health care system.

Proposals That Would Fragment Existing Health Coverage

The administration has promoted a series of proposals that would undermine existing group health coverage and segment health care markets to the detriment of sicker and older people. The most notable proposals include:

- *Individual tax credits.* The administration has introduced a proposal that would provide $1,000 in annual tax credits for individuals and $2,000–$3,000 in tax credits for families to help them purchase health coverage on their own. The White House claims that this will help low-income, uninsured people purchase insurance, but—since meaningful coverage costs three to four times as much—it is the functional equivalent of throwing a 10-foot rope to someone in a 40-foot hole. No less troublesome, this proposal would undermine employer-provided health coverage since the tax credits could not be used by employees seeking to pay for health coverage in the workplace. As a result, employers might drop or diminish health coverage, expecting that their employees would secure it on their own.

- *Association Health Plan (AHP) legislation.* AHPs are intended to enable small businesses to band together to purchase health coverage as a group and, therefore, to secure more favorable insurance premiums. Conceptually, such banding together makes good sense. However, the administration's pending legislation would exempt AHPs from state regulation—including rules that prevent discrimination based on health status. This would enable the associations to exclude companies based on health risks. As a result, insurance pools outside of these associations would become sicker and far more expensive: the Congressional Budget Office estimates that this would cause approximately 20 million people to *pay more* for their health care coverage.

- *Medical Savings Accounts (MSAs).* Although there are a variety of MSA-type plans, they generally provide tax benefits to people who select insurance plans that have high deductibles. MSAs, therefore, are attractive to healthier and wealthier people who are least concerned about high-deductible policies and who can obtain larger tax breaks because they are in higher tax brackets. Conversely, these policies are of little or no interest to people with health problems or who live on moderate wages. As a result, MSAs segment insurance markets by separating the healthier and wealthier from the sicker and poorer, thereby resulting in much higher and unaffordable premiums for those who need health care the most.

III. Solutions

The sharp ideological and partisan divisions that exist today will make it very difficult to achieve comprehensive health system reform. However, since health care is becoming increasingly unaffordable and inaccessible, meaningful action should begin as soon as possible. The following are solutions short of universal health care but which (a) would come close and (b) are capable of enactment by 2010.

• ***Improve Public Health Coverage.*** Medicaid and SCHIP are the most important safety-net health programs in America today. Medicaid, by far the program with the largest enrollment, serves approximately 51 million lower-income people, most of whom would be otherwise uninsured. The program, however, does not reach many millions of others who are uninsured and no less needy—typically low-wage workers and the dependents of those workers. This is because Medicaid's current structure creates eligibility standards that resemble a crazy-quilt.

Eligibility for Medicaid varies substantially from one state to another. It also differs quite radically based on family status. In nearly four out of five states, for example, *a child* is eligible for public health coverage (through either Medicaid or SCHIP) if that child's family income is below 200 percent of the federal poverty level. *For parents*, however, the eligibility standards are very different and considerably lower than they are for children: The median income eligibility limit for parents among the 50 states is 71 percent of the federal poverty level—a mere $10,836 in annual income for a family of three. Thus, parents of children eligible for Medicaid or SCHIP are often ineligible for public health coverage.

For *adults who are not parents*—individuals living alone or childless couples—the federal safety net is almost all hole and no webbing. In 43 states, childless adults can literally be penniless and still fail to qualify for Medicaid or any other public health coverage. Thus, contrary to public belief, there are many millions of low-income people—usually low-paid workers in jobs that provide no health care coverage—who are ineligible for safety-net health coverage.

This arbitrary eligibility system needs to be modernized. Eligibility for Medicaid should be made more uniform and should no longer be predicated on family status. Everyone with family income below a specified level—such as 200 percent of the federal poverty level—should be eligible for public health coverage, irrespective of his or her state of residence or family status, especially if he or she cannot obtain health coverage in the workplace. This step alone would reduce the number of uninsured Americans by one-half. An increment toward this goal, introduced by Senators Kennedy and Olympia Snowe (R-ME), would provide health coverage to low-income parents of children eligible for SCHIP or Medicaid coverage. It would enable approximately 7 million currently uninsured parents to gain public health coverage, *and*—in so doing—

would improve children's enrollment in such coverage by allowing them to sign up for health coverage as a family unit.

The public health programs also need to be changed because of the way they discriminate against *legal* immigrants. As a result of legislation adopted less than a decade ago, *legal* immigrants who entered the United States after August 1996 are prohibited from receiving Medicaid or SCHIP coverage for five years. After five years of residence, the law encourages states to count the income of immigrant sponsors as if their income were available to the immigrant family—a fiction that renders the immigrant family ineligible for health coverage due to "too much income." Legislation to repeal such discriminatory denials of health coverage for legal immigrant children and pregnant mothers recently received support from two-thirds of the Senate, but opposition by President Bush and the Republican House leadership has prevented its enactment.

 • **Encourage State Experimentation with Expanded Health Coverage.** Ideological and partisan rancor have resulted in national gridlock on virtually all proposals that would expand health coverage or would make such coverage more affordable. Although most policy makers believe it is important to expand health coverage, consensus about what action to take almost always breaks down as soon as the dialogue shifts to specific proposals. If this impasse is to be broken, it is crucial to find ways that transcend traditional conflicts.

One such potentially unifying proposal would build on our system of federalism. It would encourage, and underwrite, state-by-state experimentation designed to increase health coverage for all, or virtually all, state residents. It would establish coverage goals without specifying the methodology for achieving those goals. Each state could choose to expand public programs and/or to provide subsidies for expanded, private coverage—and the proposal would need to be structured in a way that genuinely encourages states to select from such diverse approaches. This concept was recently recommended by the Institute of Medicine and has received strong support from scholars at ideologically diverse think tanks.

Even though such a proposal would provide states with flexibility in expansion strategies, it would contrast quite significantly from a system of block grants. It would establish national goals for expanded health coverage and would establish specific parameters for state action. As the leading proponents of this approach have indicated, federal rules would need to be established on such matters as

- what constitutes insurance and what should be the level of coverage;

- how much cost-sharing would be permissible, and how should that change for low-income people;

- how would current Medicaid beneficiaries be protected so that they don't lose health coverage;

- what protections would be established to prevent coverage discrimination against people with health problems;

- what approval system should be established before a state qualifies for federal funding of its initiative; and

- what types of data would need to be collected to ensure that the initiative's objectives are being met.

This proposal is different in key respects from a Bush administration initiative that grants "waivers" to states so they can experiment with their Medicaid programs. Most importantly, the Bush "waiver" initiative explicitly *provides no additional money to the states.* As a result, states desiring to expand health coverage are required to do so by decreasing the health coverage of people who have it today—often the poorest of the poor who already participate in Medicaid. The federalist proposal, on the other hand, would be designed to provide significant new resources to the states, and those resources could be calibrated so that states with the greatest coverage improvements receive the largest fiscal assistance. Properly structured and adequately funded, therefore, this proposal would enable states to substantially expand coverage without doing harm to people who are happy with the health coverage they have today.

• ***Provide Reinsurance Assistance for Catastrophic Claims to Small Businesses.*** Four out of five people without health coverage today are in working families. Typically the breadwinners in these families work in small businesses whose owners feel that health benefits are too expensive and volatile—and, therefore, they don't offer health benefits at all. Unless these small businesses receive effective and well-targeted support, it is unrealistic to expect that they will introduce health coverage for their employees.

For small businesses, health costs are likely to be considerably more volatile than the costs experienced by large corporations. A serious illness for even one employee can result in very substantial premium increases for a small business, while larger businesses can absorb those unusual individual claims by spreading the cost risks over a much larger, and generally healthier, workforce. Therefore, this cost volatility is a significant obstacle for any small business.

To extend employer-provided health coverage, it would be reasonable to have a federal back-up system that reinsures the relatively few, but costly, large claims incurred by insurers of small businesses, such as individual health expenses in excess of $50,000. Seventy percent of all health care outlays are consumed by only 10 percent of the population. Such a reinsurance system would not only reduce the volatility of future premium increases, but they would also decrease current premiums that small business owners incur. This federal assistance should be conditioned on companies providing affordable health coverage to *all* their workers.

• *Fix the Glaring Deficiencies in the New Medicare Legislation.* The more seniors and people with disabilities learn about the new Medicare law, the less they like it—and with good reason. The bizarre and skimpy drug benefit package, coupled with the utter lack of efforts to contain skyrocketing pharmaceutical costs, will, over time, make drug purchases *less* affordable than they are today. At the same time, the new legislation—while enormously beneficial to drug manufacturers—will be exceedingly and unnecessarily costly to America's taxpayers. This needs to be changed.

First and foremost, the legislation that prohibits Medicare from bargaining with drug companies on behalf of program beneficiaries must be rescinded. Today the Veteran's Administration bargains on behalf of its constituency for better drug prices, and Medicare should be enabled—indeed, required—to do likewise on behalf of its program beneficiaries.

In Medicare's earliest years, the physician and hospital lobbies were successful in placing similar restrictions on government efforts to restrain unnecessary spending for outpatient and inpatient care. However, as Medicare's costs for physician and hospital care grew, succeeding Congresses established effective cost-containment regimens. All health stakeholders, save for the drug companies, are likely to support a similar change of the cost-containment prohibitions in the new Medicare law—especially seniors and people with disabilities whose drug coverage will rapidly diminish as the program's out-of-pocket requirements escalate.

Second, the drug benefit needs to be enhanced. At a minimum, the huge "doughnut hole" should be reduced, if not eliminated. Such an interruption of coverage does not exist for younger populations, and it made little sense to establish such a huge "no coverage zone" for seniors. By the time the new Medicare benefit is initiated in 2006, approximately half of all program beneficiaries will have drug costs that fall within the "doughnut hole," and many more will fall into that hole in succeeding years.

Third, the special drug subsidy help for low-income program beneficiaries in the new law is inadequate. The most significant low-income subsidies are provided to people with incomes below 135 percent of the federal poverty level ($12,569 in annual income for a person living alone). However, millions of low-income seniors will not receive this subsidy because they fail a very stringent assets test that disqualifies people from such low-income help if they have assets (including life insurance policies, burial allowances, and household effects) that exceed $6,000.

Moreover, the poorest of the poor, those approximately 6 million seniors and people with disabilities who are eligible for both Medicare and Medicaid, will be worse off under the new Medicare legislation than they are today. This is because these so-called dual eligibles, starting in 2006, will receive drug coverage through Medicare that will require higher copayments, and will make fewer drugs available in health plan formularies, than the help they receive through Medicaid today. This should be corrected immediately.

With each passing year, an increasing number of people are finding health care unaffordable and inaccessible. Even if *comprehensive* reform of America's health care system is politically unachievable in today's partisan and fractious environment, it is high time that significant remedial action be taken now. Such action should build on what works today—public programs like Medicare, Medicaid, and SCHIP as well as employer-provided health coverage. And such action should make creative use of our federalist system of governance so that far-reaching improvements can be made on a bipartisan basis. Even in the absence of comprehensive, or universal, reform, such action can move our nation much closer towards health care security.

CHAPTER TEN

Stop Environmental Darwinism:
A Program for a Renewable Economy

CARL POPE*

Restore the universality of the environmental safety net—every power plant modernized, every waterway fishable and swimmable, every chemical plant made secure—and pursue an energy independence that makes America healthier, cleaner and safer.

I. The Problem

Not since the sheets of ice first ground south had there been a biological cornucopia like the one the Europeans seized in North America. The great smallpox epidemics that swept America after Columbus arrived had drastically cut the population of native Americans. Fish, game, and forests had multiplied free of the pressures of hunting, fishing, and Indian fire. (The great white pines the British navy valued for masts in New England actually grew mainly in abandoned Indian cornfields). Settlers arriving in New England could smell the pine trees 150 miles off Cape Cod. Captain John Smith wrote of Chesapeake Bay, "We found . . . that abundance of fish lying so thicke with their heads above the water, as for want of nets we attempted to catch them with a frying pan, but we found it a bad instrument to catch fish with. Neither better fish more plenty or variety had any of us ever seene." Lobsters in Massachusetts were food for indentured servants and oysters on the Chesapeake for slaves.

Yet we squandered much of it. After 1850, two great waves of heedless industrialism swept over the continent like the coming of the glaciers.

The first was powered by steam and hammered by steel. With plow and harrow, ax and engine, buffalo gun and dredge, American settlers laid waste much of that inheritance. Gone were the pineries of the Great Lakes, the great hardwoods of Ohio and Kentucky, the riparian oak forests of California, the shad fishery of the Potomac, the oyster beds of San Francisco Bay, the white pines of northern New England, the Buffalo herds

---

* **CARL POPE** *is Executive Director of the Sierra Club.*

of the Dakotas and Kansas, the chestnut stuffed passenger pigeon flocks of Pennsylvania, the green flash of the Carolina parakeet, and the great blue stemmed grama prairie of Oklahoma.

After 1900, oil, concrete and chemistry drove the destruction. By 1970 Lake Erie was dying and the Cuyahoga River caught on fire. The old growth forests of the Rockies and the Cascades had been devastated, the bottom-land hardwoods of the Mississippi Valley leveled into soybean fields, a dead zone spread into the Gulf of Mexico, and the Everglades was re-plumbed and dying. Most of Minnesota's lakes are contaminated with mercury, the sediments of the Hudson drip PCBs, our eastern forests are blasted by air pollution and acid rain, while the landscaped is dotted with thousands of toxic waste dumps. Slowly nuclear waste makes its way through the soils of Hanford, Washingon toward the Columbia River.

But the American Republic paused, and reconsidered. Each of the great waves of industrial destruction generated a new kind of citizenship to challenge it—the conservation movement of the Progressive era, and the environmental movement of the late twentieth century.

The conservation movement, initiated in the same year that Frederick Jackson Turner declared "the frontier is closed," posed fundamental questions: "Did Americans want to hand on to their children some of that incredible biological and natural wealth and that greeted the early pioneers? Did Americans want their continent to become a second Europe, or did they want to preserve part of it wild?"

President Teddy Roosevelt sounded its great battle cry in his Natural Resources Conference of 1908. Roosevelt used his power to create National Monuments to set aside the Grand Canyon, something local officials in Arizona bitterly denounced. (Later, of course, they put the Grand Canyon on the state's license plates to recognize its economic benefits.) When Congress took away his power to create National Forests, he sprawled on his floor with Gifford Pinchot, the head of the Forest Service, creating 17 million acres of such forests just minutes before the midnight deadline when the law took effect.

The next great wave of citizen action came with the dust-bowl and the Depression. Teddy's second cousin Franklin Roosevelt put hundreds of thousands of Americans to work restoring their landscape with the Civilian Conservation Corps; Secretary of Agriculture Henry Wallace added badly overcut eastern forests to the National Forest System; Tennessee Valley Authority (TVA) began the restoration of the Tennessee Valley's forests and soils.

The petrochemical and nuclear revolution that emerged after the Second World War created a very different kind of devastation—air and and water pollution, toxic waste, radioactive hazards—which in turn spawned a new environmental movement responding with a different set of strategies. It burst like a storm onto the political landscape with Earth Day 1970. Within a few years Congress had passed a series of bold initiatives; the Wilderness Act, the Clean Air Act, the Clean Water Act, the Endangered Species Act, the Resources Conservation and Recovery Act, and the National Environmental Policy Act (NEPA). While the new Environmental Protection Agency was assigned to police industry, citizens were also involved much more directly in ensuring that these agencies were not captured by those they were to regulate. The knowledge and science of government agencies was to be laid out for public scrutiny and debate through the processes of NEPA and the Freedom of Information Act. Now not just federal bureaucrats, but concerned citizens, would be able to act to protect themselves against environmental side effects of modern industrial expansion. No longer was pollution to be an acceptable price of progress.

As we entered the new millenium, environmentalism constituted one of the great civic success stories of twentieth-century America. Air and water pollution were dramatically reduced, and society had committed to finish the job. For the first time since the petrochemical industry emerged in Pennsylvania, the number of acres contaminated by toxic industrial wastes was going down, not up, each year. Concentrations of such chemicals as lead in the blood stream of urban children was down by 93 percent. The hole in the stratospheric ozone layer was healing itself. Sixty percent of the nation's waterways were safe to swim in. And the amount of protected habitat set aside for wildlife was increasing each year, as species like the bald eagle, the gray whale, the brown pelican, the wolf, and the grizzly bear recovered, or were on the verge of recovering, some of their historic populations.

This progress had, for most American, ceased to be controversial, or even an "issue" for political debate. Americans concluded that the environmental progress they had made since 1900 had been good for them, good for their economy, and good for the country. Who could oppose it? Then George W. Bush came along.

II. The Bush Response

Most Americans know that President George Bush is not an environmentalist. Unlike 70 percent of the American public, he can't bring himself to use the e-word to describe himself. (Oddly, Vice President Dick Cheney calls himself "a good environmentalist, even if the Sierra Club may not agree.") But few Americans realize how much Bush has done, in only three years, to break with the national compact on environmental progress and turn the clock back—not years or decades but a full century. People do know that Bush is making Clean Air rules easier on industry, but haven't yet grasped that he wants to quadruple the allowable emissions of mercury into the air. They know Bush is concerned about what he considers excessive regulations, but haven't heard that he has reduced the value the government places on saving a human life through regulation by 38 percent. They've heard complaints about too much drilling, logging, and mining on public parks, refuges, and forests; but don't know that wildlife has only half as much protected habitat today as it did when Bush took office.

It is easy, in this cynical age, to chalk it all up to greed. Bush wants campaign contributions, and polluters write the checks. Americans easily connect these dots—campaign money from the oil industry means a government that sides with oil companies. When timber companies give the Bush campaign an unprecedented $1 million, our national forests are more likely to end up as two-by-fours than refuges for endangered species. When the vice president, the deputy interior secretary, and scores of other government officials have made fortunes working and lobbying for oil, mining, and timber interests prior to their government service—and sometimes during it—few are shocked when official actions happen to profit the friends of political appointees and grease the officials' own future careers.

Yet greed alone cannot explain the depth and breadth of the current assault on the environment. Something of this magnitude can only be accomplished by people in the grip of an ideological fervor. This is what the American people do not know: the Bush administration is full of influential officials who believe—from the bottom of their hearts, not just their wallets—that weaker laws on clean air, less funding to clean up toxic waste dumps, and national parks and forests run for private profit are actually good for the country.

Americans, the Bush team believes, have become soft. They expect too much safety, and a free lunch besides. If people want to hike in the wilderness, they should be willing to pay for it. If people object to the pollution where they live, they can buy an air purifier, or move. And if some children get cancer from old toxic-waste dumps, that is unfortunate but the price of progress.

Most Americans thought we had banished this robber-baron philosophy a long time ago. But it's back, as a modern variant of the Social Darwinism of the late nineteenth century, that again misapplies Darwin's concept of "survival of the fittest" to the social and economic spheres. For Social Darwinists, both nature and society were divided into winners and losers, with the triumph of the winners accorded the inevitability of natural law. In fact, having winners and losers is now once again regarded as not only inevitable, but desirable—it motivates all of us to struggle harder, to survive in a harsh and unforgiving world.

Following these beliefs the administration has managed to break completely with the American environmental tradition which stretched back a full century to Teddy Roosevelt, and which has been embraced since then by Presidents as diverse as Franklin Roosevelt, Dwight Eisenhower, Lyndon Johnson, Richard Nixon, Jimmy Carter, and George H. W. Bush.

One of the administration's first actions was to suspend federal regulations that had prevented companies that broke the law from being rewarded with additional federal contracts. (Halliburton might have lost its pipeline to contracts in Iraq without this earlier change.) When deregulation of electric power cost California electricity users billions of dollars, the Bush administration refused to stop the looting by capping prices. If Enron and others had figured out how to manipulate the electrical grid and charge thousands of dollars for a single kilowatt hour of power, they deserved to be rewarded for their ingenuity. When the Federal Energy Regulatory Commission concluded that, indeed, the shortage and the crisis had been artificially created, it fined the companies only a fraction of what they had made in a single month.

The head of risk management for the administration, Office of Management and Budget's John Graham, ridiculed the concept that before an industrial chemical was released into the environment, a community, or the food supply, it ought to be tested for safety first. America, he had warned, was suffering from "a hypochondria raging among various consumer advocates and public interest groups."

In keeping with this macho attitude, the Bush administration simply abandoned the idea that government should protect innocent people from being hurt by industrialism. Over 16,000 old and dirty power plants, petroleum refineries, chemical factories, and industrial facilities were given permanent exemptions from having to install modern pollution control technologies. Property contaminated with PCBs can now be sold and reused for any purpose—schools, housing—without government oversight. The President allowed his brother, Jeb, the Governor of Florida, to resume injecting untreated waste water into the state's drinking water aquifers. The administration allowed hazardous waste to be "recycled" into fertilizer that could then be used on playgrounds, golf courses, and parks—and then decided to allow such waste-based fertilizers to be used to grow food as well.

Faced with increasing evidence that global warming will massively disrupt the world's weather, devastate low-lying areas and countries, disrupt agriculture and water supplies, and destroy wildife and ecosystems, Bush & Co. alternately insisted that trying to prevent global warming was either premature or too late, but that in either case what we really needed to do was suck it up and get used to the idea.

One of Bush's first actions was to seek the elimination of the new national monuments declared by President Clinton. Yellowstone and Grand Teton National Parks were turned over to the snowmobile industry for winter profits at the expense of park solitude and wildlife. Timber companies were allowed to invade the Giant Sequoia National Monument and log one tree in every ten under the guise of "fire prevention." Sea turtle nesting grounds on Padre Island National Seashore were turned over to oil companies for drilling. Mining companies were allowed to dump hundreds of millions of tons of toxic mining waste on public lands without a permit. The coal industry was allowed to shear off entire mountain tops and dump them into public streams, creeks, and rivers.

Bush has taken to heart the mantra of his admired predecessor, Ronald Reagan, who in a famous malapropism once said that "Facts are stupid things." When the facts are inconsistent or contrary, no matter how well peer reviewed, science is simply bent to meet the needs of politics. The government simply cancelled studies that showed that continuing to encircle dolphins and entangle them in nets was not, in fact, a "dolphin safe" way to catch tuna. When a biologist posted data showing the location of caribou herds near proposed drilling areas, Interior Secretary Gale Norton fired him. When Interior's wildlife biologists sent the Secretary reports whose conclusions she disdained, she simply ordered them rewritten—or rewrote them herself. Distinguished scientists were bounced from National Institutes of Health (NIH) advisory panels overseeing vital federal health research, and replaced by scientists with close ties to the affected industries.

The Bush administration also realized that what citizens didn't know, they couldn't protest. So, under the guise of national security, it cut off public access to information. Websites were stripped of embarrassing information about risks that nuclear power plants or chemical factories posed to surrounding neighborhoods. Attorney General John Ashcroft advised government agencies to seek every reason to reject Freedom of Information Act inquiries, and secrecy became the norm in government agencies.

Next the administration went after the law, the lawyers, and the judges. Government regulations were rewritten to make it more difficult for citizens to step in to enforce the law, or for judges to require public officials to comply with it. The executive branch asked Congress to allow the Department of the Interior to ignore judicial rulings on endangered species. Whole categories of timber sales were exempted from the law. When judges ruled that the Navy was breaking environmental laws, the administration attempted to eliminate judicial review for anything the government did to the oceans.

It also pioneered a new way to manipulate the courts. Here's how it worked: an ally or campaign contributor who didn't like some federal law would take the government to court to block enforcement of the law. Then, rather than defend the law, as the President had taken an oath to do, the administration would come to a sweetheart settlement, often promising never again to enforce it.

The oil industry was the largest funder of the Bush campaign. So it was not surprising when not only did Bush fight the unpopular battle to open up the Arctic National Wildlife Refuge, and the coasts of Florida and California for oil drilling, but he also opened up millions of acres in the mountain west and proposed tens of billions of dollars of new subsidies. Other friends in the coal and nuclear sectors won further billions in the administration's energy proposals. Compared to the oilmen, the timber industry was a small donor. Even so, when the time came for Bush to decide whether the Forest Service would spend its limited fire prevention budget saving small towns that had voted for him, or helping pay for logging projects that benefited his donors, the small towns lost.

III. Solutions

Short-Term Initiatives

Poll after poll has shown that what the American people want and expect from their leaders is progress. They believe that a combination of common sense and American ingenuity will enable the country to solve its environmental dilemmas and enable their children to look forward to a better, not a grimmer world.

Here are ten eminently practicable steps that could, if adopted by the next administration in its first two years in office, transform the nation within twenty years:

1. *Require automakers to make cars, SUVs, and light trucks that go farther on a gallon of gas.* We do not need to wait for an all-hybrid auto fleet, much less the fuel cells of the future, because the "freedom package"—a combination of already available technologies including more efficient engines, smarter transmissions, and sleeker aerodynamics—would enable a Ford Explorer, for example, to get 35 mpg instead of 19, with no loss of roominess or acceleration. Ford, General Motors, and Chrysler have only to offer the option. In twenty years our vehicle fleet could be averaging 40 mpg, reducing the amount of oil we need to drive a mile by 50 percent from current levels, saving four million barrels of oil daily and cutting global-warming emissions from autos in half.

    We should also put a serious tax on fuel inefficiency. The proceeds from an expanded gas-guzzler tax could be used for two purposes: to subsidize the purchase of hybrids or other efficient vehicles, and to help the auto industry build new assembly lines and fabricating plants to replace the outmoded ones on which Detroit can only build inefficient, badly designed SUVs and pickups. Thus we could protect the jobs and economic base of Michigan, Wisconsin, Ohio, and Missouri while encouraging a future in which cars are still made in the United States. The alternative—our current trajectory—is to have the entire industry flee to low-wage Third World nations with low environmental standards.

2. *Reindustrialize America by creating a twenty-first-century energy indus-try.* America's energy policy is a problem desperately scrambling to escape its own obvious solutions. Policy is stuck in the 1920s, when the rapidly industrializing United States was the world's largest exporter of oil. Two generations later, our highest energy priorities are still cheap gasoline and big domestic coal and oil industries. That might make sense for Venezuela, but it is a silly energy policy for a post-industrial society that burns 25 percent of the world's oil but has only 5 percent of its population and 3 percent of its oil reserves.

    We do not have space to list all of the available solutions. The amount of electricity we could generate in 20 years from solar, wind, and other renewables is limited largely by the investments we are willing to devote to the project now. One of the most intriguing proposals comes from a group of labor unions led by the Steelworkers, the Machinists, and the Electrical Workers, called the Apollo Project. It calls for investing $300 billion over ten years into a new energy economy based on innovation and efficiency, and envisions major investments in high-performance buildings, efficient factories, energy-efficient appliances, and better mass transit as well as efficient hybrid vehicles. It should be noted that $300 billion is only a fraction of what America spends in a single year on imported oil, and economic modeling shows that these programs could create three million new manufacturing jobs.

    The Apollo Project sets the right goals and provides industry with financial assistance to achieve them. But if the public is paying the bill, we should also make clear that modernization is not optional. The Apollo Project's investment strategies need to be backed by enforceable standards and mandatory requirements. By

investing in the industries of tomorrow and rebuilding the infrastructure of our cities today, we can turn the "rust belt" into a
global hub for hybrid cars and the hydrogen future.

Besides being necessary, this is a winning political strategy. In
the fall of 2003, a poll by Greenberg Associates showed that the
single most powerful argument a Democratic candidate for president could make for replacing the Bush administration was the
need for a new energy policy to free America from its dependence
on fossil fuels.

3. *Install modern air-pollution-control equipment in old power plants, refiner-*
   ies, and factories. Many states have already done this. California has
   retired all its "grandfathered plants"; Florida makes coal-fired boil-
   ers scrub their emissions. Why should citizens of Arizona and
   Georgia breathe unnecessary and avoidable soot and smog?

   The owners of these dirty old plants have had 30 years to
   clean them up. Now it is time to pull the plug. Legislation proposed by Senator Jim Jeffords (I-Vt.) would require all power
   plants to be cleaned up by the time they are 40 years old, or by
   2014 at the latest. Cleaning up pollution just from the 51 power
   plants that the Clinton administration had already sued would save
   between 4,300 and 7,000 lives a year and prevent between 80,000
   and 120,000 asthma attacks.

4. *Restore the Superfund tax.* Getting the program back up and running—with the polluters rather than their victims paying for it—
   is the first step. There are 1,000 facilities sitting on the list today,
   and probably another 600 that ought to be added over time. If
   Congress restores the Superfund tax, we can get back to cleaning
   up 80 sites a year. In another 20 years we would be free of the
   curse of toxic waste dumps.

5. *Reinstate the environmental protections enjoyed by our national forests,*
   rivers, wetlands, wildlife habitat, and public lands as recently as January
   21, 2001. This one would not even take 20 years—it can be
   accomplished within six months of the next administration taking
   office. Restoring these safeguards will leave us with a core of wild
   country that can act as a repository and nursery for endangered

and threatened species fighting for survival, and as a sanctuary where future Americans can find renewal and inspiration. Our solution is Aldo Leopold's: "To keep every cog and wheel is the first precaution of intelligent tinkering."

6. *Restore rural America.* Right now we are spending $18 billion a year on agricultural subsidies, 70 percent of which go the largest agribusinesses—giants like Cargill and J. G. Boswell. These huge corporate conglomerates use their subsidies to drive family farmers out of business by bidding up the price of land and bankrupting small, integrated farms that combine grain and livestock production. They destroy rural communities and environments with hellish factory feedlots, virtually exempt from environmental laws. At one blow, American taxpayers finance environmental devastation and the destruction of rural communities, health, culture, and property values.

We could get back on the path we started down with the 1995 farm bill. Let's spend the $18 billion in wasteful subsidies in the current farm bill to help small farmers, restore wildlife habitat, clean up rural waterways, and reduce erosion and pesticide use. Rural America would have more jobs, rural families would have better health and more economic security, the quality of our food supply would be enhanced, and the country's air and water would be cleaner and healthier.

7. *Retire Smokey Bear.* Prevent fire in endangered communities, restore it to forest landscapes. If we refocus the Forest Service on protecting communities from fire and invest $2 billion a year to thin trees in Community Protection Zones—the half-mile perimeters around homes or towns that firefighters need to stop wildfires from destroying structures—we should be able to safeguard most communities from fire danger within five years. To prioritize community protection over timber preservation, we can embark on a program of controlled burns and—combined with careful testing—judicious thinning to reverse the damage of 50 years of misguided total fire suppression.

8. *Restore our national patrimony of public lands.* As we make progress on
    protecting communities from fire, we should shift to the next chal-
    lenge: beginning to restore the 75 percent of our national forests
    that have been logged or roaded. We should phase out the Forest
    Service's commercial timber program and begin managing our
    National Forest System exclusively for public benefits like wildlife,
    recreation, and watershed protection.

    We also need to start keeping the promise Congress made to
    use royalties from oil and gas drilling to fund the federal Land and
    Water Conservation Fund. America is not done preserving wild
    places forever as public lands. The public wants them, royalties
    from oil on public lands can pay for them, and then they will be
    ours.

9. *Clean up our waterways.* Finish the job of preventing urban storm-
    water pollution by restoring watershed quality and, where neces-
    sary, separating storm-water and sewage systems. Deal with the
    problem of runoff from farms, feedlots, and logging and develop-
    ment sites. Thousands of beaches are still closed every year because
    of inadequately treated sewage, and 40 percent of our waterways
    are still not safe to swim in. It is time to finish the job the Clean
    Water Act started.

10. *Rejoin the world.* The rest of the planet is waiting for the United
    States to join the coalition of the environmentally willing. Our
    agreement alone could put the Kyoto Protocol into effect. Then
    we need to move ahead and propose a more fundamental system
    to stabilize the global climate. (If the United States adopted the
    first two solutions in this section, we would achieve far more than
    Kyoto demands.)

In addition, we need to rejoin such international initiatives as the proposed convention to reduce emissions of mercury, to protect rain forests,
to stop overfishing, and to preserve biodiversity. On trade policy, we need
to start by fixing the North American Free Trade Agreement (NAFTA),
not by signing new trade agreements that embody all of NAFTA's flaws.
We can get rid of NAFTA's language on investment rights, which allows
foreign companies to sue state and local governments in the United States

and Mexico whenever they enforce their environmental laws against a foreign polluter. Instead, let's require U.S. companies located in Mexico to
meet the same environmental standards they would have to meet in the
United States. General Motors might still decide to locate a new plant in
Guadalajara, but it could no longer do so to reduce its environmental compliance costs.

Long-Term Proposals

The Bush administration and its cohorts have a long-range vision, one
they have used to unite and motivate their hard-right supporters. Just as the
twentieth century saw the pace of environmental progress gradually swell
and increase, they intend for the first decade of the twenty-first century to
reverse 100 years of progress. It is a breathtakingly bold enterprise: not only
to change environmental law but to do so as part of remaking the
American character and returning American society to a no-holds-barred,
winner-take-all Darwinian jungle. We're-all-in-this-alone might as well be
their motto.

If they have that much boldness, why should we have less? The ten
commonsense solutions outlined are only a short-term agenda. Just as
Bush's team did, we need to lay out our long-range vision for the twenty-
first century. That visionary path will require a good deal of collective
dreaming beyond even 2010 that will make our grandchildren proud.

First, leave behind the carbon economy of oil, gas, corrupt Saudi
princes, and Dick Cheney, not only here in the United States but global-
ly. This means having the patience to stay the course in the necessary transition to renewable energy sources while the global climate teeters and
eventually stabilizes. It is probably already too late to avoid some climate
shifts from carbon dioxide loading in the atmosphere, but a shift of two
degrees will be far less damaging than one of ten degrees. The climate will
recover more rapidly from a low fever than a high one.

Moving toward a climatic recovery will require reducing our emissions of greenhouse pollutants, principally carbon dioxide, and by more
than the 22 percent envisaged in Kyoto. We need to tax excessive emissions
of carbon dioxide and, with the payments, ensure that as villages in China
and India electrify they are able to go directly to solar and wind without
passing through a nineteenth-century dependence on coal. The planet can-

not afford a second carbon-based industrial revolution in Asia, Africa, and Latin America—but the nations that reaped the benefits of the first industrial revolution will need to pay to avoid it.

Second, substitute sustainable agriculture for the industrial model based on pesticides, herbicides, and poorly tested genetically engineered foods. Getting rid of outrageous subsidies and restoring family farms is only a first, relatively easy step. Next comes making serious public investments in agricultural research, to put the world's cumulative, sophisticated knowledge of plant ecology to work. Home gardens, for example, have provided families in Java with a huge part of their fruits and vegetables for centuries, growing hundreds of species in small courtyard gardens with neither pesticides nor artificial fertilizers. We need to develop agricultural systems of comparable sophistication, productivity, and diversity for other climates and continents—and then invest in helping farmers shift from chemical-based industrial monoculture to these new patterns. (Genetic engineering may have a place in this future—but not the place agribusiness currently imagines, where it is an excuse for driving out small farmers and expanding herbicide-dependent monocultures of quasi-corn and doctored soybeans.)

Third, amortize and retire our 200-year investment in toxic technologies based on heat and pressure applied to metals and hydrocarbons. We have the new technologies but do not want to write off the capital invested in the old ones. A green economy is now a technological reality and an economic practicality. It is penetrating the market very slowly, however, because it must compete with older, polluting technologies in which enormous capital has been invested and which enjoy tremendous subsidies from government in the form of inadequate enforcement of environmental standards. Throw-away batteries, for example, constitute 75 percent of the cadmium going into U.S. landfills. Rechargeable batteries would reduce that figure to a tiny fraction, but consumers do not pay for the toxic results of the slightly cheaper, one-time variety, so they keep buying them.

We need to stop the hidden subsidies for technologies that are poisoning the planet.

Finally—and this may seem the most outrageous suggestion yet—we need to create and measure wealth, not waste. We then should distribute it fairly enough that excess consumption is no longer the measure of either security or dignity. The connection of this principle to the environment may seem tenuous, but in cultural terms it is profound. Can we really imagine a society that would ensure the survival of obscure but important families of beetles while remaining oblivious to the welfare of members of our own species who are ethnically different, geographically distant, or educationally disadvantaged? Can we care for migratory birds while ignoring children? Can we be stewards of the earth while neglecting humanity?

CHAPTER ELEVEN

A Progressive Agenda for Metropolitan America

BRUCE KATZ*

Embrace a federal metropolitan agenda that promotes balanced growth, stimulates investment in cities and older suburbs, and connects low-income families to employment and educational opportunities.

The 2004 presidential election will take place during a period of profound change in the United States, comparable in scale and complexity to the latter part of the nineteenth century. Broad *demographic forces*—population growth, immigration, domestic migration, aging—are sweeping the nation and affecting settlement patterns, lifestyle choices, and consumption trends. Substantial *economic forces*—globalization, deindustrialization, technological innovation—are restructuring our economy, altering what Americans do and where they do it.

Together, these complex and interrelated forces are reshaping the metropolitan communities that drive and dominate the national and even global economy. Cities—while still the disproportionate home to poor, struggling families—are re-emerging as key engines of regional growth, fueled by the presence of educational and health care institutions, vibrant downtowns, and distinctive neighborhoods. Suburbs, meanwhile, are growing more diverse in terms of demographic composition, economic function, and fiscal vitality. In many respects, the differences between cities and suburbs are becoming less important than their similarities and their interdependence.

The nation's grab bag of "urban" policies—subsidized housing, community reinvestment, community development, empowerment zones—does not address or even recognize the challenges emerging from this new metropolitan reality. The almost exclusive focus of these policies on central

---

* **BRUCE KATZ** *is Vice President of the Brookings Institution and Founding Director of its Center on Urban and Metropolitan Policy. From 1993 to 1996, Mr. Katz served as Chief of Staff to Henry G. Cisneros, the Secretary of Housing and Urban Development.*

cities ignores the fact that an entire generation of suburbs now face city-like challenges. Merely renewing city neighborhoods ignores the metropolitan nature of employment and educational opportunities and, in many places, actually inhibits the access of low-income families to good schools and quality jobs. On the other hand, merely focusing on the "deficits" of communities fails to recognize that cities and older places have assets and amenities (e.g., educational institutions, density, waterfronts, historic districts) that are highly valued by our changing economy. In general, national "urban" policies are so micro as to largely ignore the major federal policies that grow economies, shape communities, and influence peoples' lives.

In shaping solutions by 2010, this chapter will contend that federal policies need to grow up and reflect the metropolitan America that is rather than the urban America that was. It will argue that, after better than a half century of sprawl, "urban" means "metropolitan"—central cities, their surrounding older suburbs, and the larger economic regions described by their effective labor market.

I. The Problem

According to the 2000 Census, eight in ten Americans and 95 percent of the foreign-born population live in the nation's nearly 300 metropolitan areas. Together, these regions produce more than 85 percent of the nation's economic output, generate 84 percent of America's jobs, and produce virtually all the nation's wealth.

Metropolitan America is also at the vanguard of our changing economy, leading the transition to an economy based on ideas and innovation. As Robert Atkinson and Paul Gottlieb have shown, the 114 largest metropolitan areas account for 67 percent of all jobs, but 81 percent of high-tech employment, and 91 percent of Internet domain names. According to Richard Florida, author of *The Rise of the Creative Class*, even fewer metropolitan areas are winning the competition for the young, talented, educated workers who form the nucleus of our entrepreneurial economy.

More and more, how metropolitan America is organized and governed determines how most Americans do in life, and how we do as a nation. Yet while the indicators cited above tell a story of economic strength and productivity, America's metropolitan areas are growing in unbalanced ways that pose significant competitive, fiscal, and social challenges that require federal action.

Despite clear signs of renewal in many central cities, a close examination of the 2000 Census and other market data shows that the decentralization of economic and residential life remains the dominant growth pattern in the United States. As Alan Berube has shown, rapidly developing new suburbs—built since the 1970s on the outer fringes of metropolitan areas—are capturing the lion's share of employment and population growth. In the largest metropolitan areas, the rate of population growth for suburbs from 1990 to 2000 was twice that of central cities—18 percent versus 9 percent. Suburban growth outpaced city growth irrespective of whether a city's population was falling like Baltimore or staying stable like Kansas City or rising rapidly like Denver. Even sunbelt cities like Phoenix, Dallas, and Houston grew more slowly than their suburbs.

Suburbs dominate employment growth as well as population growth. As Edward Glaeser and Matthew Kahn have demonstrated, employment decentralization has become the norm in American metropolitan areas. Across the largest 100 metro areas, on average only 22 percent of people work within three miles of the city center and more than 35 percent work more than ten miles from the central core. In cities like Chicago, Atlanta, and Detroit, employment patterns have radically altered, with more than 60 percent of the regional employment now located more than 10 miles from the city center. The American economy is essentially becoming an "exit ramp economy," with new office, commercial, and retail facilities increasingly located along suburban freeways.

With suburbs taking on a greater share of the country's population and employment, they are beginning to look more and more like traditional urban areas. In many metropolitan areas, the explosive growth in immigrants in the past decade skipped the cities and went directly to the suburbs. According to William Frey, every minority group grew at faster rates in the suburbs during the past decade; as a consequence, racial and ethnic minorities now make up more than a quarter (27 percent) of suburban populations, up from 19 percent in 1990.

Even with these profound changes, most metropolitan areas in the United States remain sharply divided along racial, ethnic, and class lines. America's central cities became majority minority for the first time in the nation's history during the 1990s and, while generally improving, have poverty rates that are almost double those of suburban communities. As Myron Orfield has shown, suburban diversity also tends to be uneven, with many minorities and new immigrants settling in older suburbs that are experiencing central city-like challenges—aging infrastructure, deteriorating schools and commercial corridors, and inadequate housing stock.

These patterns—of racial, ethnic, and class stratification, of extensive growth in some communities and significantly less growth in others—are all inextricably linked. Poor schools in one jurisdiction push out families and lead to overcrowded schools in other places. A lack of affordable housing in thriving job centers leads to long commutes on crowded freeways for a region's working families. Expensive housing—out of the reach of most households—in many close-in neighborhoods creates pressures to pave over and build on open space in outlying areas, as people decide that they have to move outwards to build a future.

The cumulative impact of these unbalanced growth patterns has enormous economic, fiscal, and social implications for the nation that deserve and require federal attention.

Unbalanced growth undermines the economic efficiency of metropolitan markets. Some of this is fairly obvious in metropolitan areas that are literally "stuck in traffic." Traffic congestion—a product in large part of growth patterns that are low density and decentralizing—has become the bane of daily existence in most major metropolitan areas. Such congestion places enormous burdens on employers and employees alike and substantially reduces the efficiency of labor and supplier markets. A recent study by the Texas Transportation Institute of 75 urban areas in the United States found that the average annual delay per person was 26 hours, or the equivalent of about three full work days of lost time.

Some economic consequences of unbalanced growth reflect the lost opportunities of cities and older communities that never reach their true potential. Notes *Business Week*, "cities still seem best able to provide business with access to skilled workers, specialized high-value services, and the kind of innovation and learning growth that is facilitated by close contact between diverse individuals." Indeed, as Edward Glaeser has argued, the density of cities offers the perfect milieu for the driving forces of the new economy: idea fermentation and technological innovation. These broader theories on human capital formation and metropolitan growth help explain why metropolitan areas without strong central cities—Detroit, St. Louis, Cleveland, Milwaukee—are having so much difficulty making the transition to a higher road economy.

The fiscal costs of unbalanced growth are also enormous. Low-density development increases demand for new infrastructure (e.g., schools, roads, sewer, and water extensions) and increases the costs of key services like police, fire, and emergency medical. Then there is the substantial impact of abandonment in older communities on the property values of nearby homes as well as the implications of concentrated poverty for additional municipal services in the schools and on the streets. Ultimately, these factors lead to reduced revenues, higher taxes, and over-stressed services for older communities.

Finally, unbalanced growth imposes enormous social and economic costs on low-income minority families. As economies and opportunity decentralize and low-income minorities continue to reside principally in central cities and older suburbs, a wide spatial gap has arisen between low-income minorities and quality educational and employment opportunities. Poor children growing up in neighborhoods of poverty are consigned to inner-city schools where less than a quarter of the students achieve "basic" levels in reading compared to nearly two-thirds of suburban children. Similarly, inner-city residents are cut off from regional labor markets where entry-level jobs in manufacturing, wholesale trade, and retailing (that offer opportunities for people with limited education and skills) are abundant.

Federal "Anti-Metropolitan" Policies

The metropolitan growth patterns described above are the product of many factors. Population growth, consumer housing preferences, and lifestyle choices have fueled suburbanization. Market restructuring and technological change have altered the location patterns of manufacturing, retail, and other key employment sectors. Yet the shape and extent of decentralization in America were not inevitable. Since the middle of the twentieth century, broad federal policies—the policies often ignored by "urban" initiatives—have contributed substantially to unbalanced growth patterns in metropolitan areas.

First and foremost, federal polices taken together set "rules of the development game" that encourage the decentralization of the economy and the concentration of urban poverty. Federal transportation policies generally support the expansion of road capacity at the fringe of metropolitan areas and beyond, enabling people and businesses to live miles from urban centers but still benefit from metropolitan life. The deductibility of federal income taxes for mortgage interest and property taxes appears spatially neutral but in practice favors suburban communities, particularly those with higher income residents. Federal and state environmental policies have made the redevelopment of polluted "brownfield" sites prohibitively expensive and cumbersome, increasing the attraction of suburban land.

Other federal policies have concentrated poverty rather than enhancing access to opportunity. Until recently, federal public housing catered almost exclusively to the very poor by housing them in special units concentrated in isolated neighborhoods. According to Margery Turner, more than half of public housing residents still live in high-poverty neighborhoods; only 7 percent live in low-poverty neighborhoods where fewer than 10 percent of residents are poor. Even newer federal efforts—for example, the low-income housing tax credit program—are generally targeted to areas of distress and poverty, not to areas of growing employment. We now know that concentrating poor families in a few square blocks undermines almost every other program designed to aid the poor—making it harder for the poor to find jobs and placing extraordinary burdens on the schools and teachers that serve poor children.

The effect of all these policies: they lower the costs—to individuals and firms—of living and working outside or on the outer fringes of our metro regions, while increasing the costs of living and working in the core. They push investment out of high-tax, low-service urban areas and into low-tax, high-service favored suburban quarters, while concentrating poverty in the central city core.

The second major flaw of federal policies is that they rely on states and localities to "deliver the goods." Federal policies have not recognized the primacy of metropolitan areas and have been slow to align federal programs to the geography of regional economies, commuting patterns, and social reality.

Despite the fact that the bulk of the funds for transportation programs are raised in metropolitan areas, federal law currently empowers state departments of transportation to make most transportation decisions. These powerful bureaucracies are principally the domain of traffic engineers and are notorious for disproportionately spending transportation funds raised in metropolitan areas in rural counties. Incredibly, metropolitan areas make decisions on only about 10 cents of every dollar they generate even though local governments within metropolitan areas own and maintain the vast majority of the transportation infrastructure.

Despite the metropolitan nature of residential markets, the federal government has devolved responsibility for housing voucher programs to thousands of local public housing authorities. The Detroit metropolitan area, for example, has more than 30 separate public housing authorities, greatly limiting the residential mobility of poor families. The hyper-fragmentation of governance makes it difficult for low-income recipients to know about suburban housing vacancies, let alone exercise choice in the metropolitan marketplace.

Progress During the 1990s

During the 1990s, the federal government began to recognize the importance of metropolitan areas (and cities) to national wealth and prosperity as well as the costs and consequences of unbalanced growth patterns. A series of reform efforts in the transportation and housing arenas sought to "level the playing field" between older and newer communities and devolve more responsibility and flexibility to metropolitan decision makers.

Federal transportation laws in the early and late 1990s, for example, devolved greater responsibility for planning and implementation to metropolitan planning organizations (MPOs), thus giving these areas some ability to tailor transportation plans to their distinct markets. The laws also introduced greater flexibility in the spending of federal highway and transit funds, giving state transportation departments and MPOs the ability to "flex" funding between different modes. Finally, the laws directly funded special efforts to address metropolitan challenges such as congestion and air quality, job access for low-income workers, and the linkage between transportation and land use planning.

The changes in housing policy were equally ambitious. Public housing reforms mandated the demolition of the nation's most troubled projects and supported (through the multi-billion dollar HOPE VI program) the development of a new form of public housing—smaller scale, economically integrated, well constructed, better designed. Other housing reforms enhanced the ability of low-income residents to move to areas of growing employment and high-performing schools. The rules governing housing vouchers (now the nation's largest affordable housing program) were streamlined, making this rental assistance tool more attractive to private sector landlords. Regional counseling efforts were initiated to provide voucher recipients with the kind of assistance they need to make smart neighborhood choices.

These transportation and housing reforms, while still relatively new, have already shown some positive results. Federal money spent on transit almost doubled during the 1990s and new light rail systems are being constructed in metropolitan areas as diverse as Salt Lake City, Denver, Dallas, Charlotte, and San Diego. For the first time since World War II, growth in transit ridership has outpaced the growth in driving for five straight years. The public housing reforms became the catalyst for urban regeneration as cities like Atlanta, Louisville, and St. Louis leveraged the HOPE VI funding with other private and public investments to modernize local schools, stimulate neighborhood markets and rebuild local infrastructure, parks, and libraries. The public housing reforms also contributed to one of the real success stories of the 1990s—the precipitous decline in the number of neighborhoods with poverty rates of 40 percent or higher and the number of people living in those neighborhoods.

These changes happened in the course of one decade and illustrate the kind of substantial impact a sustained course of federal action could have.

II. The Bush Response

The Bush administration's record on cities and metropolitan areas has veered between general neglect and outright hostility. It has largely just stood by while states and localities have contended with the worst budget crises since the end of World War II. The failure to provide countercyclical funding—as has been done in prior recessions—has left state, city, and suburban governments scrambling to cut spending and raise taxes at the same time that federal tax rates are being slashed.

In addition, the Bush executive branch has pursued major policy reforms without regard to their disparate impact on older, mostly poorer communities. Thus, its education efforts have imposed enormous burdens on city school systems—where the preponderance of struggling schools are located given higher poverty levels—without adequate resources. Its proposals on the reauthorization of the 1996 welfare reform law would remove much of the flexibility that city and county officials have used successfully to help welfare recipients make the transition to work. Finally, the administration's homeland security efforts have imposed costly mandates on municipalities without providing the guidance or funds necessary to upgrade the nation's first responder capacity.

Bush & Co. have also reversed course on the positive metropolitan-oriented policies tested during the 1990s. On transportation policy, President Bush has proposed rolling back many of the major bipartisan advances his father inaugurated in 1991 and President Clinton furthered in 1998. The Bush six-year transportation plan (now before Congress) would reduce the federal share for the new construction or extension of mass transit systems from 80 percent to 50 percent while retaining the federal match for highway construction at 80 percent. In fact, guaranteed highway funding would grow 24 percent from 2003 to 2009 while guaranteed funding for mass transit would actually decline by 8 percent. The Bush plan also eliminates key programs for bus facilities and clean fuels and dilutes many of the provisions for public involvement in the transportation process. These proposals would effectively penalize metropolitan areas for pursuing alternative transportation strategies and would favor road building in exurban and non-metropolitan areas at the expense of transportation solutions more suitable to cities and mature suburbs.

Perhaps most troubling, the President appears to be walking away from the bipartisan consensus that drove housing policy in the past decade. His government, for example, has been openly hostile to efforts that expand the supply of affordable rental housing, either through production subsidies or direct assistance to renters. The initial versions of the President's economic stimulus plan in 2003—by exempting corporate dividends from taxation—would have lowered the value of low-income housing tax credits, the principal tool used to stimulate affordable housing production. The Bush HUD budget for fiscal year 2004 operated along the same lines, recommending no funding for both the HOPE VI program and incremental rental vouchers, the principal means by which the federal government ensures affordability in housing assistance. The administration also has not pushed its campaign proposal for a new homeownership tax credit program, failing to include it in any of the three major tax bills since taking office.

Finally, the Bush administration has proposed substantial changes to the governance of the voucher program in ways that undermine it. Specifically, it sought in 2003 to convert the voucher program to a block grant to the states, a move that would ultimately result in the reduction in the number of vouchers over time.

III. Solutions

It is time to develop a federal metropolitan agenda that takes account of the new spatial geography of work and opportunity in America. A progressive metropolitan agenda is necessary to help shape growth patterns that are economically efficient, fiscally responsible and environmentally sustainable. It can also revitalize central cities and older suburbs and connect low-income families to broader educational and employment opportunities.

A federal metropolitan agenda should cover many aspects of domestic policy, ranging from workforce development to economic development to homeland security. It should be closely coordinated with major federal policies on immigration, working families and the environment. Reform of current transportation and housing policies, however, is at the core of the new metropolitan agenda.

A New Transportation Agenda for Metropolitan America

Metropolitan America faces a daunting set of transportation challenges—increasing congestion, deteriorating air quality, crumbling infrastructure, spatial mismatches in the labor market—that threaten to undermine their competitive edge in the global economy. Three reforms are essential.

The federal government should continue to expand the responsibility of metropolitan transportation entities. These institutions are, after all, in the best position to integrate transportation decisions with local and regional decisions on land use, housing, and economic development. At the same time, states should be required to tie their decisions more closely to the demographic and market realities of metropolitan areas. Both states and metropolitan areas should be encouraged to work together on major commercial corridors and to knit together what are now separate air, rail, and surface transportation policies.

Besides governance reform, a Metropolitan Transportation Fund should be created to provide metropolitan areas with the predictability of resources required for long-term planning and the flexibility necessary to tailor transportation solutions to individual markets. The fund and all other federal programs should treat highway and transit projects equally in terms of financing and regulatory oversight. New resources, including tax credits, should be made available to stimulate development around existing light rail and other rail projects. At the same time, transportation reform should encourage the greater use of market mechanisms—such as tolls and value pricing—to ease congestion on major thoroughfares at peak traffic times. London's recent experimentation with congestion pricing, in particular, offers lessons for large American cities and metropolitan areas.

Finally, a metropolitan transportation agenda should hold all recipients of federal funding to a high standard of managerial efficiency, programmatic effectiveness, and fiscal responsibility. To that end, transportation reform should establish a framework for accountability that includes tighter disclosure requirements, improved performance measures, and rewards for exceptional performance. Transportation reform should also increase the practical opportunities for citizen and business participation in transportation decision making. States and metropolitan areas should be provided the funding to experiment with state-of-the-art technologies for engaging citizens in public debates.

A New Housing Agenda for Metropolitan America

Federal housing policy must also be recast to fit the new metropolitan reality. As discussed, the uneven residential patterns in most metropolitan areas are placing special burdens on older communities and limiting the educational and employment opportunities of a wide cross section of families.

A new federal housing agenda must expand housing opportunities for moderate- and middle-class families in the cities and close-in suburbs while creating more affordable, "workforce" housing near job centers. Ideally, federal policies should help regional elected leaders balance their housing markets through zoning changes, subsidies, and tax incentives so that all families—both middle class and low income—have more choice about where they live and how to be closer to quality jobs and good schools. A new federal housing agenda can build on the balanced housing strategies that are already emerging in the metropolitan areas of Minneapolis, Portland, Seattle, and Washington, D.C.

To achieve these ends, federal tax incentives should be expanded to boost homeownership in places where homeownership rates are exceedingly low. Incentives could include a tax credit that goes directly to first time homebuyers (as in Washington, D.C.) and a tax benefit that entices developers to construct or renovate affordable homes (like the existing tax credit for rental housing). Such incentives would enhance the ability of working families to accumulate wealth and contribute to the stability of neighborhoods by lowering the costs of homeownership.

In addition, the federal government should continue its efforts to demolish and redevelop distressed public housing and promote economic integration in them. The successful HOPE VI program should be renewed for another decade of investment and its reach should be extended beyond public housing to distressed housing projects financed by the federal government. The federal government should also make it easier in all housing programs to serve families with a broader range of incomes, particularly in neighborhoods with high concentrations of poverty.

To enhance housing choice, the federal government should invest more substantially in vouchers. A national goal of a million more vouchers over the next decade sets an ambitious, but achievable, target. Vouchers have consistently proven to be the most cost effective and market-oriented of federal housing programs and, more than any other housing program, enable low-income parents to base their housing decisions on the performance of local schools.

Besides these additional investments, more substantial governance and statutory reforms will be necessary to promote greater housing choice for low-income families. The federal government should, for example, shift governance of the housing voucher program to the metropolitan level. As noted, the federal voucher program is administered by thousands of separate public housing bureaucracies operating in parochial jurisdictions. Competitions should be held in dozens of metropolitan areas to determine what kind of entity—public, for-profit, non-profit, or combination thereof—is best suited to administer the program.

The federal government should also make it easier to allocate low-income housing tax credits to areas of growing employment, not only to areas of distress and poverty. And existing funds should be invested in creating a network of regional housing corporations to develop and preserve affordable housing in suburban areas. A national network of regional housing corporations can build on the achievements of community development corporations, many of which can naturally graduate to operate at the metropolitan level.

The most important action, however, will be the hardest. Many wealthy communities will only open up their communities if they are denied something they want. To this end, the federal government should prohibit lucrative federal highway investments in communities that have been found in violation of federal civil rights laws or otherwise have engaged in exclusionary housing practices.

The metropolitan agenda described could have a transforming affect on the physical and social landscape of metropolitan areas. For example, obsolescent freeways that currently block access to urban waterfronts and other valuable real estate can be removed, as in Milwaukee, Boston, and Portland. At the same time, new, dense residential communities can emerge along commuter rail, light rail, and rapid bus lines (as in Dallas and Arlington, Virginia), giving commuters greater residential and transportation choices and responding to the changing demographics of the country.

Providing affordable housing throughout a region will also produce substantial benefits. It should help workers live closer to suburban areas of employment and reduce congestion on roadways. It should help reduce the concentration of poverty, thereby making school reform and educational achievement real possibilities. It should help cities and older suburbs create mixed-income communities, thereby revitalizing neighborhoods and generating markets. By strengthening older communities, it will take the pressure off of sprawl, thereby improving the quality of life in outer exurban areas.

Some of the reforms described above are feasible in the current political environment and should be enacted in the near term. The homeownership tax credit idea, for example, has already received broad bipartisan support.

Yet other reforms and investments may take toward the end of this decade. State departments of transportation will oppose the further devolution of responsibility to metropolitan entities as well as greater levels of federal oversight and accountability. Some neighborhood advocates will oppose additional efforts to demolish distressed housing and provide low-income residents with greater choice in the metropolitan marketplace.

Some low-income housing advocates will oppose efforts to promote economic integration in federally assisted housing. Many suburban areas will surely resist the production of affordable housing. In general, the constrained fiscal environment created by Bush policies will make any new housing investments extremely difficult.

This new metropolitan agenda, therefore, will require not just new policy ideas but new political coalitions that span jurisdictional, ideological, and party lines. Existing local constituencies will have to think differently about metropolitan issues and make connections between policies— housing, workforce, education, transportation—that are now kept separate and distinct.

To a large extent, this change is inevitable. Urban policy in America can no longer be exclusively about cities or neighborhoods. It must be about the new metropolitan reality that defines our economy and society and the larger government rules that help shape that reality. The next administration has an historic opportunity to design and implement a metropolitan agenda that promotes balanced growth, stimulates investment in cities, and older suburbs and connects low-income families to employment and educational opportunities.

JUSTICE:

TOWARD A MORE JUST AMERICA

Terrorism and the Rule of Law: Maintaining Security and Liberty

DAVID COLE

Don't strike the balance between liberty and security by exploiting the most vulnerable among us, which is morally wrong, ineffective, and makes us less secure by breeding anti-American resentment.

I. The Problem

In 1919, the United States suffered a series of terrorist bombings, including mail bombs addressed to Supreme Court Justice Oliver Wendell Holmes, Attorney General A. Mitchell Palmer, senators and other government officials, and financial barons John D. Rockefeller and J. P. Morgan. An observant mail clerk intercepted most of the mail bombs, but not before one detonated, causing the maid to Senator James Hardwick to lose both her hands. The mail bombs were followed one month later by a coordinated set of bombings in eight cities in a single day, including one that destroyed the front of Attorney General Palmer's private home in Washington, D.C.

The government responded with a nationwide dragnet targeting foreign nationals and using immigration law. It arrested several thousand individuals in coordinated raids, and charged them not with the bombings but with technical immigration violations and guilt-by-association membership in various Communist groups. It held them incommunicado, denied them access to lawyers, and interrogated them under coercive conditions. In the end, over 500 were deported. The bombers were never found. Louis Post, who as Acting Secretary of Labor personally intervened to reverse more than 1,000 deportation orders, later wrote that the force of the delirium turned in the direction of a deportation crusade with the spontaneity of water seeking out the course of least resistance.

In the wake of the terrorist attacks of September 11, 2001, the federal

---

DAVID COLE, *a professor at Georgetown University Law Center, is author, most recently, of* Enemy Aliens: Double Standards and Constitutional Freedoms in the War on Terrorism.

government has again pursued the course of least resistance, targeting foreign nationals for treatment that we would not tolerate for U.S. citizens. As with the Palmer Raids of 1919–1920, the government's domestic enforcement efforts have sacrificed some of the most basic principles of American liberty *without* achieving much in the way of safety. The world today, more than two years after September 11, is very likely a more dangerous place for Americans than it was on September 11 itself. Our response to the war on terrorism has not only failed to generate much in the way of cognizable gains in security but has also contributed to what is almost certainly the greatest threat we face today—the unprecedented level of hostility and resentment directed toward the United States around the world. That anti-Americanism, prompted in significant part by the double standards with which we have waged the war on terrorism, simultaneously aids our enemies and makes our friends less eager to cooperate with us as we struggle to maintain our security.

A more just and effective response to the problem of national security after September 11 is possible. Indeed a more just response will be more effective precisely because it is more just. Combating terrorism is a legitimate end, but unless we adopt legitimate means effectiveness will be compromised. If our measures are seen as principled, fair, and reasonable, they will encourage others to work with us, and will reduce support for our enemies. But if we are seen as overreacting, and especially as more willing to sacrifice others' rights rather than our own, the legitimacy of the campaign will be seriously compromised, and so too will our safety.

II. The Bush Response

It is difficult to name a right that the Bush administration has *not* sacrificed in the name of the "war on terrorism." First Amendment rights of speech and association have fallen prey to ideological exclusion of foreign visitors and guilt-by-association for anyone who supports a group the administration labels as terrorist. The Fourth Amendment right of privacy has given way to data-mining, political spying, and the USA PATRIOT Act's authorization of secret searches and wiretaps without probable cause of criminal conduct. The Fifth Amendment right to due process has been denied by preventive detention, in some cases without any hearings whatsoever, in others with only secret hearings from which public, press, and family members are excluded. The Fifth Amendment's prohibition on coercive interrogations has given way to assertions that the government can hold suspects incommunicado indefinitely for purposes of rendering them hopeless and entirely dependent on their captors, as well as by the patently immoral and illegal practice of sending suspects to particular countries precisely because we know they are likely to be tortured there.

The Sixth Amendment rights of the accused to a fair criminal trial have been undermined by attempts to impose the death penalty while denying the defendant the right to call witnesses in government custody who would exonerate him, and by military tribunals that permit defendants to be convicted and even executed on the basis of secret evidence that neither the defendant nor his chosen lawyer is able to see. The right to counsel has been obstructed by concerted efforts to deny detainees access to lawyers, the monitoring of attorney-client communications without probable cause of criminal conduct or a court order, and the outright denial of any access to lawyers for anyone declared an "enemy combatant." Habeas corpus has been denied to over 700 persons held without charges or hearings in military custody in Guantanamo Bay, Cuba, and denied in all but name to the U.S. citizens held in the United States under the same asserted authority. And perhaps the Constitution's most essential guarantee—equal protection of the law—has given way to the most extensive campaign of ethnic profiling since the treatment of Japanese immigrants and Japanese Americans during World War II.

The only right the administration has not been willing to curtail is the right-wing's favorite (although never recognized by the Supreme Court)— the right to bear arms. Attorney General Ashcroft was willing to lock up thousands of suspected terrorists without any individualized evidence of terrorist activity, and to deny many of them access to lawyers while trying them in secret, but he drew the line at checking suspected terrorists' gun purchasing records.

But of course these rights have not been sacrificed across the board. For the most part, the government has sacrificed the rights of foreign nationals, while implicitly or explicitly assuring Americans that they need not sacrifice their own rights. To the extent the sacrifices have extended to citizens, it has been primarily citizens who are or appear to be Arabs or Muslims who have felt the brunt of the measures. But mainstream Americans should take no solace in the fact that they have not been targeted, for history shows that what the government does to foreign nationals in the name of security inevitably gets extended to U.S. citizens.

What do we have to show for these sacrifices in basic liberties? The government has locked up over 5,000 foreign nationals, nearly all Arabs and Muslims, in a campaign of preventive detention designed to capture suspected terrorists, take them off the streets, and prevent the next terrorist attack. Yet as of February 2004, more than two years into that campaign, the government has not charged *any* of these detainees with being a member of al Qaeda, nor with any involvement in the attacks of September 11. It has charged only three of the foreign nationals subject to preventive detention with any terrorist crime, and two of those three were acquitted of the terrorist charges. So it has only one terrorist conviction to show for over 5,000 detentions. (And the legality of even that conviction, obtained after a lengthy trial in Detroit, has recently been called into question by evidence that the prosecution failed to disclose to the defense evidence showing that its principal witness lied on the stand.)

The government has compelled over 80,000 men from Arab and Muslim nations to register with the government and be questioned, fingerprinted and photographed, and selectively subjected some 200,000 more to similar measures at the border. The FBI has attempted to interview about 8,000 men, solely because they are from Arab or Muslim countries. Immigration authorities have prioritized the detention and deportation of some 6,000 foreign nationals with outstanding deportation orders, again simply because they hold passports from Arab and Muslim countries. And during the war with Iraq, the government adopted a policy of automatically detaining all foreign nationals seeking asylum from Arab or Muslim countries, without regard to whether there was any reason to believe that they were in fact dangerous or a risk of flight. Yet of all these individuals singled out for their ethnic or religious identity, not one has been accused of being an al Qaeda member, not one has been indicted for involvement in the September 11 attacks, and not one has been charged with any terrorist crime of any kind.

Thus, when Attorney General Ashcroft claims credit for the fact that there has not been another terrorist attack in the United States since September 11, one has to wonder how or whether his initiatives have had anything to do with that fortunate fact. The military, by contrast, can credibly point to results from its campaign in Afghanistan that may well have made us safer. The military offensive closed al Qaeda's base of operations and training camps, killed and/or captured many of its members, and retrieved valuable information from its headquarters that has made possible the capture abroad of many of the group's leading figures, if not Osama bin Laden himself. These measures undoubtedly have made it much more difficult for al Qaeda to attack us. But on the domestic side, our efforts appear to have netted virtually no real terrorists, while generating substantial animosity and criticism from the very groups with which we need to be working most closely.

It is true that the Justice Department has filed a number of high-profile criminal indictments, and has obtained a number of guilty pleas. But with the exception of Zaccarias Moussaoui, shoe-bomber Richard Reid, and Iyman Faris, charged with a conspiracy to bring down the Brooklyn Bridge with an acetylene torch, the Justice Department has charged no one with actually engaging in or even planning to engage in any specific terrorist activity. Moussaoui, of course, was picked up *before* the September 11 attacks, and while Faris pleaded guilty to the Brooklyn Bridge plot, his was not the most plausible of terrorist scenarios. And Reid was captured not through any investigative work by the government, but by an observant fellow passenger.

Most of the criminal cases actually alleging "terrorism" that the Justice Department has filed since September 11 are based on 18 U.S.C. 2339B, which makes it a crime to provide "material support"—broadly defined to include any tangible thing of value, as well as personnel, training, and expert advice and assistance—to any group the Secretary of State has labeled "terrorist." Under this statute, significant parts of which have been declared unconstitutional by several federal courts, the government need not make any showing that an individual's support had any connection to any terrorist acts of the recipient group. The defendant may not challenge the designation of the group as terrorist. And it is no defense to show that one's support was designed to further the group's lawful, as opposed to its illegal, terrorist ends. This sweeping statute allows the government to use the terrorist label against persons who have never engaged in or supported violence. It essentially resurrects guilt-by-association in the name of cutting off funding for terrorists.

Six young men in Lackawanna, New York, pleaded guilty to having

violated this statute by merely attending an al Qaeda training camp (before
September 11). There was no allegation that the young men intended to
undertake any actual terrorist activity, nor that they gave anything of value
to the group. The government closely monitored them for a substantial
period of time after they attended the training camp, but found no evidence that they were planning to undertake any terrorist or even criminal
activity. The defendants' lawyers maintained that the young men were simply recruited by a charismatic religious leader, and then wanted no part of
al Qaeda's campaign against the United States. On the government's theory, however, this was no defense; merely attending the camp, without more,
was sufficient to constitute material support in the form of personnel to al
Qaeda, and was therefore enough to warrant criminal punishment.

The same material support statute has been used in prosecutions in
Seattle, Portland, New York City, Tampa, Brooklyn, Minneapolis, and
Alexandria, Virginia. What unites all of these cases—the government's most
high-profile terrorist prosecutions—is that the government alleges not terrorist activity, not conspiracy to commit terrorist activity, not even material support for terrorist *activity*, but material support for an *organization*. Had
this law been on the books in the 1980s, the tens of thousands of
Americans who contributed to the African National Congress's (ANC)
lawful, nonviolent opposition to apartheid would have been vulnerable to
prosecution as terrorists for providing material support to a terrorist organization. The State Department officially designated the ANC a terrorist
organization every year until it came to power in South Africa. But would
prosecution of those individuals have made us safe from terrorism?

Federal courts in California have declared unconstitutional the "material support" statute's prohibition on the provision of "training," "personnel," and "expert advice and assistance" to designated groups. A federal
court in New York similarly ruled the ban on providing "personnel" and
"communications" unconstitutional. These courts reasoned that the law's
terms are so vague that they conceivably encompass pure speech and advocacy protected by the First Amendment.

The Attorney General often asserts that his criminal terrorism prosecutions could not have been pursued without reforms introduced by the
USA PATRIOT Act. But again, Ashcroft's claims are not backed up by the
evidence. The two principal examples he cites are the Lackawana prosecution and the prosecution of Sami Al Arian, a University of South Florida

professor charged with aiding the Palestine Islamic Jihad. But the Lackawanna men were identified, tracked, and wiretapped before the PATRIOT Act was even enacted. And Sami Al Arian's indictment is based on more than a decade of wiretaps, some conducted by Israeli intelligence forces in Israel; the legality of those wiretaps will stand or fall without regard to the PATRIOT Act.

So as we pass the two-year anniversary of the attacks of September 11, there is strikingly little evidence that our domestic initiatives have in fact thwarted terrorist acts here. It is of course possible that the harsh measures adopted have deterred some would-be terrorists from attempting to enter the United States to attack us. But the still porous character of our borders, especially those with Canada and Mexico, makes it unlikely that a committed terrorist would not be able to enter the United States if he chose to do so. And to the extent that these measures were undertaken on the theory that there was a fifth column of Arab and Muslim terrorists in the United States ready and willing to attack us, the dragnet has produced no evidence to confirm that theory, and much to contradict it. Yet the administration has not significantly revised its tactics, despite the failure of these policies to identify real terrorists.

Meanwhile, the administration has compromised many of the most basic principles of our democratic society. To take just one example, it has conducted a campaign of preventive detention on a scale matched by the Palmer Raids. In this campaign, monumentally unsuccessful in terms of identifying actual terrorists, the government locked up people without charges, based on such information as an anonymous tip that too many Middle Eastern men were working in a convenience store. Over seven hundred arrests were secret, and the detainees remain unidentified to this day, even though the FBI has cleared virtually all of them of any connection to terrorism. Over six hundred detainees were tried in secret immigration hearings, without any showing that classified information was involved. The government adopted policies and practices designed to deny detainees access to lawyers, and to keep detainees locked up even after immigration judges ordered that they could be released. When some detainees held on immigration charges admitted that they had violated immigration law and offered to leave the country, the government adopted a "hold until cleared" policy under which they were kept behind bars for months, without probable cause of criminal activity or any legitimate immigration purpose, while the FBI sought to satisfy itself that they were unconnected to terrorism. Some of the detainees were beaten. Yet when the Justice Department's own Inspector General issued a highly critical report on these abuses, the Justice Department's official response was "we make no apologies."

And the domestic detainees were the lucky ones. Consider the plight of Maher Arar, a Canadian citizen apprehended by U.S. immigration authorities as he was changing planes at New York's JFK Airport on his way back to Canada after a trip abroad. Exploiting the fact that he technically had to enter the United States in order to make his connecting flight, U.S. officials detained him, interrogated him, denied his repeated requests for a lawyer, and then ordered him expelled on the basis of secret evidence. When he asked to be expelled to Canada, his home of sixteen years, the authorities denied that request, and instead spirited him to Syria, where he was tortured and incarcerated without charges for nearly a year. What possible interest would the United States have in stopping a Canadian citizen on his way home to Canada and sending him to Syria instead? We certainly have better relations with Canada than with Syria. But Canada does not have a record of incarcerating people without charges and torturing them; Syria does. The Convention Against Torture, which the United States has ratified and incorporated into federal law, categorically forbids sending persons to countries where there is a substantial likelihood that they will be tortured. So does basic morality. In Arar's case, federal authorities violated both.

The more than 650 persons still detained at Guantanamo Bay, Cuba, have it even worse. The government contends that because they are foreign nationals being held outside U.S. borders, they have no constitutional rights whatsoever, and no access to legal courts. It further claims that it can hold them as "enemy combatants" for the duration of the war on terrorism, or, as Donald Rumsfeld put it, until there are no longer any effective global terrorist networks left in the world. Everyone has global reach these days, and the prospects for ending political violence worldwide are dim, to say the least, so the administration in effect claims the power to impose life sentences without trial. The sentences are served incommunicado, and without any hearings or trials. Is it any wonder that there have been more than 30 suicide attempts at Guantanamo thus far? The Supreme Court has agreed to decide whether federal courts can even entertain challenges to the legality of the Guantanamo detentions, but the government's essentially lawless actions there have already incurred widespread international condemnation.

The government should be able to hold enemy combatants during wartime. But when war is defined in the administration's terms, it is not a temporary measure but a permanent condition. And the Geneva Conventions, which recognize the authority to detain enemy combatants, also require that where there is any doubt as to their status, they must be afforded a hearing. The United States has routinely provided such hearings in prior conflicts. Yet the administration has held not a single such hearing for the Guantanamo detainees. President Bush says he's sure they are all bad people. But as Stuart Taylor has pointed out, he was also sure on May 29, 2003, that we had found Iraq's weapons of mass destruction.

The administration is planning to subject some of the Guantanamo detainees to trials before military tribunals. But the rules for these tribunals appear to be designed not to distinguish the innocent from the guilty, but to stage show trials targeted at a small segment of the detained population. As of February 2004, more than two years after the first detainees were brought to Guantanamo, the administration had selected only eight persons as eligible for trial, and had not yet begun those trials. The rules for the tribunals permit imposition of the death penalty but deny defendants *any* independent judicial review. The President authorizes the prosecutions and is the final stage of review, with only a military apparatus (subject to his command) in between. What's worse, defendants may be convicted on the basis of evidence that neither they nor their chosen attorney has any opportunity to confront or rebut.

The Bush White House defends its actions on Guantanamo by emphasizing that the detainees are foreign nationals held outside our borders, implying that American citizens' rights are not threatened. It defends its campaign of preventive detention by broadly asserting that most of those detained were illegal aliens, again suggesting that citizens need not worry about being similarly treated. And it has limited the military tribunals' jurisdiction to noncitizens accused of terrorism, explaining that those who come here to attack us do not deserve the same rights and guarantees that American citizens do. But the government's ultimate argument for these authorities is not the passport the detainees happen to carry, but the war power, which is in no way limited to foreign nationals. It is now holding two American citizens—Yasser Hamdi and Jose Padilla—under the same authority it initially invoked only as to foreign nationals on Guantanamo. Hamdi was allegedly captured in Afghanistan; Padilla was arrested at Chicago's O'Hare Airport. Both have been held incommunicado in military brigs for more than a year. Thus, the administration now claims that the President can declare anyone—American or Pakistani—anywhere in the world, from Iraq to Idaho, as an "enemy combatant," and thereby subject him to indefinite incommunicado military detention without access to lawyers or the courts. The Supreme Court has also agreed to review Hamdi's and Padilla's cases, after a federal court of appeals in New York City ruled that the President lacked the power to detain Padilla without express congressional authorization.

The administration's war on terrorism has little to show in the way of improvements in security, and much to explain in terms of lost liberties. In particular, its tendency to pursue the course of least resistance has contributed to a world more virulently anti-American than ever before in our nation's history. There was and is a better way to assure that we are both safe and free.

III. Solutions

If law enforcement should not broadly target Arab and Muslim foreign nationals, what can be done to make the United States more secure? At the outset, it is important to acknowledge that no combination of measures will ever eliminate the threat of politically motivated violence. This phenomenon has been with us since time immemorial, and cannot be eliminated, even by the toughest security measures imaginable. If President Bush is correct that the war on terrorism will not end until "every terrorist group of global reach has been found, stopped, and defeated," it will never end. As Tom Ridge, head of Homeland Security, has said, the scope of the undertaking is daunting: "Airports, borders, development of partnerships with the state and local governments, mapping critical infrastructure with the private sector, focusing on cybersecurity, developing plans to enhance our capacity to respond to weapons of mass destruction, enhancement of our public infrastructure—I mean it is an endless list." So endless that

Atlantic Monthly writer David Carr has argued, only slightly hyperbolically, that "homeland security is the national version of the gas mask in the desk drawer—something that lets people feel safer without actually making them so." As Carr elaborates:

> In 2000 more than 350 million non-U.S. citizens entered the country. In 1999 Americans made 5.2 billion phone calls to locations outside the country. Federal Express handles nearly five million packages every business day, UPS accounts for 13.6 million, and until it became a portal for terror, the Postal Service processed 680 million pieces of mail a day. More than two billion tons of cargo ran in and out of U.S. ports in 1999.

Weapons of mass destruction could be smuggled into the country relatively easily in a cargo container, yet before September 11 only two percent of all containers coming into the country were actually inspected, and we do not have the means now to increase that percentage substantially. In addition, as drug smugglers have shown, a few well-placed bribes can defeat virtually any inspection scheme. And if terrorists decide to turn on us the suicide bombing tactics that Palestinians have employed in Israel, there will be little we can do to stop them.

This is not to say that we should throw up our hands. While no measures can guarantee absolute safety, we can be made safer. But at the same time, we must accept the reality that we have to live with a considerable amount of risk. As former National Security Council officials Daniel Benjamin and Steven Simon argue, "Technology and better information sharing within the United States government and between the United States and other countries can improve the probability of finding the needle in the haystack from zero to 'just maybe.'"

There are a range of steps that can be taken to make us more secure without compromising our basic principles.

Sharing and Analyzing Data

First and foremost, efforts to improve information sharing within the government and with other nations are critical. But by most accounts, the barriers to information sharing prior to September 11 were more bureaucratic than legal in nature, so amending laws will not solve the problem.

The FBI reportedly used legalistic arguments to rationalize its reluctance to share information with others, but the source of the reluctance was its own institutional culture, not law. Similarly, internally the FBI's problem was not so much that it was legally hampered by restrictions on its investigatory powers as that it was disorganized and decentralized, and did not sufficiently reward intelligence analysis. According to former National Security Council officials Benjamin and Simon, "New York doesn't talk to Headquarters. Headquarters doesn't talk to itself. Operations doesn't talk to the analysts. Field offices don't talk to each other.... From the inside, the FBI was a disorganized jumble of competing and unruly power centers; from the outside it was a surly colossus." These problems require changes in institutional culture and organization, not an expansion of investigative authority. The PATRIOT Act did not do it; a bipartisan commission of national security experts concluded more than two years after the PATRIOT Act was enacted that the federal government had made little progress in facilitating information sharing on matters of national security.

As virtually all assessments of the government's failure to detect and prevent the September 11 attacks have concluded, the principal problem was not the government's lack of legal authority for gathering information, but its failure to analyze the massive troves of data it had. As so many have said, the government did not "connect the dots." Some of this criticism is unfair; it is always easier to see connections in hindsight than while events are developing. But if the problem is that the government failed to analyze the information it had, laws and programs that will inundate authorities with still more information are not likely to provide a solution. The difficulty is that there are already too many extraneous dots. According to a Markle Foundation Task Force comprised of national security and technology experts, "Those who have called for endless mining of vast new government data warehouses are not offering the promise of real security. They instead evoke memories of the walls of clippings collected by the paranoid genius, John Nash, in *A Beautiful Mind*."

For this reason, freeing the FBI from the requirement that it limit its investigations to individuals and groups with some basis for concern about criminal activity—or for that matter, creating a separate domestic intelligence agency along the lines of Great Britain's MI5—is unlikely to make us safer. The nominal requirement that the FBI's activities have some connection to federal crime serves to focus the agency on those who pose the greatest threat, and to forestall the expenditure of scarce resources on individuals and groups with neither an intention nor a capacity to commit a federal crime. This is hardly an onerous threshold; before Ashcroft relaxed the FBI guidelines, a preliminary inquiry could be instituted where there was any indication of concern about criminal activity, and required nothing like probable cause. Thus, contrary to popular wisdom, the FBI was never prohibited from investigating groups that had not yet engaged in criminal activity, and could investigate as long as there was some basis for believing that they had the potential to do so.

Controlling Access to Weapons of Mass Destruction

One important measure that can make us safer without infringing on civil liberties is limiting the threat posed by access to weapons of mass destruction. As Jessica Stern, former National Security Council official and author of *The Ultimate Terrorist*, has argued, it is essential that we help secure vulnerable stockpiles of nuclear weapons and weapons components, especially those in the former Soviet Union; that we shore up security measures in the states of the former Soviet Union to forestall smuggling, theft, or sale of such weapons; and that we do much more to prepare for attacks with chemical and biological weapons or industrial poisons. With respect to the latter, Stern argues, it is relatively impossible to prevent their entry into the United States, but many lives can be saved if emergency responders are better prepared to detect the attacks, and to take protective measures to treat victims and to limit the spread of harmful viruses or pathogens.

Other responses to the dangers posed by weapons of mass destruction do present constitutional concerns, but are nonetheless warranted. Prohibitions on the publication of information about how to build such weapons may be justified, even though they would restrict speech not necessarily intended or likely to incite imminent illegal conduct (the usual standard for criminalizing advocacy of criminal conduct). It is difficult to see what value such publications add to the "marketplace of ideas" that the First Amendment is designed to protect, and the dangers they present grow exponentially with each technological advance. Similarly, efforts to limit widespread public access to information about the vulnerabilities of critical infrastructure, such as water and energy supplies, Internet and communication networks, and nuclear power plants, make a great deal of sense, even though they may also impede some access to that information for legitimate purposes. Because such measures do not target any particularly vulnerable minority, and affect in some measure the informational rights of us all, one can be more sanguine that the political process will ensure that it is an appropriately limited infringement.

Protecting Targets

We need to protect potential targets of terrorism through limitations on access, metal detectors, concrete barriers, and the like. These measures create inconvenience for many in the name of creating inconvenience for terrorists, but again, precisely because they inconvenience us all, the measures adopted are likely to reflect a fair balance between security and freedom. Strengthening cockpit doors and placing air marshals on some planes are more likely to deter another terrorist hijacking than ethnic profiling, and do not rely on a double standard. Of course, the sheer number of potential targets makes target protection a necessarily partial measure, but it is nonetheless an important one.

Border Control and Adapting to Advances in Technology

Increased border control and information gathering about foreign guests also makes sense as a security matter. There are legitimate questions about how effective the collection of such information will be, but constitutional concerns are presented not by registration itself but by its selective targeting at certain ethnic and religious groups. In addition, modernizing information gathering techniques to take account of technological advances, such as authorizing "roving wiretaps" to address the problem of suspects regularly changing their cell phones, are not objectionable, and may be essential to tracking down terrorist suspects.

Working with—Not against—Arab and Muslim Communities

But if we are to have a real chance at finding the proverbial needles in the haystack, human intelligence is critical, and for that we must seek to work with, not against, those communities in which there is reason to suspect al Qaeda threats might exist. It is not a prejudicial stereotype to acknowledge that al Qaeda is made up principally of Arab and Muslim foreign nationals. But instead of treating all males within those communities as presumptively suspect, we should be seeking to build bridges to Arab and Muslim communities here and abroad, to encourage the law-abiding and security-loving members of those communities to work with us to identify any terrorists among them. The Bush administration has paid lip service to the need not to alienate these communities, but its actions have spoken louder than words. Its massive ethnic profiling campaign could hardly have been *less* successful in identifying actual terrorists. We would do far better to work with Arab and Muslim communities cooperatively rather than profile them coercively.

Beyond Law Enforcement

Finally, we must not make the mistake of focusing exclusively on law enforcement and intelligence measures. Security is affected by a wide variety of domestic and foreign policies and actions. As the longstanding, terror-ridden conflicts in Great Britain and Israel painfully illustrate, nations cannot police themselves out of politically motivated violence. Israel has cracked down on civil liberties in ways that thus far still seem unimaginable in the United States, and yet it continues to be plagued by terrorist violence. If we are to reduce the extent of terrorist violence aimed at us, we must understand its root causes and address them.

We cannot negotiate a peace settlement with al Qaeda, nor should we appease terrorists. But we must recognize that the seeds of political violence thrive in discontent and despair, and that our policies affect those conditions. Thus, for example, two of al Qaeda's biggest recruiting pitches focused on the stationing of American troops in Saudi Arabia, and U.S. support of Israel's occupation of the West Bank. More deeply, we need to address the massive inequalities in global wealth and resources from which we inordinately benefit, and which breed much poverty and resentment.

The roots of Islamic fundamentalism lie in truly desperate situations; the fact that some of the 9/11 hijackers were middle class does not refute the reality that people are generally driven to desperate actions by desperate situations. We are the richest nation in the world, yet we are dead last in terms of the amount of foreign aid doled out to other nations as a percentage of gross national income.

Most importantly, we must not lose sight of the costs of "American exceptionalism," both in our foreign policy abroad and in the double standards we employ at home. The perception that the United States feels free to operate by its own set of rules, is not bound by the rule of law, and is willing to impose on foreigners burdens and obligations its own citizens would never tolerate, has generated an unprecedented wave of resentment that both impedes cooperation in the struggle against terrorism and further incites those already hostile to us.

The events of September 11 have for good reason prompted widespread concern about the United States' ability to predict and prevent future terrorist attacks. That concern may well justify recalibrating the balance between liberty and security. But when we seek to strike that balance by targeting foreign nationals, and especially foreign nationals of Arab and Muslim identity, we undermine security by simultaneously creating enemies and losing the assistance and cooperation of potential friends.

CHAPTER THIRTEEN

From Affirmative Action to Affirmative Opportunity

CHRISTOPHER EDLEY JR.*

Complete the unfinished anti-discrimination law enforcement agenda and then move on to the "opportunity agenda" that will target racial and ethnic disparities in education, health, criminal justice, and other areas.

I. The Problem

The Michigan Cases

A meaningful assessment of racial justice should begin with analysis of the data concerning continuing levels of discrimination, deepening patterns of residential and school segregation, and persistent racial and ethnic disparities in vital social and economic indicators. For better or worse, however, discussion of the politics of civil rights now begins with an assessment of the affirmative action wars.

In the June 2003 *Michigan Cases,* the U.S. Supreme Court ruled that race-sensitive affirmative action in admissions to public higher education, if done properly, is constitutionally permissible. The central opinion by Justice Sandra Day O'Connor, writing for a 5-4 majority, was an implicit affirmation of President Clinton's 1995 "mend it, don't end it" stance on affirmative action. It was also a repudiation of conservative and revisionist arguments that affirmative action is morally and constitutionally indefensible.

Critically, the constitutional ruling does not *require* that institutions adopt affirmative action; it merely confirms that there are constitutionally acceptable justifications and means available. We are left with the continuing debate in institutions and communities around the country over

* CHRISTOPHER EDLEY JR. *is a Professor at Harvard Law School, Co-Director of The Civil Rights Project at Harvard, and Dean-Designate of the University of California at Berkeley Law School (Boalt Hall). He was in charge of President Clinton's Review of Federal Affirmative Action Programs. He is grateful for the help of Marilyn Byrne, Taj Clayton, Jia Cobb, Laurent Heller, and Johanna Wald in preparing this paper.*

whether and when race-conscious measures are *desirable*. As a practical matter, the question is not whether progressives will continue to support the Clinton formulation; even a majority of the Supreme Court has, in effect, done just that. The question is whether progressives will be willing to spend capital to defend race-sensitive affirmative action in the face of continuing challenges in the political and policy realms.

Affirmative action is worth fighting about for at least three reasons.

First, it is a tool that enables us to take qualified individuals who are standing at the threshold of some opportunity (educational, employment, business) and help them get across that threshold in the face of individual or structural bias—be it old fashioned bigotry, informal networks, or innocent "comfort level" judgments. Second, affirmative action is a tool that helps particular organizations—such as a university, a newsroom, the military, a corporation, or a police force—pursue excellence because diversity is critical to success in some aspect of that mission. Third, this is a fight about values that we also bring to bear on a host of other race-related social and policy matters. If retrogression is victorious in one setting, it is more likely to triumph elsewhere. Call it the domino theory of race relations.

Affirmative action is also a *transitional policy*, in the sense that someday the ordinary opportunity mechanisms of society will be repaired so as to make the policy unnecessary, as both President Clinton and Justice O'Connor suggested in different ways. More than this, however, it is a transition policy because its practice and its justification lead us beyond the unfinished, traditional *anti-discrimination agenda* for racial progress toward an emerging *opportunity agenda* that focuses on education, employment, home ownership and asset-building, health care, immigrant rights, and the deepening of democratic engagement—starting with voter participation.

Beyond the Michigan Cases

The Court's opinions in *The Michigan Cases* left many legal questions unanswered, some of them quite important not only for debates over affirmative action in employment and elsewhere but also for the broader national struggle to deal fairly and productively with our growing diversity. For example, one step away from the cases, and quite clearly implicated by them, is the matter of K-12 school integration—what costs if any are we prepared to bear in pursuing it notwithstanding persistent residential segregation? We face a confluence of challenging trends.

First, increasingly conservative federal courts are growing more aggressive in dissolving long-standing court orders against racial segregation, declaring that the constitutional violations and their legally material "vestiges" are over, or that no further remedial effort is practicable. (Many civil rights advocates believe that these courts have simply lowered the standard and declared a remedial victory when schools remain separate and unequal because officials simply have not tried hard enough, and courts prefer not to be bothered any longer.) Second, while racial and ethnic diversity are growing nationwide, all too frequently this dramatic change is accompanied by economic and racial segregation in housing patterns, and hence in neighborhood-oriented public schools. Third, the standards-based school reform movement initiated by the 1983 report, *A Nation At Risk*, is in full flower as policy across the nation at every level of government.

One dimension of reform is an emphasis on test-based accountability for education achievement. So, at the same time that schools in many areas are growing more segregated or at risk of becoming so, there is an ever-growing body of quantitative evidence that education opportunity and achievement are color-coded. On the one hand, this increases the incentives for achievement-oriented families to seek out communities or school settings in which they will be segregated away from under-achieving populations. On the other hand, it leads everyone, including minorities, to be more focused on the goal of measurable achievement rather than the ethnic demography of school buildings or classrooms. Local newspapers rate schools based on standardized test scores, not quality of preparation for life in increasingly diverse communities.

The question for progressives and everyone else, then, is not whether school integration is desirable, for surely it is. The question is whether we care enough to actually *do* something, and whether federal judges appointed by Presidents and confirmed by the Senate will consider such voluntary efforts to fight racial segregation in our schools to be constitutionally permissible. And, finally, the question is whether the President's appointees at the Justice Department, who with their staff appear in courts on behalf of the United States, will take sides in our national ambivalence around the integration ideal.

Taking another step away from *The Michigan Cases* then brings us to the still broader agenda not just of K–12 and college but also the full foundation of opportunities required for genuine equality and social justice. The question for progressives is not whether we are committed to expanding opportunity for all, for again surely we are. But will we demand accountability from leaders and institutions not only for ending discrimination but also for affirmatively equalizing opportunities in the face of inherited and structural disadvantages? Or was our moral and political commitment to racial progress limited to merely one generation of struggle, and in only the most noxious dimensions of American apartheid and color caste?

The Legacies of American Apartheid

It was only 50 years ago that the Supreme Court held unconstitutional America's version of racial apartheid, although it was over a decade before any real progress was made desegregating schools in the south and a few districts elsewhere. It was only 40 years ago, in the Civil Rights Act of 1964, that Congress prohibited rank discrimination in private sector employment, hotels, and public accommodations. Nor would Congress have moved on those issues even then had it not been for the mass protests and mobilization of the civil rights movement, the assassination of a president, and the extraordinary force-of-nature determination of President Johnson. Then, within the next few years, the Voting Rights Act of 1965 and the Fair Housing Act of 1968 completed a 15-year period of affirmative progress, with each of the three branches of government contributing important elements to the struggle. Since then, however, there has never been a moment when all three branches can be said to have worked in concert to undo the lasting damage from America's legacy of color caste.

The Nixon administration, for example, set to work against court-ordered school desegregation and constructed the modern Republican Party's "southern strategy" of appeals to disaffected Whites resentful of the racial disruptions caused by Martin Luther King, Lyndon Johnson, Earl Warren, and their ilk. Congress hesitated as well, allowing too many of the Great Society initiatives to wither which might have been the opportunity-creating complement to the formal legal equality promised by civil rights statutes. And the courts, with a newly conservative Supreme Court and increasingly conservative lower courts, began to hesitate and then, by the 1980s, switch sides and become, more often than not, obstacles to racial justice.

But at the same time we have seen dramatic demographic developments that make the issue of race in America even more complex. By the middle of the twenty-first century, there will be no majority racial group, and the common media portrayal of the "typical" American as a Euro-Caucasian should have long-since been abandoned. Latinos now outnumber African Americans, and both Latinos and Asians are becoming significant population subgroups in an ever-growing list of communities and states. For example:

- The 2000 Census of Population counted nearly 29 million immigrants living in United States metropolitan areas, representing a 10 million-person increase since 1990. In the period between 1980 and 2000, the White population in the United States grew by 14 million people but dropped from over three-quarters to less than two-thirds of the metropolitan total.

- In recent years, there has been significant demographic change within the Black population. The number of Black Americans with origins in sub-Saharan Africa nearly tripled during the 1990s. The number of Black Americans with recent roots in the Caribbean increased by over 60 percent. In some major metropolitan regions, these groups amount to 20 percent or more of the Black population.

- Schools within the United States are steadily becoming more non-White. Minority student enrollment is nearly 40 percent of all American public school students. In the western and southern regions of the United States, almost half of all public school students are non-White. After a steady decline in racial segregation from the mid 1960s through the late 1980s, public schools have been resegregating for the past 15 years. This is particularly notable in the South, where school desegregation has receded the most rapidly. Since 1988, there has also been a steady increase in the number of Black and Latino students attending 90–100 percent minority schools. In the West, the typical Latino student is currently attending a school that is almost 75 percent non-White, an

increase of 13 percentage points over the last two decades. Among
public schools where Black and Latino students are the majority,
over 70 percent are concentrated poverty schools. (And, of course,
schools with concentrated poverty are far less likely to be educationally effective.)

- There are six states in which Anglo public school children are less
  than a majority, including California and Texas (the others being
  Hawaii, New Mexico, Louisiana, and Mississippi) and of the 25
  largest central city school districts in the country, only one has a
  majority White student population.

The cliché that we must move beyond the Black-White paradigm of
race relations provides only the thinnest hint of the dimensions of the challenge. The diversity sweeping America will have profound affects on language, popular culture, politics, and even religion. The size of the continuing immigration from Latin America, but also from Asia and Africa—much
of it the inexorable result of global economic forces in combination with
our own democratic traditions—assures that the patterns we now see so
clearly in the data are here to stay, and will grow. We see it most clearly in
our schools, but soon it will transform the workforce and every arena of
national life.

The challenge, of course, is not simply one of newness and change. The
demography is combined with deep divisions and disparities along lines of
color, raising questions about whether we are one community of equal
stakeholders in the grand American experiment of multiethnic, liberal,
market-oriented democracy. For example:

- A study based on data from the 2000 Census revealed that non-
  Hispanic Blacks remain the lowest-income minority group with
  household incomes that are only 63.7 percent as high as non-
  Hispanic Whites. And wealth disparities are far greater, even, than
  income disparities.

- With respect to health care, racial and ethnic minorities are more
  likely than Whites to be enrolled in "lower-end" health plans,
  characterized by higher per capita resource constraints and more
  severe limits on covered services. In fact, hundreds of studies reveal
  that African Americans, Hispanics, Native Americans, and Asian

American/ Pacific Islanders receive less care and lower quality of care than comparable Whites.

- There is a strong correlation between uncounted, or "spoiled," election ballots and the percentage of Blacks in the voting district's population. Of the 100 counties with the highest spoilage rates, 67 have Black populations above 12 percent. Of the top 100 counties with the lowest spoilage rates, only 10 have sizeable Black populations, while the population of 70 of these counties is over 75 percent White. A study by the House Committee on Government Reform found that votes cast for president in low-income, high-minority congressional districts throughout the United States were three times more likely to be discarded as spoiled than votes cast in more affluent, low-minority districts; in balloting for congressional candidates, voters in the less fortunate districts were 20 times more likely to have their votes go up in smoke.

- A study of the criminal justice system revealed that when White youth and minority youth were charged with the same offenses, African-American youth with no prior offenses were six times more likely to be incarcerated in public facilities than White youth with the same background, and Hispanic youth three times more likely. It is estimated that 28.5 percent of Black males born today will serve time in a state or federal prison compared to 4.4 percent of non-Hispanic, White males.

- By 1998, while Black and Latino youths represented about one-third of the country's adolescent population, they accounted for two-thirds of all youths confined to juvenile or detention and correctional placement.

- Nationwide, Black students are nearly three times as likely as White students to be labeled mentally retarded and almost twice as likely to be labeled as having emotional disturbances. Once labeled, these students are much more likely to be isolated in substantially separate classrooms from their non-disabled peers. (Note that since these are national averages, they mask much more dramatic racial disparities in particular states and school districts.)

- In our 100 largest cities, 58 percent or more of ninth grade students in schools with a high population of minority students do not graduate four years later. Tragic achievement disparities persist; scores in mathematics and reading from the National Assessment of Educational Progress indicate significant differences between Latinos and Whites and between Blacks and Whites, with no over- all statistically significant narrowing of these gaps since 1990. Despite an overall decline in the dropout rates for the past 30 years, Black students drop out at nearly twice the rate of Whites, and Latinos drop out at nearly four times the rate of Whites.

- Disparities with respect to public transportation are prevalent throughout the United States. Inequities in investments, expendi- tures, and service quality exist between bus service, which tends to serve more low-income riders, and rail service, which tends to serve higher-income riders. Furthermore, many transportation planners and policymakers, concerned primarily with the needs of suburban commuters, have focused on constructing highways and commuter rail lines that do little to serve the needs of minority and low-income communities, which depend on public trans- portation.

Finally, we face a new and more complex agenda without having com- pleted the first agenda, that of combating persistent discrimination and bigotry. For example:

- A recent experiment in Boston and Chicago revealed that resumes randomly assigned "White-sounding names" received 50 percent more callbacks for interviews than identical resumes assigned "African-American sounding" names.

- A HUD Housing Discrimination Study conducted in the early 1990s revealed strong evidence of racial steering and discrimina- tion in the housing market. Twenty audit cites were randomly selected from among metropolitan areas having a central city pop- ulation exceeding 100,000 with Blacks constituting more than 12 percent of the population. Whites received more favorable credit assistance in 46 percent of sales encounters.

- The HUD 2000 Housing Discrimination Study conducted by the Urban Institute in 23 metro areas showed important improvements since studies in 1977 and 1989, but continuing strong evidence of discrimination and steering. For example Black renters receive consistently unfavorable treatment in 21.6 percent of their inquiries, down 4.8 percentage points since 1989. Hispanic renters receive consistently unfavorable treatment in 25.7 percent of their inquiries, essentially the same as 1989.

- Investigators at Tufts University, who exposed research subjects to digitally manipulated faces identical except for skin tone, found that both Blacks and Whites associate intelligence, motivation, and attractiveness with light-skinned Blacks, and poverty and unattractiveness with darker-skinned Blacks.

- Numerous studies have revealed that police routinely use a person's race in calculating whether, or to what extent, to subject that person to surveillance, questioning, or search.

These social and economic disparities mean that demographic change, if it continues to reinforce those disparities, portends ever-worsening strains and, eventually, calamitous adjustments. For America is not immune to the miseries of tribalism and intolerance. In the measure of history, slavery was not long ago, and Jim Crow was only yesterday. Only moments ago, lynching was a sport and racial intermarriage a crime. There is little reason to believe that America's long history of race riots is finished.

II. Recent Developments

Today, all three branches pose dire threats both to hard-won victories of a generation ago and to the opportunity agenda that must complement the anti-discrimination agenda if that legacy is to be undone. Occasional victories can be better understood as tactical victories against a growing conservative retrenchment in matters of civil rights policy and law.

Consider two of the most noted "progressive victories" for civil rights in the past decade: President Clinton's successful "mend it, don't end it" defense of affirmative action in 1995, and the Supreme Court's 2003 ruling in *The Michigan Cases*. Each development was, in fact, merely a successful defense of a widely used practice, not a material advance. Indeed, these political and judicial decisions were, in some respects, conservative and limiting, effectively reigning in some practices that many advocates believed entirely defensible and desirable.

More broadly, the recent developments in litigation, policy and politics all reinforce this pattern of limited successes in the face of a serious loss of momentum, if not outright erosion in progress. Even as we search out bold but feasible new directions, we cannot avoid being reactive; much of our new agenda is mortgaged to the defense of earlier gains and the reversal of recent setbacks.

1. Litigation and the Courts

Notwithstanding *The Michigan Cases,* there were a string of judicial decisions during the 1990s that created obstacles to racial justice litigation in voting rights, employment discrimination, housing discrimination, school desegregation, and elsewhere (see the table of cases). Put broadly, there are several troubling and substantial developments in Supreme Court doctrine, combining breadth of impact with difficulty of overturning legislative or administrative action. In voting rights, the Supreme Court in its *Shaw v. Reno* line of cases beginning in 1993 has established guidelines that make it more difficult to defend districts that will likely elect minority officials, and more difficult to attack redistricting and other election procedure changes that arguably erode minority electoral power. Concerning congressional power, in *City of Boerne v. Flores*, the Court announced novel restrictions on the power of Congress to adopt legislation to remedy violations of the Equal Protection clause. A cluster of cases raise barriers to the efforts of private plaintiffs to take states to court and to congressional efforts to make states subject to civil rights damages suits by individuals. In the crucial case of *Alexander v. Sandoval*, the Court cut off access to court for private victims of "disparate impact" or "effects-based" discrimination based on the regulations implementing Title VI of the Civil Rights Act of 1964. Simultaneously, some of the Court's language and reasoning raised questions about the legitimacy of the regulations themselves, even if limited to grounds for agency-driven administrative enforcement of the act, which bans discrimination by recipients of federal grants, contracts, and aid.

SOME KEY CASES IMPOSING LIMITATIONS
ON CIVIL RIGHTS STATUTES

- *Buckhannon Board & Care Home, Inc. v. West Virginia Dept. of Health and Human Services*: Eliminated the catalyst theory of attorneys fees, making it more difficult for individuals to obtain legal representation to vindicate their civil rights in court.

- *Alexander v. Sandoval:* Prohibited the private right of action to sue under the disparate impact regulations of Title VI of the 1964 Civil Rights Act and questioned the validity of disparate impact regulations; possible implications for other civil rights statutes.

- *Hoffman Plastic Compounds, Inc. v. NLRB:* Undocumented workers are not entitled to post-discharge back pay remedies under the National Labor Relations Act.

- *Circuit City Stores v. Adams and Gilmer v. Interstate/Johnson Lane Corp.:* Civil rights claimants can be forced to give up their right to bring claims in court and instead be required to seek relief through arbitration procedures that lack most of the protections of court proceedings.

- *Kimel v. Florida Board of Regents:* State sovereign immunity bars claims against states by employees for damages under the Age and Discrimination in Employment Act (ADEA); possible implications for other civil rights statutes.

- *Alden v. Maine:* Constitutionally founded state sovereign immunity means no right to bring an action for damages against a state under the Fair Labor Standards Act; possible implications for other civil rights statutes.

- *Barnes v. Gorman:* No right to punitive damages for intentional violations of Section 504 and the Americans with Disabilities Act; possible implications for other civil rights statutes.

- *Gebser v. Lago Vista Independent School District:* No damages for sexual harassment under Title IX unless there is "actual notice" to the

school district and "deliberate indifference" to the claim; possible
implications for other civil rights statutes.

- *Hazen Paper v. Biggins: In dicta*, the Court utilized language subsequently interpreted by some lower courts that the disparate impact
  standard of proof is not available under the Age Discrimination in
  Employment Act; possible implications for other civil rights
  statutes.

- *West Virginia University Hospitals v. Casey*: No right to recover
  expert witness fees under Section 1988.

The table lists examples of several cases that are troubling for racial justice, but that can be reversed or at least mitigated by congressional action.
This inventory illustrates the importance of effective political participation,
absent which there is no reason to expect congressional action, no matter
who is President. More broadly, however, the difficulty is in the very conservative turn of the Supreme Court and many of the lower federal courts.
Again, the "remedy" is political: the stakes in presidential elections are often
high, but especially so when the Supreme Court hangs in the balance.
Although the major parties may want to avoid making race an explicit
issue in the 2004 presidential election, voters interested in racial justice
should discuss it given how much is at risk.

2. Policy Developments

Outside the courts, on the policy front the difficulties seem as pronounced. For example:

- *Civil rights enforcement.* Since the Carter administration, federal
  enforcement expenditures across the agencies have declined
  approximately 40 percent in real terms, even though civil rights
  enforcement has broadened far beyond racial justice to the point
  where most agency litigation also involves disability or age discrimination. This is not because racial discrimination has vanished;
  the evidence, of course, is that it has not. The budgets are an index
  of political and perhaps even moral commitment to the anti-
  discrimination imperative, and the signal is dismaying.

- *Racial profiling.* Advocates and researchers succeeded over the 1990s in raising the visibility of racial profiling and bringing policymakers and police officials to realize it is both a rights abuse and an ineffective law enforcement tool. By the end of the decade, there was bipartisan agreement, at least at a superficial, rhetorical level, that racial profiling is unacceptable. The consensus, however, never extended to include immigration and border enforcement, on the debatable logic—supported by the Supreme Court—that profiling based on "national origin" is less objectionable even if correlated with color (or religion), especially near our borders. (That argument is rarely embraced, for example, by Latino communities in the Southwest who might be expected to question a "liberty tax" imposed on brown-skinned people for the privilege of living within a few hundred miles of the border.) In any case, this awkward consensus was dealt a mortal blow by the tragedy of September 11, 2001, and the politically popular anti-terrorism measures adopted in its aftermath.

- *Sentencing, incarceration, and prevention.* Perhaps the most dramatic civil rights setback in the criminal justice arena has been the steady march towards punitive incarceration as the public safety tool of choice. The trend, building since the 1980s, has accelerated as state and federal policies alike emphasized mandatory minimum sentencing, "truth-in-sentencing" laws, 3-strikes rules, a proliferation of death penalty offenses, limitations on post-conviction judicial relief through habeas corpus, and—compounding matters—cuts in prevention and diversion strategies. Violent crime rates peaked and retreated in most communities, but many analysts find little reason to think that incarceration rates are the principal explanatory factor. Minority communities want freedom from victimization as much if not more than middle-class communities. *The question is whether a just society should make a community pay for safety by enduring the burden, cost, and disruption of the highest incarceration rates in the developed world.* Moreover, there is increasing concern about the back end of the criminal justice system: the high incarceration rates mean that large numbers of ex-felons return to their communities, often concentrated in particular neighborhoods—but without the needed array of social services from job training to drug treatment. Yet with overwhelmed and chaotic parole systems, they too often become repeat offenders.

- *Felon disfranchisement.* One concomitant of the high incarceration rates is that a growing proportion of minority voting-age citizens are barred from voting because of state disfranchisement laws. Nationally, 1.84 million African Americans are disenfranchised, which represents 7.5 percent of the African-American voting-age population; this is roughly *seven times* the rate for voting age citizens as a whole. In six of the states that disenfranchise ex-felons, one-in-four Black men are permanently denied the right to vote.

- *K-12 education equity.* There are countless education-related issues that must be part of the racial justice agenda, including school resegregation, resource inequity, abusive high-stakes testing, teacher quality in needy schools, opportunity for English Language Learners, racial disparities in school discipline, and more. There are cosmic questions to be faced about whether nineteenth century models for the organization, funding, and governance of schools will work for the diversity and complexity of the twenty-first century, with the dangerous trends in deep inequality. Less ambitiously and more immediately, however, we must answer the question of whether school reform will serve to advance or derail our racial justice efforts in the years ahead.

This last point bears added emphasis. In 2002, some observers believed there was a major advance in the bipartisan, federal No Child Left Behind (NCLB) Act, the most recent reauthorization of the Elementary and Secondary Education Act of 1965. This optimism was based on several features of the new law, including the requirement that states and districts disaggregate district and school-level student achievement data by racial and other subpopulations, and that accountability for school improvement be determined with respect to the annual progress towards student proficiency made by each subgroup. In short, there was a national commitment, at least in statute, to the proposition that a successful school and school system must succeed with poor and minority students, not just with middle-class and Anglo students.

In two short years, however, many of the hopes that accompanied enactment have been dashed by federal and state budget cuts that make the NCLB reforms all but unachievable, together with feckless implementation and excessively rigid technicalities in the complex law. All of this is compounded by requirements for massive increases in testing and analytically flawed use of the testing for determination of school progress, which many expert observers from all ideological camps consider a prescription for disaster.

Thus, it remains to be seen whether the national movement for standards-based school reform can indeed be harnessed to advance the racial justice agenda, rather than transformed into a stalking horse for privatization and the dismantling of public education. This is the single most important opportunity component of the civil rights agenda for the coming decade.

3. Political Developments

Over the past 15 years, the evolution of the two major national parties has complicated the political images presented to those voters concerned with racial and ethnic justice. Each political party has always had within it contrasting tendencies on race, progressive and reactionary. Ironically, as the absence of immediate crises of blood or protest has permitted race to recede into a secondary issue in national political life, each party has had latitude to fashion an image less centered on racial matters, thereby allowing the competing intra-party tendencies on race to harden and co-exist. For those observers to whom the race issues remain primary, the party's images are perhaps as fractured as they have been since the civil rights era a generation ago.

The Republican Party's "southern strategy" mobilized a combination of racial resentment and cultural conservatism to achieve political dominance throughout most of that region. Today, in the wake of that success, the hard-edged civil rights revisionism of the Reagan administration has given way to a "kinder, gentler" message from many national GOP leaders. On affirmative action, for example, the effectiveness of Clinton's centrist formulation in the mid-1990s quelled the interest of the congressional wing of the GOP in dismantling federal affirmative action (though not edgier conservative GOP factions elsewhere). More recently, Colin Powell and Condoleezza Rice, African-American senior appointees in Bush's government, are commonly thought to have played central roles in moderating the influence of administration conservatives on the subject.

In the Supreme Court, the Bush Department of Justice argued somewhat moderately as a "friend of the court" only that the Michigan plans were not "narrowly tailored" because they were allegedly too quota-like; the government did not contest the university's asserted "compelling interest" in diversity. The "quota" label was libelous, but the implied concession concerning the compelling interest in diversity was momentous. On racial profiling, prior to 9/11, Attorney General John Ashcroft made statements condemning the practice. In its K–12 education reform legislation in 2001, the Republican administration was initially more forthcoming about the importance of accountability for closing racial disparities in achievement than the Clinton administration had been (while at the same time, however, substantially curtailing the effectiveness of civil rights enforcement in the Department of Education, and later breaking its funding promises on school reform).

To be sure, beneath this softer message the policy actions of the Bush administration and Republican-controlled Congress are a plethora of legislative, regulatory, budgetary and enforcement choices attempting to turn back the clock, though with less fanfare and zealotry than in the heyday of Reagan civil rights revisionism. For Republicans, the "Rockefeller wing" of the party was traditionally more supportive of civil rights and uneasy about the southern strategy. Now this centrist strand, a decidedly lesser voice within the party, is especially intent on courting the growing Latino vote. The question is whether such a socially tolerant, economically pragmatic, politically strategic perspective will carry the day in GOP circles increasingly dominated by staunch conservatives.

While it still seems undeniable that Democrats are generally more attuned to the anti-discrimination and opportunity agendas, and polling indicates that this is the perception among minorities, many Democratic Party leaders are loathe to concede the South but unable to devise an effective counter-strategy. Their prescription since the 1988 cycle has been to move to the right on social issues and reposition the Democratic Party on race. More specifically, some of these conservative Democrats counsel abandoning race-sensitive affirmative action (gender is different). Others want to purge concerns about racial justice from the policy agenda altogether in a politically craven reincarnation of Moynihan-Nixon "benign neglect." Simultaneously, these conservatives discount the political importance of building or mobilizing the party base within minority communities.

During the Clinton administration, for example, some champions of the center-conservative Democratic Leadership Council urged the President and his advisers to abandon traditional affirmative action, or at least change its name, and focus on income to the exclusion of race-sensitive strategies. Later, when Clinton pondered and then conducted his "Race Initiative," including a blue-ribbon Advisory Board chaired by Professor John Hope Franklin, these and similar voices at first counseled against any initiative focused on "race"; later, their fallback position was to minimize the time, energy and policy investment of the White House in actually pursuing the initiative. They were largely successful, although the initiative had some successes.*

For Democrats, this conservative strain contrasts with the traditional loyalty to the LBJ legacy and to minority groups within the party base. In some respects this dissenting, conservative caution is a latter-day version of the Southern Democrat opposition to JFK-LBJ-Warren Court advances, but updated to be more civilized, less region-specific, and cautious rather than oppositional. Unlike the anti-integrationists, however, and unlike today's (mostly) GOP proponents of "anti-preference color blindness," these Democratic revisionists are less committed to particular principles, at least rhetorically. Instead, these conservative Democrats usually voice opposition or caution to race-related initiatives based on coarse electoral tactics: race-talk will allegedly drive away swing White voters in battleground states. Their highest principle is pragmatism, which is perhaps what

---

* The principal success was in stimulating countless programs and initiatives related to racial dialogue or exploration of race-related themes in both public and private institutions around the country. There were waves of campus-based initiatives, and innumerable special projects in newspapers and other media. On the policy front, however, there were only a handful of initiatives directly traceable to the President's Race Initiative. Among them: an official publication from the President's Council of Economic Advisors documenting racial disparities in a variety of economic and social measures; an initiative to cut racial disparities in a set of key health indicators by 50 percent over ten years; a major research conference organized by the National Academy of Sciences to assess racial issues; an executive memorandum concerning racial profiling; and creation of a White House Office for One America.

one expects in political operatives. But the history of racial progress is that pragmatism must be lieutenant to principle, not master of it. Operatives and leaders of this stripe can only be, at best, fair-weather friends of civil rights workers. (Interestingly, every candidate for the Democratic presidential nomination in 2004 rejected this conservative Democratic strategy and seemed intent on competing vigorously for minority community support through policy, message, and organizing activity. The harder test comes, however, in the general election strategy.)

III. Solutions

The Opportunity Revolution

Simply put, the challenge today is two-fold. First, we must rededicate ourselves to completing the difficult *anti-discrimination agenda*—combating racial and ethnic discrimination in its myriad forms, including the subtle manifestations of prejudice and distrust that may be difficult to detect but that nonetheless amount to the denial of equal opportunity under law. Old-fashioned discrimination is all too alive and well, with wily descendants that often elude traditional enforcement tools.

Second, we must build the *next* civil rights and racial justice movement—an *opportunity revolution*—giving policy and political expression to the plea of Martin Luther King in his later years that we progress beyond the elimination of legalized apartheid and state-sanctioned oppression to create the positive conditions of social and economic justice. In this revolution, political leaders and governmental institutions will be agents of our collective moral commitments and our righteous aspirations. Our political leaders must be dedicated to active pursuit of a long-term vision of communities in which there is no color-coding of opportunities in education, housing, employment, and commerce; nor color-coding for the tragedies of victimization, incarceration, environmental poisoning, chronic disease, homelessness, and illiteracy.

In the broadest terms, of course, the greatest contribution to the social and economic condition of minorities will come from the same thing that all Americans want—a growing, vibrant economy that produces good, secure jobs and rising real incomes. In this fundamental respect, the contrast between the Clinton-Gore record and the Bush-Cheney record, as detailed elsewhere in this volume, is as stark as one might imagine. Our racial justice goal, however, is not only progress in ensuring minimum material needs and access to the middle-class American dream. The deepening inequality of recent years demonstrates that when the Great American Economy cranks up to produce opportunity, those that already have much tend to get more than those clinging to the lower rungs of the ladder.

Viewed with the perspective of historical subjugation, racial fairness can only be understood to involve direct consideration of both absolute and relative well-being. If 150 years ago one observed that a rising tide lifts all boats, this would have given little comfort to the African American who found his boat rising, while he remained chained in the galley decks below. Fifty years ago, a Black worker locked into low-wage work in a Jim Crow workplace would have wanted the tide to help his employer prosper, but would also have wanted a fair share of the dividend check. Today, slavery and Jim Crow are gone, but the color line remains. Indeed, now with our more complex demography, there are multiple color lines.

The implication of this—and it is a bitter message for White centrists eager to retire race from political discourse—is that prescriptions for benign neglect of racial and ethnic equity in favor of race-blind or race-ignorant policy strategies must be judged in part by the effectiveness of those policies in racial terms. Race-neutral strategies are important to consider on political and ethical grounds, as well as constitutional grounds. But we must ask whether the policies serve to heal our history, or merely to hide it.

What we stand for is a commitment to turn America back onto the path toward racial and economic justice—not just a commitment to end discrimination in its ever-mutating manifestations, but to create opportunity and bring about the day when the only evidence of our terrible racial legacy will be found in history books and the memories of elders, not in the social and economic condition of our communities and families.

The next president therefore can lead America in several new ways to face this oldest of challenges—what W. E. B. DuBois called "the problem of the color line" a century ago:

Completing the Anti-discrimination Agenda:
- Adopt legislation to respond to civil rights setbacks in the federal courts regarding: access to courts, attorneys' fees, expert witness

fees, remedies for undocumented workers, and the definition of
discriminatory "harassment."

- Adopt regulations and, if necessary pursue legislation, to eliminate
any uncertainty that the "disparate impact" method for establishing illegal discrimination is as broadly available as the Constitution
permits.

- Adopt stronger anti-discrimination regulations under Title VI in
education, health care, social services, transportation, and the environment to make clear that the continuing patterns of racial disparities will not be tolerated; and institute aggressive administrative and judicial enforcement efforts.

- Strengthen enforcement budgets of federal anti-discrimination
agencies, and adopt bold, new grant-in-aid programs to assist state-level civil rights enforcement efforts by state attorneys general and
other officials.

- Ban racial profiling by federal law enforcement, and use existing
Title VI authority to ban the practice by state and local officials—
and establish effective data collection and monitoring to put teeth
in the ban.

Building the Opportunity Agenda:
- Move forward aggressively with standards-based school reform,
including a focus on holding states and districts accountable for
closing racial and ethnic disparities in achievement and attainment.

- Pursue legislative, regulatory, and litigation strategies to attack
sharp inequities in education resources that result from unfair state
school finance structures, as is now occurring in New York State
following the successful Campaign for Fiscal Equity lawsuit showing that the state failed to provide a "sound basic education" for a
New York City school system of 85 percent minority students.

- Adopt specific education strategies targeting immigrant students
and English Language Learners, especially in communities facing
abrupt demographic change.

- Enact criminal justice reforms that will improve community safety while reducing reliance on incarceration—by investing in prevention, by dramatically reforming state probation and parole systems to cut recidivism, and by emphasizing such measures as "coerced abstinence" linked to drug treatment for all individuals under criminal justice system supervision.

- Aggressively support immigrant rights and immigration reform, taking special care to rationalize the economically inevitable flow of future workers, and to do so in a way that avoids worker exploitation and anti-immigrant discrimination.

Creating Public Understanding and Consensus

- Invest in research of several kinds—on the nature and extent of discrimination in various sectors; on effective strategies for raising minority and low income student achievement; on strategies to eliminate racial discrimination by health care providers; and on what kinds of experiences or education influence racial and ethnic tolerances.

- Invest time, as President, in using the bully pulpit to teach and lead on issues of race and ethnicity, because no domestic challenge facing America is more important to our future.

- Appoint people throughout the administration who will be committed to this agenda, and hold them accountable for advancing it.

A President pursuing these three related agendas would be declaring that he stands for all Americans, and for One America.

CHAPTER FOURTEEN

A Progressive Agenda for Women's Rights

ELLEN CHESLER[*]

Advocate immediate U.S. ratification of the Convention to Eliminate Discrimination against Women (CEDAW), the U.N.'s visionary global treaty for advancing women's rights and opportunities in all aspects of life—and insist that U.S. domestic law and foreign policy accord fully with the treaty's aspirations for civil, political, social, and economic equality for all women.

Nowhere in the Bush administration is the gap between rhetoric and reality greater—nowhere is the sheer hypocrisy and outright deceit more pronounced—than on the subject of women's rights. "No society can succeed and prosper while denying basic rights and opportunities to women," the President observed in the spring of 2003 in a much ballyhooed speech at the University of South Carolina. "The advancement of women is critical to achieving open and prosperous societies." Lest we doubt the sincerity of his convictions, the First Lady made a rare appearance at a conference of women judges in Washington in October and earnestly repeated them: "There can be no justice in the world unless every woman has equal rights."

True enough that George Bush is not against letting women vote, or own property, or get an education, or hold a job. What he is against, however, are the core public policies and legal remedies that have been central to the advancement of those rights by women in the United States and abroad during the past thirty years. If given his way, he would overturn or weaken affirmative action and overall employment rights enforcement, along with reproductive rights, federal legislation against domestic violence, and a host of other fundamentals. He offers no new programs for child care, paid family leave, or flexible work arrangements to help women

---

[*] **ELLEN CHESLER** *is a Senior Fellow at the Open Society Institute (OSI), where she has directed its program on reproductive health and rights. She is author of* Woman of Valor: Margaret Sanger and the Birth Control Movement in America. *The views in this article are hers personally and do not necessarily represent those of OSI.*

balance work and family. And though his administration is modestly funding new programs for women abroad, especially in Afghanistan and Iraq, it openly opposes the major conventions, treaties, and other instruments of international law in which the rights of women around the world are enshrined. Look at the actual record, and it simply is not as advertised. Bush talks one way and governs another.

I. The Problem

In a single generation American women have made extraordinary advances in education and employment. Today, 46.5 percent of the labor force, more than half of all college graduates, and nearly half of those with advanced degrees, are female. Just a generation ago, women tended to be less well educated than men, made up a third of the labor force but were typically employed episodically and, once married, still identified primarily as housewives. Today women work through the life cycle and take little time off for childbirth. More than 70 percent of all families are headed by two working parents or a single parent. And in nearly half the households with two incomes (sadly, a diminishing proportion of the total) the woman is earning as much or more than the man.

Profound shifts in the economy—away from agriculture, heavy industry, and manufacturing and toward information and services—have eroded the traditional advantages men enjoyed and opened competition to women. A powerful second wave of women's rights advocates drove necessary changes in cultural norms. But whatever the larger historical trends at play, the gains women have experienced would never have happened without the full force of law and without the watchful eye of the federal government.

Beginning with the civil rights acts of the 1960s, women have won hard-fought battles for equality through affirmative action and other measures to end discrimination in education, employment, government contracting, and the military. Their gains expanded when there was aggressive enforcement by the Department of Justice, the Department of Education, the Equal Employment Opportunity Commission, and by the courts. The results have been stunning. The proportion of women aged 25–34 in executive, management, and administrative jobs in this country has reached 51 percent of the total. Women now comprise just under a third of all lawyers and 40 percent of doctors, up from negligible numbers in 1970. Small businesses owned by women are growing at twice the rate of those owned by men, with a recent tally of 6.2 million establishments employing some ten million workers—famously more jobs than the number provided by all the Fortune 500 companies combined. Many of these entrepreneurs have been helped by loans from the federal Small Business Administration under the Clinton administration, when women beneficiaries outnumbered men by six-to-one. Even in non-traditional fields of employment, the government's holding steadfast in hiring and procurement policies has helped advance gains for women in such unlikely areas as federal highway construction and the military.

Where does the Bush administration stand on affirmative action? Most prominently, through its Solicitor General's brief in *Grutter v. Bollinger,* the White House opposed the University of Michigan in its landmark case upholding the principle of selective admissions for women and minorities. In typically Orwellian fashion, this did not stop the President from congratulating the university on its victory, of course, but his position in opposition is a matter of public record.

Less well known is the fact that government filings of employment discrimination complaints have reached record lows in this government. In its first two and a half years under Attorney General John Ashcroft, the Justice Department filed only eight Title VII cases, or three a year, compared to an average of 13 a year over the Reagan, Bush I, and Clinton presidencies. There are many egregious examples of further stalemating on women's employment rights. The Justice Department has decided not to defend a Clinton administration consent decree put in place to advance opportunity for women in coveted and highly paid positions as custodians in New York City Schools. It also changed course and dropped a four-year effort to challenge discriminatory hiring practices by the Southeastern Pennsylvania Transportation Authority and an on-going suit challenging unfair employment tests used by the City of Buffalo police department, to cite just a few. Long-time senior civil servants at Justice have been reassigned, some say in retaliation for their loyal commitment to these employment discrimination cases.

Elsewhere in the name of cost cutting, Bush has de-funded programs to advance opportunities for women. He shut down the White House Office for Women's Initiative and Outreach, which has long coordinated policies on women. He closed the women's equity office at the

Department of Education, along with programs to advance women within the Department of Defense and the Environmental Protection Agency, and tried with only partial success to dismantle the regional women's offices of the Department of Labor.

Most disingenuous of all, the administration launched a two-year review by the Department of Education of long-standing policies under Title IX athletics policies responsible for the tremendous gains women and girls have experienced in sports—and the larger benefits that ensue from teamwork and competition, such as improved health, better grades and graduation rates, and preparation to succeed in the workplace. It gave every sign of its intention to weaken the law and then suddenly reversed itself under pressure from a broad coalition fighting to save it. Advocates worry, however, that this apparent capitulation to the voting power of "soccer moms and dads" could easily be reversed should there be a second Bush term.

Sustained commitment to education and employment rights remains important because while much has changed for American women and their families, so much still remains the same. While it is true that the gender wage gap has narrowed in nearly half of all coupled households, the percentage of those couples in the total population has declined markedly. American women overall—many more of whom are single heads of households today—still earn only about 76 cents on the male dollar. Despite high-profile gains in fields like medicine and law, wage stagnation for most workers combines with the dogged persistence of sex segregation in many sectors of the workplace to hit women especially hard. Men continue to have greater opportunities in the most reliable and highly compensated trades, and wages remain most depressed in fields where women typically predominate, like primary and secondary education and home health services. Women face unique challenges because they are more likely to be employed in non-standard jobs, part-time, freelance, or self-employed, and this has adverse consequences for wages, health care, and pension coverage.

Just over a quarter of all white women, a third of African-American women, and fully half of Latinas who work full-time still earn wages that fall at or below the poverty level. Even more disturbing is a recent finding that since 1977, the number of hours worked by dual or single wage earning couples has increased by an average of 12 hours a week, and yet median family income grew by only about 2 percent a year between 1995 and 2000, and is actually now declining as a result of job losses and slower economic growth. Meanwhile, health premiums for those lucky enough to have insurance, along with the costs of child care, college tuitions, housing, and other necessities, continue to skyrocket, while, of course, 20 million Americans who work full-time still lack health benefits for themselves and their dependents.

Even where women start out on equal and stronger footing, they tend to lag behind over time as a result of cultural stereotypes that persist in trivializing women's work and reward men with positions of greater prominence and pay. This is a high-profile "glass ceiling" dilemma for women in the corporate and professional sectors, where they rise to only a fraction of the top slots. But it is typically true as well for middle-income and working-class women whose earnings also level off at age 35.

Women get stuck because the burden of balancing work and family obligations still typically rests with them, granting less flexibility to move along, let alone move up, in their jobs, unless they choose not to have families. Alone among advanced industrial nations in the world, the United States still provides little public funding and few tax incentives for child care, deploys only scattered and inadequate resources for after-school and summer school programs, and mandates no paid leave or flexible work arrangements. Fortunately, as a shining if lone exception in this area of social insurance, millions of families have now made use of the Family and Medical Leave Act, which provides at least three months of unpaid absence for pregnancy or other emergency family obligations to men and women in all but the smallest workplaces.

Most women with children are making do under these circumstances, cobbling together child care and juggling other responsibilities because they have no other choice. The elite media may feature the stories of a prosperous few who reject the stress of trying to have it all, retreat from the workplace and idealize old-fashioned family virtues. But the phenomenal rate of women's growth in the economy has slowed by only a negligible percentage point or two, demonstrating that most continue to look instead for balance in work and family life. A recent survey of American women by Lifetime Television reported striking dissatisfaction with the level of attention being given to issues of greatest importance to them, including most prominently, equal pay, child care and family leave, women's health, and sexual violence.

The Bush administration has promoted no new policy on work and family balance. It does not support expanded or paid family leave and mandates no child care obligations, though 28 states have now offered local programs to these ends. It has offered no plan to end the "parent penalties" in the tax code by providing tax exemptions for secondary earners or meaningful credits to cover child care costs. By refusing to consider increases (even to cover inflation) for the Child Care and Development Block Grant and for Head Start, the nation's premier pre-kindergarten program for children in poverty, the administration even neglects the needs of low-income women trying to move from welfare to work (and has been overruled by a coalition of Democrats and moderate Republicans in Congress). Its Social Security policies contain no new provisions to secure women in old age or to compensate for formulas that discriminate against working women in two-income households who do not receive the full benefit of their contributions and their spouses, if as is typically the case they are the survivors. Moreover, even as tensions in families grow and domestic violence increases, the administration's 2004 budget proposes to streamline a number of critical law enforcement, crime prevention, and crime victim assistance programs, including the Violence Against Women Act grant programs, whose budgets have been cut. Key Bush appointees to the National Advisory Council that advises the administration on these matters, moreover, are officials of the conservative Independent Women's Forum, on record against the act on the grounds that the battered women's movement "has outlived its usefulness."

So too, Bush assaults on reproductive rights continue to be persistent and unsettling, despite the undeniable reality that women's autonomy and labor force participation rest on the ability to plan and space childbirth. The President signed the so-called partial birth abortion law, though it is patently unconstitutional and was immediately enjoined in three federal courts. He authorized Justice Department warrants for hospital records on abortion, many of which have also been enjoined as privacy infringements. He refuses to acknowledge that restricting access to safe and legal abortion here and abroad will result in increased death and injury from unsafe procedures and will heavily burden public health capacity. He has denied abortion services to women in the U.S. military. He has refused to release the $34 million dollars authorized by Congress for the United Nations Fund for Population Activities on the specious grounds that UNFPA endorses abortion in China. He has reinforced existing prohibitions on U.S. funding for abortion at home and abroad and, through the imposition of the so-called Global Gag Rule, has further censored speech about abortion by any foreign contractor receiving U.S. funds. This action so seriously compromised the provision of family planning services in a number of countries surveyed that Democrats and Republican moderates in Congress got together and tried to soften the impact in this year's foreign operations authorization bill by including a provision expressly authorizing a full range of counseling options at least in those places where abortion is already legal.

Less well known, but equally serious, are direct efforts to undermine family planning and to promote sexual abstinence at home and abroad. Let's remember that without contraception, a typical woman would become pregnant from 12 to 15 times in her lifetime. Even today in the United States nearly half of all pregnancies remain unintended, and nearly half of those in turn result in abortion. Yet, the Bush administration tried and failed to strip contraceptive benefits from federal employees, only because a few moderate Republicans in Congress objected. It tried and failed to reduce Medicaid coverage of contraception for poor women in 14 states. It has allocated no new money for the Title X program that provides birth control to working women just above the poverty line and no new funds for family planning abroad, though both programs have seen little growth for years and are seriously under-funded. It has worked to block federal legislation that would require private insurance coverage of contraceptives. All this, while hundreds of millions of dollars are spent on flawed programs promoting sexual abstinence that do little good, and indeed may cause harm by undermining condom use among adolescents, despite widespread evidence that comprehensive sex education, including birth control, has led to significant declines in U.S. teen pregnancy in recent years and has expanded opportunities for young women. This did not stop the administration, however, from saddling recent funds provided for HIV/AIDS prevention abroad with a similar abstinence-only provision that will attach to $148 million this year and will increase gradually over the five-year life of the program.

Apparent political intervention recently delayed and may threaten a decision by two professional advisory boards to the Food and Drug Administration in support of increasing access to emergency contraception through direct pharmacy distribution, requiring no prescription. The delay was granted though physicians representing all of the major medical associations testified that the so-called morning-after pill works to prevent pregnancy by suppressing ovulation and implantation, and, if widely distributed, would cut rates of abortion in half. Opponents nonetheless insist that it will encourage promiscuity, comparing it to the birth control pill in the 1960s, though studies show that the pill's principal clientele have been married women for whom it has made work possible, not sexual license.

Granted, the President, after intense advocacy by women's organizations and women members of Congress, did sign a 2004 appropriations bill that earmarks several hundred million dollars for women's programs in Afghanistan, Iraq, and elsewhere in the developing world, programs slated to improve access to education, economic opportunity, and maternal and child health services and to develop women's leadership capacity. Bending to interest from religious conservatives, budgets for efforts to stop trafficking of women in the international sex-trade have actually increased, but there remains no recognition of the need to address the underlying cultural conditions in which the sex trade is rooted. New monies announced but not yet appropriated under the $5 billion Millennium Challenge Account are bound by Senate provisions demanding gender integration and linking eligibility to assessments of how countries invest in women and girls.

Still, the gap between rhetoric and reality remains substantial. In Iraq, the U.S.-appointed Governing Council in early 2004 voted to replace secular laws governing marriage, divorce, custody, child support, inheritance, and all other aspects of family life under traditional Islamic or Shariah Law, an action that provoked major protest from Iraqi women's rights activists and has been put on hold without resolution, despite the adoption of a constitution with language guaranteeing women's political participation. Likewise, in Afghanistan an equal rights provision was written into the country's new constitution, but the new chief justice of the high court has pledged not to enforce it on religious grounds. Maternal health dollars in Afghanistan are not directed to family planning so levels of fertility and of maternal and infant mortality remain deplorably high, preventing progress on other fronts.

Elsewhere U.S. policies also fail to protect or directly harm women. Trade liberalization agreements do not address the critical problems of women factory workers with minimum job safety standards, wage and

hour regulation, or protections from sexual harassment. Conscience claus-
es and abstinence-only curricula deny women important protection from
HIV-AIDS. Over and over again, eagerness to embrace fundamentalism at
home repeatedly undermines progress in attacking it abroad by preventing
important interventions on behalf of women. Moreover, our insistence on
unilateral efforts addressing women—our absence from the table where
the rest of the world sits—compromises our effectiveness.

Yet Bush continues to get away with these policies because few
Americans apply a women's lens to public policy. We know more than we
need to about John Kennedy's women, of course, but not one of the popular books on the Kennedy presidency I have read analyzes its landmark
achievement in creating a Commission on the Status of Women chaired by
Eleanor Roosevelt. This historic institution mobilized working women in
every state to fight for federally guaranteed equal pay and left in place the
infrastructure that became the National Organization for Women, the first
of the modern women's rights groups to advocate for legal action against
sex discrimination and for subsequent legislation that expanded these protections to education and other sectors.

Americans may also identify Lyndon Johnson as a ladies man, but who
remembers that he was also the first President who dared to incorporate
family planning into America's public health and social welfare programs?
That he also committed the first foreign policy resources to population
investments that have since had palpable consequences in advancing
women's status (not to speak of their happiness)?

How many know that muscular implementation of U.S. affirmative
action programs for women actually began under a Republican, Richard
Nixon? Who today would believe that Nixon's Labor Department first
applied goals and timetables to break away from historic practices that
harmed women in government contracting, and that Nixon's Justice
Department vigorously enforced hiring plans for women and minorities in
universities and the private sector?

And, sadly enough, who still credits Bill Clinton with the Family and
Medical Leave Act, which became the centerpiece of his second-term reelection campaign, brought so many "soccer moms" into the Democratic
column, and has since benefited millions? Who recalls that fully half of the
Clinton administration's government appointments went to women, altering
at least temporarily the cultures and the agendas of many federal agencies?

Mix up women and foreign policy, and the situation is even worse. In the last days of his presidency, Jimmy Carter signed CEDAW, the U.N. Convention on the Elimination of All Forms of Discrimination Against Women, and sent it to the U.S. Senate for ratification, where it has languished ever since, held up by intransigent conservatives. One hundred seventy five countries have now signed the treaty, leaving the United States among a handful of "rogue" states like Iran, Somalia, Syria and Sudan, refusing to be bound by the global framework that has defined women's equality in civil, political, economic, and social life for 25 years. Yet George Bush refuses to stand behind this covenant or use his political capital to ratify it, even as he justifies his wars against fundamentalism in the name of advancing women's rights.

What's a progressive to do? We need, of course, to pursue specific legislation and policy and to litigate when necessary. To these ends, readers should look to tenacious policy and advocacy orgainzations like the National Partnership for Women and Families, the National Women's Law Center, and the New America Foundation, which offer well-developed proposals on a range of issues from workplace equity to paid family leave and child care. But the biggest challenge derives from this very incrementalism. We suffer from the tendency that my colleague, Gara LaMarche of the Open Society Institute, bemoaned in a recent speech. We spend so much time fending off attacks on our hard-won gains that we lose the capacity to think big about how best to preserve and advance our most cherished values and institutions. Or citing linguist and moral theorist George Lakoff: "You don't win by using the other guy's terms and putting a 'not' in front of it or a 'stop' in front of it." We need what Lakoff calls a positive frame.

For American women, at this moment in history, that frame exists in CEDAW. The world's so-called "bill of rights for women" must also be ours here in the United States. While championing human rights abroad, Americans have for too long either assumed that these rights were already fully protected at home or resisted their application here in response to conservatives who refuse to hold our own country accountable in global forums to the highest standards of behavior in protecting human rights and advancing social justice.

No, I haven't forgotten what a frenzy ensued when American women tried to pass an equal rights amendment to the United States constitution, yet now I'm recommending that we get behind an equivalent statute whose authority rests in international law. But times are different now, I would argue, and the stakes are higher too—so we should aim very high.

II. Solutions

Since the ERA battles of the seventies, American women have achieved significant incremental gains but no irrevocable guarantee of equality. In these same years the world community has come together under the umbrella of the U.N. and agreed that opening opportunity to women must be a priority, not just for women but for everyone's good. Empowering women is now seen as essential to expanding economic growth, reducing poverty, improving public health, sustaining the environment, and consolidating democratic transitions in societies long beholden to tyrants. This is no small matter. In the name of progress, a near-universal consensus has been achieved calling for fundamental changes in practices that have denied rights to women and held them back for centuries. But the United States, once the world's leader in advancing women's rights, is not an official party to this agreement.

Drafted by the United Nations in 1979, with active participation by the United States, CEDAW commits countries to overcome barriers to discrimination by taking concrete action to advance women's status. It acknowledges the importance of women's traditional obligations as mothers responsible for the raising of children and the preservation of families, but it also establishes new norms for women's participation in all dimensions of society. The Convention catalogues a broad range of rights in marriage and family relations, including property, inheritance, and access to health care, with an explicit mention of family planning (though not of abortion). It demands equality for women as citizens with full access to suffrage, political representation, and other legal benefits—it also declares their right to education, including professional and vocational training and the elimination of gender stereotypes and segregation. Last, it establishes their rights as workers deserving equal remuneration, social security benefits, and protection from sexual harassment and from workplace discrimination on the grounds of marriage or maternity.

In a number of countries including South Africa, Brazil, Australia, Zambia, Sri Lanka, Uganda, and most recently Afghanistan, treaty provisions have been incorporated into constitutions or bills of rights for women. Elsewhere the treaty has been used to pass specific laws governing workplace practices and property rights, improving access to girls' education, extending maternity leave and child care, requiring legal protection for victims of domestic violence, outlawing female genital cutting, expanding family planning access, and curbing sexual trafficking.

Like all international covenants, the treaty respects national sovereignty and does not impose legal obligations. Intended to guide, not to supercede national law, CEDAW is not "self-executing" but requires instead that national laws be passed to implement its provisions. It also provides for the granting of "reservations, understandings, and declarations" if necessary to accommodate local variations from its standards, but establishes no benchmarks of any kind. Indeed, many signatories do not live up to its obligations, which is an admitted weakness of it and many other human rights statutes. Still, ratifying countries are obliged to submit regular reports to the United Nations, where a CEDAW Committee semi-annually reviews country-by-country progress toward implementation and reports to the General Assembly with strong suggestions and recommendations for improvement.

Conservative opponents of the treaty in the United States regularly misrepresent and ridicule the work of this committee. Their most common canards repeat the same specious claims that defeated the Equal Rights Amendment—that CEDAW abridges parental rights; threatens single-sex education; mandates combat military service for women; demands legal abortion; sanctions homosexuality and same-sex marriage; prohibits the celebration of Mother's Day; and the like—all not true, of course.

Ratification in the United States requires only a two-thirds majority, or 67 votes, in the Senate, but the treaty has never come before the full body for a vote. Having languished during the years of the Reagan and first Bush administrations, it was sent to the Senate by the Clinton administration in 1994 with a number of reservations and understandings to allay conservative concerns about women in combat, comparable worth, paid maternity leave, universal health care, and abortion. The Foreign Relations Committee held hearings and sent the treaty to the floor, thinking they had the votes, but Jesse Helms exercised his right to put a hold on it. In 1999, a group of women on Capitol Hill called again for ratification, but Helms responded by attacking the treaty as the work of "radical feminists" with an "anti-family agenda." "I do not intend to be pushed around by discourteous, demanding women, no matter how loud they are or how much they are willing to violate every trace of civility," he said in widely quoted remarks on the Senate floor.

When the Senate briefly changed hands in 2000, the new Democratic Foreign Relations Committee Chair Joe Biden and Senator Barbara Boxer opened a hearing on CEDAW by reading poignant testimony in support from Dr. Sima Samar of Afghanistan on behalf of the women of her country. A broad U.S. coalition supported ratification, representing more than 190 national organizations and millions of individuals from religious, civic, labor, women's, and human rights communities from AARP to Zonta International. The matter was widely covered by the press and received substantial editorial endorsement. The Bush State Department initially notified the Senate that it would not object to ratification, but the White House then changed course and sent the treaty to the Justice Department for review, where it has remained ever since.

Instead, last fall the Bush administration disingenuously proposed a toothless U.N. Resolution on "Women and Political Participation," which promotes women's right to vote and hold political office and vaguely encourages their equal access to education, property and inheritance rights, information technology, and economic opportunity. It avoids mention of anything remotely more controversial, however, pledges no new funds to support its goals, and obligates no enforcement mechanism of any kind. The U.S. delegation browbeat enough countries to get the resolution passed at the General Assembly, but most have since simply ignored it as yet another example of unorthodox diplomatic behavior under this president. Nothing has been as shocking, however, as the Bush administration's refusal to reaffirm the Platform of Action of the 1995 World Conference on Women in Beijing because it endorses women's rights to reproductive health information and sevices. In this brash action at the United Nations in March (the day before the President gave another speech extolling his record on women's rights), the United States stood alone, without support from any other country.

CEDAW ratification has been caught on the horns of a dilemma. In the words of former Ambassador Linda Tarr-Whelan, the Clinton administration's representative to the U.N. Commission on the Status for Women: "If CEDAW is presented as essential for women here, there is immediate, powerful, and vocal opposition. If it is presented as 'nice' for us but essential for women around the world, there has been considerable apathy."

This is what must change. With heightened attention by U.S. citizens to international affairs and especially to the low status of the world's women—with increasing concern over the threat that the Bush administration poses to women's rights here at home—there may never be a better moment to begin an effort to ratify CEDAW.

U.S. Supreme Court Justices Stephen Breyer and Ruth Bader Ginsburg have both spoken widely of the positive benefits of applying international standards in pursuing equality under U.S. law. Their concurring opinion in the recent case upholding the use of affirmative action by the University of Michigan cited the International Convention on the Elimination of all Forms of Racial Discrimination, which the United States has ratified, and which obliges governments in judging racist practices to look not only at intent, but also at outcome. In a recent article, Justice Ginsburg highlighted CEDAW as an argument for increasing government's obligation to promote women's full workforce participation and to protect parenting. She positioned it in defense of affirmative action policies in employment and as an argument for paid family leave and child care. Many advocates make similar arguments. LaShawn Jefferson of Human Rights Watch looks to CEDAW for guidance in rationalizing U.S. law on marital property distribution and as an argument for toughening laws on access to credit for women. Leila Milani of the Working Group on Ratification of CEDAW points out that since the U.S. Congress and all executive agencies are exempt from affirmative action laws, CEDAW may be a vehicle to encourage more equal representation of women in government here. This is particularly important since, despite substantial gains, women hold only 14 of 100 seats in the Senate, 59 of 435 in the House of Representatives, and approximately 20 percent of state legislative positions, nowhere near parity.

Awareness of CEDAW is growing nationally. A September 2003 Zogby poll for the Foreign Policy Association show that seven in ten Americans assign high importance to the CEDAW treaty—ranking it above the Kyoto Protocol and on par with agreements addressing the regulation of nuclear weapons. Several states have already passed resolutions urging Senate action. And in San Francisco, a young women's group called WILD (for Women's Institute for Leadership Development for Human

Rights) passed a local ordinance implementing its principles in relation to municipal laws and demanding a gender audit of city hiring and contracting. Similar efforts are underway in New York and Iowa.

CEDAW cannot by itself resolve the myriad problems women still face at home or abroad. Realizing its full potential as a tool for interpreting U.S. law and influencing policy will require repeated—and sure to be contested—applications in legislatures and courts over many years. But for social activists looking to educate and activate the public around women's issues, a campaign to ratify CEDAW now offers a potentially inspiring and unifying tool, one that will help point out the inadequacies and inconsistencies of Bush administration policies and the common threat they pose to American women and those in even worse circumstances abroad. As a new report from the Ford Foundation points out, "an instinctive desire to reassert the common human dimension of all social justice work" is combining with increased awareness of the importance of U.S. multilateralism to nurture a vibrant human rights movement in the United States that bonds us the rest of the world and refuses to accept arguments about our own exceptionalism.

The grassroots campaign for CEDAW has extended its reach considerably in recent years. There is a sizable organizational infrastructure already in place. Media strategies have also been developed through an initiative underway by the Communications Consortium Media Center in Washington. Lobbying strategies are also being developed there through the CEDAW Working Group and the Women's Edge Coalition, both of which report growing interest from Democrats and Republican moderates in the Senate, including Richard Lugar, the highly considered Foreign Relations Committee Chair, who replaced Jesse Helms when he retired. The logjam remains in the Bush executive branch, but a resolute electorate, pushed by a public education and mobilization effort with real muscle behind it, may be able to change that.

A campaign to ratify CEDAW would start America talking about the centrality of women's issues to America's collective interests at home and abroad. We owe it to ourselves and to women around the world.

CHAPTER FIFTEEN

No Compromise on Crime

CHRISTOPHER STONE*

Ensure a professional, respectful, and effective police service that is provided locally but meets new national standards of training, accountability, and integrity.

I. The Problem

The problem of crime in the United States today is a trap for complacent officials. Official statistics tell us that Americans are safer from serious crime than at any time in recent memory and that public confidence in the criminal justice system is at a ten-year high.

While accurate, those statistics can easily induce mayors, governors, members of Congress, and even a President to cut budgets for crime prevention and cut corners in the administration of justice. Just as an unprecedented budget surplus can quickly become a record deficit, America's newfound safety can be lost tomorrow if we compromise either our commitment to reduce crime or our commitment to strengthen justice. Indeed, there are already worrying signs that crime may again begin to rise, and it will be tempting for nervous officials to sacrifice justice in response.

The United States has no comprehensive national crime policy: We are instead committed to local control and initiative in dealing with crime and administering justice. Still, the federal government has selectively but increasingly intervened on certain issues over the last half century, and in the last decade those interventions have displayed remarkable consistency across parties and administrations. The result is that we are developing a common, national vocabulary for discussing crime policy and the proper administration of justice, and good policies regularly attract bipartisan support. Whether we think of President Bush's pledge in his first year in office to end racial profiling in police work or his proposal in the State of the Union address in January 2004 to invest in easing the return of ex-offenders to their communities after release from prison, it is useful to recall that the same pledges and proposals could have come from President Clinton.

---

* **CHRISTOPHER STONE** *is the Director of the Vera Institute of Justice.*

The challenge for the next Congress and presidential administration is to pursue these and other sensible policies, to build on their successes, to learn from their weaknesses, and to cement America's commitment to crime policy that strives for safety and fairness together. But national policy should remain deferential to states and localities. However tempting it may be for good people newly invested with national authority to use federal law to impose their particular vision of justice, the administration of justice generally benefits from seeing its subjects up close, where the humanity of victims, suspects, and offenders is most vivid.

Nonetheless, while preserving local control and initiative, the next administration can and should draw on the best local practices to articulate the highest national aspirations and, at the same time, insist on compliance with a set of minimum structural standards that assure all Americans that key institutions—police oversight bodies, community corrections agencies, victim services, and public defenders—are in place and performing well.

II. Recent Developments

The good news on crime is very good, indeed. The two most widely used measures of crime trends nationally have been registering reductions in crime for more than a decade—the most sustained decline in serious crime ever recorded. The percentage of households victimized by crime in 2002, based on household surveys by the federal government, was about half what it was ten years earlier for both personal and property crimes (see Figure 1). Similarly, the overall rate of serious crimes recorded by police departments was at a 20-year low in 2002 (see Figure 2), and the preliminary figures for the first half of 2003 are showing a further decrease.

Figure 1. U.S. Crime Victimizations per 1,000 Households, 1993–2002

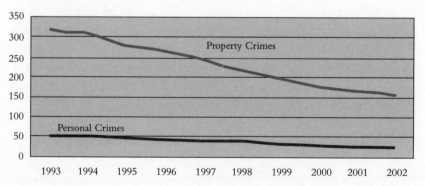

Figure 2. U.S. Index Crime Rates per 100,000 People, 1983–2002

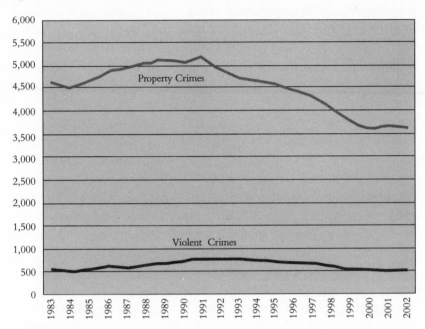

Not only are Americans safer from serious crime than we were ten years ago, but more Americans appear to have substantial confidence in the criminal justice system. Twenty-nine percent of adults surveyed in 2003 had "a great deal" or "quite a lot" of confidence in the criminal justice system, a huge improvement over the merely 15 percent of adults who expressed such confidence ten years ago (see Figure 3).

Figure 3. Public Confidence in Criminal Justice, 1993–2003

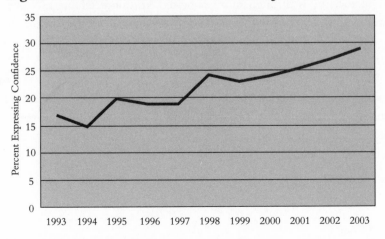

Even a quick look at the good news, however, begins to reveal some disquieting facts. While confidence in the criminal justice system may be rising, the absolute level of confidence is still dangerously low. The 29 percent in 2003 is well below the 40 to 50 percent of Americans who have confidence in other institutions, including the banking system, the medical system, organized religion, and the public schools. Confidence in the criminal justice system is still lower than that in almost any institution other than big business.

A closer look at the crime figures also reveals signs that crime could quickly return to haunt daily life and political debate in the United States. After declining for six consecutive years, the number of murders has now risen, albeit modestly, for four years in a row (see Figure 4). Moreover, the number of Americans who notice more crime in their neighborhoods than the year before has been growing for the last two years, as has the number saying that they cannot walk safely alone in their neighborhoods at night.

These up-ticks in crime indicators might tempt some officials to ratchet-up the aggressiveness of local policing, but two additional indicators warn of the dangers in such a blunt enforcement strategy. First, large numbers of Americans simply do not trust the police to be able to distinguish guilty people from innocent people. A striking 21 percent of adults surveyed in 2002 are at times afraid that the police will arrest them even when they are completely innocent of any crime. This percentage grows to 36 percent among those between 18 and 24 years old—more than one-in-three young adults. Among Hispanic and Black respondents, the percentage grows even further to 39 and 42 percent, respectively.

Second, a large majority of Americans no longer believe that the way to reduce crime is through more policing. An unprecedented 69 percent of adults surveyed believe that the best investment in further crime reduction is to attack the social conditions that comprise the underlying causes of crime rather than invest in more law enforcement.

In short, we must not compromise our efforts to reduce crime and at the same time not further compromise the integrity of the administration of justice. Fortunately, the knowledge and resources to improve safety and justice together are readily available, and the federal government has the means to put them in the hands that best use them.

Figure 4. Annual Change in Number of Murders in the United States, 1984–2003

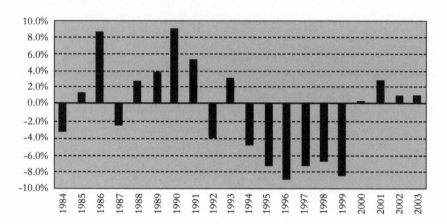

III. Solutions

What is most surprising about federal crime policy over the last two presidencies and the last six Congresses is how consistent that policy has remained. The 1994 Crime Act, passed into law with overwhelming bipartisan support, set the course for federal policy regarding local crime that has changed only in a few details through the present day.

Moreover, many parts of that bipartisan policy have been rational, progressive, and successful. The exceptions are important: From 1994 forward, the legislative and executive leadership of both parties have shown a barbaric enthusiasm for the death penalty, a disgraceful bias against immigrants, and a reckless embrace of absurdly long prison sentences. Nevertheless, over this same period, Republicans and Democrats have together committed the federal government to reducing violence against women, making schools safer for students and teachers, ending racial profiling in police work, establishing drug courts to ensure accountability in drug treatment, expanding "community policing," and successfully integrating ex-offenders back into their communities once their punishment is over.

These are the policies and practices from which we have much to learn, and it is here that the best local practice can help us articulate ambitious, achievable aspirations.

Reducing Violence against Women

Most violent crime in the United States takes place between people who know each other, and this is especially true for violent crimes against women. Indeed, women are victims not only of friends and acquaintances, but frequently also of their intimate partners. For example, of all homicides in 2002 in which the relationship between the offender and the victim is known, husbands and boyfriends murdered 32 percent of all women victims, whereas wives and girlfriends murdered less than 3 percent of male victims.

In 1994, as part of the larger Crime Act, Congress passed the Violence Against Women Act, committing the federal government to the most ambitious and expensive effort ever to reduce the incidence of domestic violence, sexual assault, and other violent crime against women across the country. Since then, bipartisan support for the effort has remained strong and funding has increased to the point where Congress appropriated $390 million for the fiscal year that began in October 2003.

Inside the Justice Department, the Office on Violence Against Women has spent more than a billion dollars over the last ten years to sponsor programs in every state that (a) educate police, prosecutors, and judges about the seriousness of domestic violence, (b) deploy technologies that can identify persistent offenders and alert victims about possible danger, (c) strengthen the enforcement of orders of protection, and (d) encourage partnerships between law enforcement and women's advocates in every aspect of the effort.

In 2003, President Bush increased funding by $100 million for this Clinton-era program. About a fifth of that increase will go to support construction of family justice centers, modeled on a center in San Diego where victims of domestic violence can go to talk to police, prosecutors, probation officers, counselors, doctors, and representatives of community organizations. The San Diego model puts the district attorney at the center of the effort to coordinate the many public and private agencies that respond to incidents of domestic violence. Other federal initiatives are testing the idea of putting judges in the coordinating role. Regardless of who plays the pivotal role, strengthening a coordinated community response to domestic violence is one of the more powerful ideas backed by both the Clinton and Bush administrations.

This wide array of activities promoted by the Violence Against Women

Act has certainly helped to improve the awareness and sensitivity of law enforcement agencies and judges to the victimization of women and may also have contributed to an actual reduction of violence. Reliable data on the rate of violence against women are difficult to collect because so many people are reluctant to report domestic violence to the police or mention it to researchers. Nevertheless, the best measure we have of violent crime trends—the National Crime Victimization Survey—shows that the rate of violent crime against women has declined every year since the mid-1990s.

The bad news, however, is that the reduction in violence against women has been slower than the reduction in violence against men in these same years. Indeed, if we focus on completed crimes of violence (excluding threats and attempted crimes), *the rate of violent victimization of women exceeded that of men in 2002 for the first time since statistics have been compiled* (see Figure 5).

In sum, the federal government has mobilized unprecedented resources to reduce violence against women and spurred a wide range of innovation in enforcement, services, and prevention. But we know little about which of these strategies have worked, and the combined effects have not yet produced impressive results on a national scale. After ten years of wide-ranging experimentation, it is time to adopt a more evidence-based approach to reducing violence against women.

Figure 5. Rate of Completed Violent Victimizations by Gender, 1996–2002

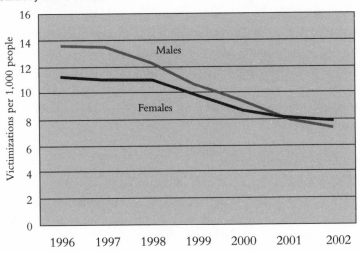

Our aspirations here are clear. Every American will receive care, compensation, and assistance when they are the victim of a violent crime; we must eliminate the bias persisting in some minds that violence against women is not a crime; and to reduce the level of violence against women requires more objective, less ideological assessment of what works. Sometimes what works will be law enforcement, but we must be willing to test other solutions as well, such as batterer treatment and mediation.

At the same time, the federal government should insist that a minimum set of institutions are available for victims everywhere. Today, the treatment that victims receive—both women and men—remains widely inconsistent. Compensation is haphazard, and assistance in reducing the risks of victimization rarely available. Experiments with the counseling of sexual assault victims are beginning to show that the high risk of re-victimization can be reduced, and experiments with "parallel justice" more effectively provided, when they are not tied to the traditional justice system that focuses on arrest and prosecution.

Experiments with comprehensive community responses to domestic violence are also showing some promise in their integration of offender supervision, counseling, and treatment. Counseling, compensation, and other assistance independent of law enforcement should be available to victims in every community, particularly those with low incomes who are disproportionately victimized. In addition, every community should measure the rate of re-victimization for crimes like sexual assault, aggravated assault, and other completed acts of violence. By insisting that states and localities report the rates of re-victimization separately for men, women, and children, the federal government would ensure accountability of local institutions while leaving responsibility and initiative to local officials and residents. These could be the elements of a new federal-state partnership, in which federal financial assistance for victim compensation is conditioned on a state's provision of basic services and the publication of relevant data.

Making Schools Safer
The 1999 killings in Columbine are only the most notorious of dozens of incidents over the last decade when students have shot and killed other students and faculty at school. Those tragic, persistent incidents focus

national attention on the daily challenge faced by schools across the country to keep their children and staff safe.

The Bush and Clinton administrations have consistently responded with funding for school districts to improve safety, guidance about the design of violence prevention programs, and encouragement to deploy more police personnel in schools. Most recently, the No Child Left Behind act has imposed new requirements on states to identify persistently dangerous schools and either make them safer or allow their students to transfer to safer schools.

All of these efforts are sensible and well-intentioned, but none of them have yet proved particularly effective. For example, the number of uniformed security personnel and police officers assigned to schools on a permanent basis has risen steadily over the last decade, but they are often poorly deployed, trained, and supervised. Similarly, many schools have implemented a wide range of ambitious violence prevention programs over the same time, but evaluations suggest that most are poorly conceived, executed, and managed. While a few model programs have been favorably reviewed, federal efforts to improve the quality of prevention programs have had very limited effect.

The No Child Left Behind act tried to address this lack of accountability by insisting that each state establish a definition of "persistently dangerous schools" and then give parents the right to transfer children out of schools that met that definition. But even where individual schools or school districts have good local systems for measuring school safety, it turned out that there were no good measures that could work consistently across an entire state. Without decent measurement systems, the designation of persistently dangerous schools has been idiosyncratic, with 46 states identifying no such schools anywhere.

In sum, as with the federal effort to reduce violence against women, the effort to improve school safety has produced a wide array of creative experimentation and has focused some principals and superintendents on the importance of engaging all adults in their schools in creating a climate of safety. Some of this federal activity may also have contributed to a modest decline in school violence in the 1990s, but the decline has not been sufficient and the numbers of violent crimes in schools since 2000 have remained stagnant or started to rise again (see Figure 6).

Figure 6. School–Related Violent Crimes, 1996–2002

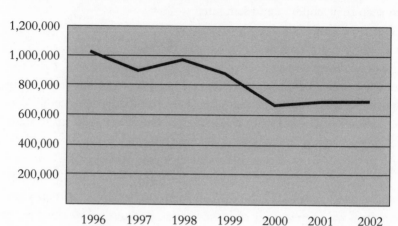

Here, too, our aspirations are clear: Every American family should have access to public schools that are safe environments for learning. Students should feel confident that they can approach any adult in their schools when they are concerned about their safety, and those adults should be skilled in how to prevent violence and intimidation, not merely keep it off school grounds. There are many such schools, including many in America's most impoverished communities, and the federal government should celebrate their success.

At the same time, the next Congress and presidential administration should strengthen the minimum requirements in federal law. Any law enforcement officers deployed inside schools should receive specialized training in how to police in these unique environments, and training in basic elements of school safety should be required of all principals and superintendents. States should remain responsible for setting their own criteria for designating a school as "persistently dangerous" but all school systems receiving any federal aid should be required to use the same indicators of school safety.

What indicators of safety should the federal government require to be measured? Merely counting the number of box cutters seized at the door of a school or the number of students suspended for fighting will not tell parents or the public which schools are safe or help principals and school districts maintain safe environments. Law enforcement, metal detectors, and effective discipline can all play important roles in keeping schools safe, but they only work when they are reinforcing the efforts of all the teachers and administrators to create a positive, safe environment for learning. Schools should be measuring that environment directly, easily done with annual, standardized surveys of students and staff.

In short, the federal government should not dictate how schools are policed, but it should assure all Americans that their local schools are taking advantage of the tools and proven strategies that are available.

Ending Racial Profiling

When President Bush and Attorney General Ashcroft pledged to end racial profiling, they joined a long list of elected officials who have recognized that the use of race instead of suspicious *behavior* as a trigger for extra attention from police is a destructive force in American society. Racial profiling persists, however, on two different levels.

First, racial profiling can find its way into explicit policy and training. For example, police commanders can tell their patrol officers that there has been a pattern of robberies by young Hispanic men in a business district, which officers may take to mean that they should stop and question all the young Hispanic men in that area. Or a training video can picture criminals as belonging to a certain race or ethnic group, apparently endorsing the use of race as a trigger for suspicion. There are some who argue that these uses of race are rational and legitimate; there are others who argue that they are irrational and illegitimate; and there are still others who argue that they may be "rational" but the nation's history of racism and constitutional commitments preclude police from relying on race as a trigger for stopping or searching people of color. Despite unequivocal promises from President Clinton and then President Bush to end the practice, police officials continue to debate the acceptability of relying on race to form suspicions.

But even if official endorsements of racial profiling could be eliminated, profiling would persist on the individual level. The problem, of course, is that hundreds of thousands of individual law enforcement officers make their own judgments many times each day about what is suspicious, and it is very difficult for officials to guide those judgments. Removing race from official policy pronouncements and training videos is easy compared with changing the racial presumptions on which individual police officers find their suspicions aroused.

The response of both the Clinton and Bush administrations has been to encourage, and in some cases require, police agencies to collect data in which patterns of racial profiling might be detected. There is little agreement about how these data should be analyzed, but their collection alone has provoked discussion and debate in communities across the United States about the hugely elevated risk that innocent Black and Latino Americans run in encounters with police, compared with innocent White Americans.

In some states and cities, the federal government has detected what it believed to be a pattern of racially biased policing and has used new powers to sue those jurisdictions in federal court. The 1994 Crime Act gave the U.S. Justice Department authority to bring these lawsuits alleging a pattern and practice of illegal policing, and both the Clinton and Bush administrations have used that authority to negotiate agreements with cities and states to monitor and eliminate racial profiling. Independent monitors are now in place to oversee such agreements in cities such as Los Angeles and Cincinnati, as well as the entire state of New Jersey.

Despite the heightened concerns with terrorism after September 2001, the agreements that the Bush administration has negotiated with police agencies have remained remarkably consistent, insisting on the collection and publication of data about racial differences in the numbers of civilians whom police stop and search.

In contrast to most countries in the world, where the primary police function is organized at the national or state level, the United States has evolved a uniquely local approach to policing, where most police work is organized under municipal and county control. The United States has less than a hundred prison systems, about 3,000 prosecution offices, but approximately 19,000 police agencies. That makes American policing uniquely responsive to local concerns, but it also produces wide disparities in the quality, professionalism, and integrity of policing in America.

While the federal government should not try to dictate how police work is performed across the country, it can harvest the lessons of the last ten years of bipartisan police reform to set new minimum standards. Those standards already exist in the agreements signed between the U.S. Justice Department and more than a dozen cities and states across the country. They require clear policies on the use of force and on the conduct of traffic and pedestrian stops, independent mechanisms for reviewing complaints against the police, and independent monitoring of key aspects of police performance including any disproportionate policing of minorities.

Oversight of police operations is crucial to this process. Again, that oversight must be organized on a state or local basis but should operate consistently across the country. Today, civilian complaint review boards operate in some cities but not others. There are statewide ombudsmen to receive complaints about the police in some parts of the country, but not in others. If policing is to remain local in this country, as it should, then oversight must be vigilant and consistent.

Continued support for community policing is also crucial to this process. The definition of community policing may have become unhelpfully broad, but it continues to convey to citizens across the United States that police treat them as their customers, responding to the persistent problems that residents identify and engaging those residents in the solutions.

Integrating Ex-Offenders

In the 1990s, Attorney General Janet Reno began to focus attention of other federal officials on the challenge of "re-entry": the difficulty of reintegrating hundreds of thousands of ex-offenders returning every year to their communities from jails and prisons. With an unprecedented two million people incarcerated in the United States, the numbers of people leaving jail and prison each year is also at an all-time high. At the beginning of 2004, calling the United States the "land of the second chance," President Bush focused the country's attention on this same issue, proposing a $300 million re-entry investment in programs to assist those completing their sentences to rejoin their communities.

Over the last decade, the federal re-entry initiative has spurred many states to develop a wide range of new programs, in part with federal funding. Prisons have enhanced their pre-release services, expanded their parenting and family support programs, and increased drug treatment and employment training. Parole and probation departments have developed new ways to engage entire families in the support of returning ex-offenders and have tried to reduce the numbers of prisoners who become homeless upon release. And legislators are reconsidering state laws that prevent ex-offenders from voting or otherwise participating in community life. The "invisible punishments" that accompany criminal convictions in the United States, and that should be removed, are legion—statutory exclusions from many lines of employment, exclusion from many forms of public housing, exclusion from various benefit programs. At the least they are now being more carefully catalogued and debated.

A significant blind spot in federal re-entry initiatives has been the hundreds of thousands of Americans annually completing local jail sentences. In New York City, for example, the number of people returning home from a jail sentence exceeds those returning from prison. But while the federal government has focused on prisons, the New York City administration (also Republican) has focused on the more numerous repeat petty offenders leaving jail. In the last year, a crusading city corrections commissioner has begun programs that not only better prepare inmates for release but also provide transportation to take them directly from jail to a work site where they are guaranteed a temporary job. The enthusiasm of everyone involved from Mayor Bloomberg to the jail wardens defies political convention and should be a spur to widening the scope of federal policy.

As with the other federal initiatives discussed here, there is very little evidence that the attention to re-entry has yet made a substantial dent in the problem of crime and recidivism. About half of all people released from state prisons are back inside within three to five years. We have only begun to collect evidence about which re-entry programs are successful at reducing this proportion, and which ones are affordable on a large scale. As with programs to reduce violence against women, improve school safety, and end racial profiling, programs to ease re-entry require a cultural and normative shift among hundreds of thousands of law enforcement officers who deal with prisoners and parolees. Despite attention to this issue across two administrations, we are only beginning to see signs, like those in New York City, that the culture is changing.

Achieving World-Class Standards of Safety and Fairness
In the quest for safety and justice, Americans are no different from the citizens of democracies anywhere. In Paris, Buenos Aires, Cape Town, and Mumbai, citizens feel the same double threat—the fear of rising crime on one hand and the erosion of justice on the other. And those citizens want the same professional policing, safe schools, and victim services that we do.

As Americans work with others around the world to define and strengthen democratic institutions, we should recognize that safety and justice are integral to that project. Not only should continued improvement in these fields make us safer at home, but sharing what we know and borrowing the best practices from others can make us safer in the world as well.

For example, American policy on gun control seems stuck in domestic politics. Despite the bipartisan consensus on many crime policies since 1994, the assault weapons ban, the Brady Bill, and similar efforts to restrict the proliferation of guns have been blocked by partisan intransigence. Gun violence remains the most preventable cause of death in America, yet our government is paralyzed by the power of narrow interests.

Other countries with similarly daunting problems of gun violence are adopting solutions like the recent ban on all private gun ownership in Brazil. Examining the results of that new law—what it actually accomplishes and where it fails—may provoke new thinking in the United States about how to end the scourge of gun violence. Another example arises with police oversight: a patchwork in the United States but a comprehensive, national function in most other countries.

Indeed, as our federal government sets more institutional standards and articulates our highest aspirations, we can and should see ourselves in an ever wider context, building a system of justice that, in both its fairness and effectiveness, is truly world-class.

CHAPTER SIXTEEN

Beyond Money: Making Democracy Work

MARK SCHMITT*

Renew democracy by enacting "clean money" public financing laws and by reforming voting, representation, and congressional procedures.

I. The Problem

The rules that govern American democracy have a single objective: to ensure that power is always subject to challenge, change, and renewal. From the right to free expression—which Justice Louis Brandeis said was meant to ensure that we do not become "an inert people"—to the checks and balances between the major institutions of government, through the rules governing lobbying, campaign contributions, and other influence, all are intended to prevent power from becoming entrenched in the hands of a few. These rules are the means by which we prevent democracy from destroying itself.

There are two ways that power can become entrenched in a free society. One is when those who win power through the political process abuse it to claim lasting advantages for themselves, their allies, and their economic class. The other is the risk that, in a society based on both capitalism and democracy, the inequalities that are inevitable in the economic system will be reinforced by or even exacerbated by the political process. While many believe that economic inequality cannot co-exist with fair democracy, some level of inequality is an inevitable outcome of a dynamic market economy but should be managed by a political process to maintain competition, protect the weak, and invest in public goods. Justice depends on keeping the sharpest inequalities of the market from entering the domain of democracy so that public deliberation can effectively make these decisions, which may require forbearance or even sacrifice from currently advantaged economic interests.

---

* **MARK SCHMITT** *is Director of Policy and Research for the U.S. Programs of the Open Society Institute.*

Over the last several years, however, power has become more entrenched in the United States. Although there is reason to think that public opinion among those who vote is split about evenly between liberal and conservative viewpoints, a tiny shift in public opinion has produced a huge effect on the actual configuration of power, one that will have lasting consequences and bind many future generations to unpleasant choices. The projected fiscal deficit, the mishandling of our relationships with most of the other nations of the world, the reversal of longstanding principles of environmental protection, and the packing of our nation's courts with far-right ideologues who would resurrect the obsolete legal theories used to invalidate the New Deal are just four of the ways in which those in power today have converted their narrow margin into long-term entrenched power.

Several factors in the political process itself are reinforcing this tendency toward entrenched power—factors that must be radically reformed if we are to maintain our democracy in fact and not merely in speeches:

1. *Money in politics.* Political competition is more expensive than ever, and is controlled by those already in power. Virtually unavailable to most challengers until they are deemed to have a good shot at winning, money has much to with the stasis of our current politics, as well as with the corruption of decision making.

2. *The broadcast monopoly over democratic communications.* Although they have been granted a public trust to use a currently scarce common resource—the broadcast spectrum—radio and television broadcasters reap huge profits by assuming the role of gatekeeper over most of the communications between candidates and voters. And the increased concentration of media ownership has given certain economic interests a power, which some have not hesitated to use aggressively, over the way Americans perceive news and events.

3. *A limited electorate.* Both parties assume that the population of voters will not change dramatically, and are generally not eager to deal with the unpredictability that would ensue if it did. They invest little effort in broadening the electorate and, in many cases, strive to limit it. That Democrats as well as Republicans would prefer the

voting population to remain basically as it is can be shown by former California Governor Gray Davis's opposition to an initiative
to allow would-be voters in that state to register on election day,
which was defeated. One measure of the narrow electorate is that
the inequality of income between voters and non-voters has been
even greater than the general rise in inequality: a recent study
found that the family income of the average voter rose from the
53rd percentile in 1964 to the 59th percentile in 2000.

4. *Incumbent protection in redistricting.* It is unprecedented that the first
    congressional election after a redistricting cycle, as the 2002 elec-
    tion was, should produce almost no turnover in the House of
    Representatives. But redistricting has become so partisan, the
    techniques so sophisticated, and the natural compromise in close-
    ly divided state legislatures so likely to involve protecting all
    incumbents that only about 40 congressional races were even
    remotely competitive, and a good number of those were in those
    states where population decreases had forced two incumbents to
    face each other. (On the other hand, where a legislature is not
    closely divided, as in Texas, partisans chose the unprecedented
    move of redistricting in the middle of the election cycle, in order
    to wipe out several Democratic incumbents, an example of prob-
    lem 5, below.)

5. *A ruthless willingness by some to manipulate the rules at will.* House
    Majority Leader Tom DeLay has been quoted as telling lobbyists,
    "If you want to be part of our revolution, you have to play by our
    rules." In this case, he meant his rule that, to be given access to
    Congress, lobbyists would have to stop contributing to Democrats
    or hiring Democratic lobbyists. But the principle of changing
    many of the underlying rules of politics to gain advantage pervades
    our politics in a way that is entirely without precedent in our his-
    tory. Although the margins by which the Republican party gained
    control of both legislative bodies, the executive branch, and much
    of the courts were narrow or nonexistent, this party has created a
    set of rules that can perpetuate their own power. Examples include
    the redistricting of Texas congressional districts in 2003, the three-

hour late-night vote in the House on the Medicare bill during which dissenting Republicans were cajoled, worn down, or bribed into going along, and the misuse of special congressional budget procedures intended to reduce deficits to instead push through legislation, with very limited opportunity for debate and amendment, which has given away $3 trillion largely to the wealthiest Americans.

It is these five pillars, and not the actual opinions of American voters, on which the self-perpetuation of entrenched power rests. Except for the last, the radical rewriting of rules—which is entirely unprecedented and entirely the work of one party—both parties are responsible for much in these trends. And these pillars reinforce one another, locking politics into a degrading and diminishing cycle in which the fullest possibilities of democracy go unrealized. For example, the broadcast monopoly on political communication exacerbates the pressure on money and the exclusion of candidates who can't raise it. The malleability of candidates' claimed positions on issues encourages voters to think there are not major differences between the parties, which deepens the cynicism that, in turn, compounds the problem of a withdrawal from democratic participation. The limited electorate also increases the relative payoff to strongly negative advertising, which in turn requires an advantage in broadcast time and thus money. The paucity of competitive seats, because of redistricting, allows the parties to concentrate resources on just a few, which then become showdowns between outside financial resources, rather than the candidates themselves. And so it goes.

Further, these forces lead to a concentration of political attention on that marginal voter at the fiftieth percentile, who has some real possibility of switching votes or staying home. The concerns of millions of voters who are taken for granted as either loyal voters to one party or another, or as non-voters, go virtually unheard in the election process. For this reason, politics focuses on issues such as the Patients' Bill of Rights, protecting those who have health coverage through HMOs, rather than the 43 million people without health insurance at all.

We are facing a great confrontation in American politics. It is not so much between Democrats and Republicans, or liberals and conservatives. And it is not even between an ideal of "clean" politics and a corrupt system, since no political system is free of the temptations of private interests. Rather it is a confrontation between the closed politics of entrenched power, and an open politics in which there is more opportunity for new candidates, new ideas, new voters, and new majorities to emerge. The closed politics of our time occurs when all the anti-democratic forces in our politics come together.

These forces form a vicious circle, and the challenge for advocates of more robust democracy is to break the cycle, turning one or two of these forces around. That alone might be enough to create a virtuous circle, in which the strengths of American democracy reassert themselves and reinforce others, as they have done so many times in the past.

II. Recent Developments

The goal of a political reform agenda should be to address each of the self-perpetuating causes of entrenched power and dismantle them. Perhaps most important is the role of money in politics. Reformers have often focused principally on direct corruption, the implicit corruption of large contributions, or the unequal access and power of large contributors. All these concerns are important. But the goal of opening the system must also be a part of the agenda for campaign finance reformers. In the last several years, there have been major breakthroughs in campaign finance reform, at both the federal and state level, many of which will open the system and others that may not.

The most recent crusade to confront political corruption and the distortion of democracy by money began in 1996. It was in that year's presidential elections that unlimited contributions from individuals, as well as money from corporations and labor unions, made their unwelcome return. These contributions to the political parties and independent groups, which were known as soft money, challenged not just the limits on contributions put in place after the Watergate scandal, but even the prohibitions on corporate funding of politics that dated to 1906. Although the outrage was immediate, it took six more years and an intensive legislative effort for Congress to finally ban these contributions in the Bipartisan Campaign Reform Act (BCRA), more commonly referred to as McCain-Feingold.

As we approach the first national election held under these new rules, some perspective is in order. In 1996, all the soft money raised by both parties put together, for all elections, totaled $271 million. Eight years later, a single candidate for President, the incumbent, expects to raise and spend some $200 million just for the presidential primaries, in which he faces no opposition. Individuals who could raise more than $200,000 for this candidate were given special designation as "Rangers," and, based on past practice, were likely to receive preference for presidential appointments and government contracts. Independent organizations on the left, right, and center were looking for ways to attract the funds that formerly went to political parties, with the promise of influencing the election. And the price of a seat in the U.S. House of Representatives remains out of reach to any candidate without the connections to raise at least a million dollars. The average House freshman elected in 1976 raised and spent $87,000, and in 2002, $1.1 million.

More to the point, money has distorted the decisions of government in ways that make 1996 look like the age of innocence. Virtually every major policy initiative in the last three years has, either at its inception or as it moved through Congress, become embedded with special benefits for specific donors or for the industries that provided financial support to the party in power. The Energy Policy Act of 2003 was drafted by industry lobbyists working with the White House and emerged from a House-Senate conference with $31 billion in new tax breaks for industry.

A rare window on the way Washington works opened when an unrelated lawsuit forced a Kansas company, Westar Energy, Inc., to make public internal e-mails. A Westar executive asked why he was being asked to find $56,000 in corporate and individual contributions for various House candidates and a political committee run by House Majority Leader Tom DeLay with the purpose of electing Republicans to the Texas legislature, even though the company did no business in Texas. The response came back from his superior that the contributions were the price of "a seat at the table" in the negotiations over the energy legislation, and, indeed, Westar won a special exemption in the House version of the bill.

Under these circumstances, during the six years between the identification of the problem of soft money, and the passage of BCRA, the influence of money metastasized in ways that will require a more radical solution. As discussed below, the next steps in reform of the democratic process call for an entirely new and more imaginative approach. Which is not to say that passing the McCain-Feingold legislation banning soft money was not a significant improvement to the political process. It was, for several reasons.

First, it proved that there is a vocal, voting segment of the public that really does care about the political process and about reducing the influence of money. Many politicians doubted that, and reform opponents still do. Passage of BCRA was one of the signal legislative achievements of the modern era. It stands as the only significant piece of legislation on any topic to pass into law over the fierce opposition of the Republican leadership during the Bush years.

Second, the lengthy congressional debate and the legal challenge that followed its passage provided substantial evidence of what had been widely, if inexplicably, doubted: that money not only influences elections, but influences the outcome of legislative decisions. This may seem to be common sense and uncontroversial, but for decades, there was a consensus among political scientists, journalists, politicians and fundraisers that money might help contributors gain access to power but that (a) legislative decisions were driven as much by other forces, (b) spending does not decide election outcomes, and (c) restrictions on money would do more to distort democracy than money itself. But the evidence gathered during the legislative and litigative battles leaves no room for any doubt that money has a direct effect on legislative decisions.

The Supreme Court majority summed up this evidence quite succinctly:

> Plaintiffs argue that without concrete evidence of an instance in which a federal officeholder has actually switched a vote (or, presumably, evidence of a specific instance where the public believes a vote was switched), Congress has not shown that there exists real or apparent corruption. But the record is to the contrary. The evidence connects soft money to manipulations of the legislative calendar, leading to Congress's failure to enact, among other things, generic drug legislation, tort reform, and tobacco legislation. Donations from the tobacco industry to Republicans scuttled tobacco legislation, just as contributions from the trial lawyers to Democrats stopped tort reform. To claim that such actions do not change legislative outcomes surely misunderstands the legislative process.

Third, BCRA will eliminate the types of financing that have the most potentially corrupting effect on government: huge contributions from a single individual, as well as contributions of any amount directly from corporate or union treasuries. The latter reflect exclusively economic interests and not the political inclinations and decisions of individual voters. The "bundling" represented by Bush's Rangers, as well as political action committees that take in small contributions and can in turn make gifts of up to $5,000 to federal candidates, are disturbing but at least it can be said that they represent sizable numbers of individuals making their own choices, whether based on ideology, economic interest, or personal friendship.

Finally, and in the least well-understood benefit of the new law, it will encourage the parties and other organizations to revitalize politics by engaging actual voters. Soft money was created by the Federal Election Commission in the early 1980s with the admirable purpose of strengthening political parties. Instead, as political scientists Jonathan Krasno and Frank Sorauf have shown, by inducing parties to shift their attention to television advertising on behalf of specific candidates, soft money actually weakened the parties by diverting them from the task of building strong state and local organizations that command the loyalty of voters and engage citizens at the ground level of democracy. Removing this distraction will force parties to rediscover their traditional strengths as participatory institutions for ordinary citizens. What we have learned from the twenty-year experiment with soft money is that rich parties are not necessarily strong parties.

Likewise, while much of the soft money that had been going to parties will undoubtedly shift instead to independent organizations working on voter turnout and on particular issues, those organizations will generally be prohibited from running ads that are obviously intended to influence the election in the final weeks, those notorious ads that evaded previous laws by saying things like, "Call Congressman Jones and ask why he thinks criminals shouldn't go to jail," instead of "vote against Jones." Now they may actually reach out to voters, face to face, and talk about real issues—all of which is far healthier for democracy than the hit-and-run politics of television advertising.

On December 10, 2003, the Supreme Court upheld almost all of McCain-Feingold. Huge soft money gifts were not regarded as constitutionally protected speech; "independent" ads implying who to vote for within 30 or 60 days before a primary or general election could be prohibited; and an "anti-millionaire's provision" allowing a candidate an increased maximum gift if running against a self-financed candidate was upheld.

The fact that the upheld law tracks so closely with the Supreme Court's outline of what's permissible, at least when it comes to limits on contributions, means that it will be very difficult to get much further in a future law. As compromised as McCain-Feingold was, this may be as far as it goes. Absent a major transformation of America's courts, it is unlikely that *Buckley v. Valeo* will soon be reversed to allow spending limits, or to allow further restrictions on independent groups. Even supporters of campaign finance reform should have some trepidations about the consequences for free expression of an effort to close everything that appears to be a loophole in the law. For example, outside groups will always be able to influence elections by focusing attention on issues, such as the environment or national security, that might tend to shift the election agenda in one direction or the other. But to restrict the right of organized groups, even if corporate- or union-funded, to speak out on any issue would quite obviously restrain the give-and-take of ideas on which democracy depends.

In short, we may have reached the limit of limits. Further progress toward a fair political system cannot be achieved by attempting to *restrict* the role of money in politics. But that does not mean accepting a world in which contributors write legislation, or in which less than 10 percent of congressional races are competitive. Further progress toward freeing politics from the grip of money will have to take a different approach. It will not only have to follow different legal lines, but also develop a new and clearer sense of the purpose of reform.

III. Solutions

Newt Gingrich, the former Speaker of the House, was not entirely wrong when he said in 1995 that the problem of money in politics was not that there was too much money, but too little. Too much money in the wrong places, too little money to allow other voices to be heard or enable candidates who aren't connected to big donors. For that reason, the most important step forward to make democracy work is a system of reasonable, voluntary public financing, such as are being pioneered in the states of Arizona and Maine, and in several cities, including New York City.

In Arizona Governor Janet Napolitano in 2002 became the first state executive to win office through a system of full public financing. Rather than spending the first months of the campaign chasing big donors in the state's major industries, she instead raised 6,000 five dollar contributions to show a broad base of support. Like hundreds of other candidates, she held "five-dollar parties" on Native American reservations, in the poor African-American and Latino neighborhoods of Phoenix, in rural southern Arizona—in short, she raised money in the very same places she was campaigning for votes, where most candidates live very different lives when they are looking for money than when they are reaching out to voters.

Similarly in New York City, the innovative campaign finance system works by providing a public match of $4 for every dollar raised in contributions of $250 or less. A candidate can ask for a reasonable sum, such as $100, knowing that it will be worth $500 to the campaign. Like the Arizona system, candidates can reach out to the very same people for financial support that they want to appeal to for votes. This campaign worked well in city council races in 2001, many of which had six or seven well-qualified candidates, and in the Democratic mayoral primary, but not in the general election for mayor, where the self-financed candidate Michael Bloomberg chose not to participate in the system and spent an astonishing $74 million. Other than that, participation in the system, which requires candidates to abide by spending limits, was close to 100 percent and many fresh faces entered government.

These successes are threatened, unfortunately, by the impending unraveling of the presidential public financing system, in which President Bush has refused to participate. That is, he has declined to participate in the first part, the matching funds program, under which his spending for the primaries would be limited to about one-quarter of what he is likely to raise, but he is happily taking advantage of the public subsidy for the second part, the general election. Concerned about being outspent, two major Democratic candidates for president, Howard Dean and then John Kerry, opted out themselves in order to be able to compete with Bush in the general election.

If the presidential system, which provides a one-to-one match on the first $250 in contributions and full public financing for the general election, is perceived to have failed, it will be a black eye for public financing of all kinds. But there are specific reasons why this system does not work.

For one, public financing should never allow a candidate to opt out of one part and not out of another, as Bush did in 2000 and is doing again. Second, it should provide a match that is generous enough to encourage most candidates to participate. With the increase in individual contribution limits to $2,000, a match on the first $250 means that a candidate might receive as little as one-eighth of her total campaign funds in public dollars, not a strong incentive. Third, the presidential system places limits on spending on the primaries in each state, and in New Hampshire the limit of $730,000 is simply too low, given the importance of that first primary. But all of these are reparable problems, and this is a system that can be fixed, not abandoned.

Just as limiting money in politics is no longer a sufficient solution, limiting our purview to the role of money in politics cannot by itself open up the system. Systemic reforms must address each of the pillars of entrenched power, one by one.

Media Democracy

Since the power of money in politics is ultimately a problem of public information, the broadcast media must be open to competition, and broadcasters must to live up to their obligations to the public. Currently, broadcasters receive what is quite literally a license to print money, much of which they make from politics—more than $1 billion in the 2002 elections alone, according to a study by the Alliance for Better Campaigns. The Alliance also found that broadcasters raised advertising rates for candidates by 50 percent in the days before the election, further increasing the pressure to raise money.

The Bush administration in 2003 attempted to rewrite the rules for broadcasters to allow even greater concentration of media ownership. As adopted by the Federal Communications Commission, a single company would be permitted to own a newspaper and a television station in a single market, even if they were the only paper and the only station in that market, and to own stations that reach up to 45 percent of the nation's media markets. Surprisingly, a bipartisan backlash against these proposals led to passage in both the House and Senate of amendments to reverse the FCC. The congressional leadership, backed by a White House veto threat, effectively blocked the will of these majorities.

The fight over the media ownership rules demonstrated that there are voters and activists who understand the issue and are willing to at least call their representatives. But these specific provisions are not nearly as important as requiring broadcasters to respect the responsibilities they owe to the public in exchange for the right to use a public good. Even with media ownership widely dispersed among companies, the result may be that public issues receive little attention, as the various broadcast owners all seek the same lucrative viewers. But the airwaves are a public good—a "commons"—and with the right to use them for profit should come responsibilities. Chief among those responsibilities should be an obligation to improve democracy. More specifically, broadcasters should be required to provide time for candidates to speak to voters, and to cover local issues and events.

The backers of BCRA, shortly after its passage, introduced legislation to require broadcasters to meet their public obligations, which some of them described as "the next McCain-Feingold." In order to be fair to broadcasters who are less profitable than others, the "broadcast time bank" established under this bill would require broadcasters to make time available in the form of vouchers that candidates could use to buy ads, but the broadcasters would be compensated.

Voter Participation

There are many academic theories about why people don't vote, and even about whether the preferences of non-voters would be dramatically different from those of voters. Regardless, an electorate that was expanding rather than shrinking, and that was unpredictable rather than predictable, would provide a healthy incentive for parties and candidates to broaden their message. It would also encourage candidates to present positive visions rather than narrow attacks aimed at swing voters.

To broaden the electorate, election-day voter registration should be a top priority reform. At a time when people can sign up on line and within minutes buy and sell thousands of dollars worth of stocks, there is no reason that we cannot create a system that would allow people to decide on the day of the election that they want to vote, and appear at the polling place with some reasonable proof of address, which can then be entered into a computer to prevent people from voting twice. When people take the test to become naturalized citizens of this country, one of the questions is, "What is the most important right granted to American citizens?" The correct answer is "the right to vote." So why do we still cordon that right off behind barriers, delays, and bureaucracy? Shouldn't we do everything possible to make that right universally available? That would include same-day registration, or perhaps even elimination of the unnecessary barrier of voter registration altogether. It should include elimination of the laws in many states that permanently disenfranchise citizens who have been convicted of a felony and served their time. It should include aggressive enforcement of laws against intimidation of voters. Citizens of the District of Columbia should have full voting rights for senators and voting representatives. And backing it all up, we should consider amending the constitution simply to guarantee what we now call "the most important right," which for some reason doesn't happen to be mentioned in our founding charter.

Redistricting, Representation, and Voting Procedures

Other reforms that would revitalize the political process would include changes to redistricting procedures, not just to prevent the raw exercise of power such as the forcible rearrangement of Texas's congressional districts in 2003 but also to prevent the zero-sum game whereby electing more minority members of Congress and state legislatures comes at the expense of white Democrats. In Iowa, a non-partisan commission draws the districts, more of which are competitive than in any comparable state.

Another approach to redistricting and representation, which is a longer-term vision, involves proportional representation. Using a proportional system, such as one under which candidates rank their preferences among several candidates, large multi-member districts can be created which might elect a minority candidate, a white Democrat and a moderate Republican, instead of three white Democrats.

The agenda of procedural reforms is crowded, however, with reform ideas that, while they have some public support, do not fundamentally restore the promise of an open, rule-based democracy. One of these is instant-runoff voting (IRV), which some believe shares the advantages of proportional representation. In an instant runoff, the voter chooses both a first and second choice candidate; if a candidate does not win a majority on the first ballot, second-choice votes are added automatically until one candidate does prevail. This would allow voters to register support for a third-party or independent candidate, without the risk of spoiling the election for an acceptable major party candidate, such as occurred in 2000 when voters who wanted to show support for Ralph Nader had the effect of costing their preferred major party candidate, Vice President Al Gore, the election.

However, IRV would add very little to our politics because those third-party votes would be symbolic. In the typical situation in which the third candidate is either to the left of the Democrat, or to the right of the Republican, his or her votes are likely to be almost automatically delivered to the ideologically closest candidate. As a result, the main candidates can take these supporters for granted. The most likely effect of IRV is to allow major-party candidates to ignore outside voices even more than they already do, which may be good or bad for the parties but adds little to democracy.

On the other hand, there are reforms that can allow third parties to function constructively within the political process, as New York's Working Families Party does today. Representing some labor unions and community organizations, the Working Families Party often endorses Democrats, occasionally reformist Republicans, and infrequently sees a need to run its own candidates, including a candidate who won a special election to the City Council in 2003. The party's second ballot line is a valuable asset to Democratic candidates, and encourages them to respond to the issues being raised by the party. The Conservative Party plays a similar role on the right. But the option of endorsing another party's candidates is only available in seven states, and only in New York is it a routine part of the political culture. Expanding the number of states in which such "fusion" parties are allowed to cross-endorse would be a far better means to give voice to those who are not in the center of politics than IRV or other procedural reforms.

Congressional Democracy

Most political reform efforts focus purely on electoral politics, whether on money, voting rights, or redistricting. Very little attention has been paid to legislative politics and the urgency of reforming Congress. The most fundamental rules that try to balance the rights of minorities against the fleeting power of majorities have been completely eviscerated in just three years, making Congress an instrument of the raw power of a few leaders.

Consider what's happened to the congressional budget process. A carefully balanced system developed over more than 50 years in order to give Congress freedom to make decisions in a context of planning for the long-term has been corrupted into an instrument that forces Congress to take action without debate or consideration of alternatives. Tax cuts have been pushed through under rules intended principally for deficit-reduction measures that limit debate and stymie most amendments. Congressional votes to raise the debt ceiling have been blocked. Hearings on major legislation are rarely held. Congress attempted to force the Congressional Budget Office to adopt a controversial procedure called "dynamic scoring" in order to suggest that tax cuts would produce economic growth and greater revenues, and backed off only when they found that even this procedure did not yield the results they wanted.

Perhaps the most egregious example of rewriting the rules is still playing itself out in the battle over judicial nominations. Having failed to block a filibuster on several extremely conservative nominees, Senate Republicans prepared to propose a rules change to say that the institution's rule of unlimited debate, which is what permits filibusters, would not apply to such nominations. Failing to win that rule change, some Republicans— beyond a couple of presidential "recess appointments" good only until that Congress adjourns—said they were prepared for what they called the "nuclear option": overruling the Senate parliamentarian to declare that judicial nominations are exempt from the rule of unlimited debate, even though nothing in the 2000 pages of Senate rules supports that position. This comes after the same group had fired an earlier Senate parliamentarian for rulings they did not like during the budget process.

This is not an area where significant new rules are needed, but rather a change in the culture, to respect the spirit of the existing rules. A deeper public understanding of just how far Congress has drifted away from democratic deliberation and toward autocratic control should be part of the public conversation in 2004.

The five pillars that have caused power to become entrenched in the United States—money in politics, media monopoly, noncompetitive elections, a narrow electorate, and the congressional culture of rewriting the rules to suit the powerful have also brought a deeply poisonous element to our politics. They add up to what journalist Ron Brownstein has described as "an age of total war." "The only rule is that there are no longer any rules."

Brownstein describes the consequences well:

> No one really wins in a political climate where the end always justifies the means. Both parties suffer when their competition has no restraints. The public suffers the most because the intensity of modern political combat makes it tougher, often impossible, for the two major parties to work together to solve problems when the shooting stops. If it ever does stop.
>
> The political warriors need to remember what the real generals learned a long time ago: The reason to accept rules for warfare isn't to be nice to the other guy. It's to protect your own side from the atrocities that are inevitable when there are no standards except survival.

The mission of political reform is not the narrow agenda of putting restrictions on campaign contributions, although reducing the influence of money is the top priority. It is not even the somewhat broader mission of restoring trust and encouraging broader participation, although such measures are the next step. The real mission is to restore the sense that democracy must be governed by *our rules*, that is, rules that bind all of us to an open process of deliberation and debate, rules that we all accede to whether they give us a momentary advantage or not. The alternative to the closed circle of big-money politics, low-vote politics, and politics-as-warfare is a democracy that opens to all the possibilities of renewal and change.

Endnotes

Chapter Two: Containing Nuclear Proliferation

p. 13: **Eisenhower on "preventive war":** McGeorge Bundy, *Danger and Survival* (New York: Random House, 1988), p. 252.

p. 14: **Gen. Leslie Groves:** Nina Byers, "Physicists and the 1945 Decision to Drop the Bomb," *Physics/0200158,* vol.1, October 13, 2002.

p. 14: **Ted Sorensen:** Fred Kaplan, *The Wizards of Armageddon* (New York: Simon & Schuster, 1983), p. 299.

p. 15: **"We have to assume that they might have one or two":** State Department, Secretary of State Press Releases, "Interview on ABC's *This Week with George Stephanopoulos,*" October 20, 2002.

p. 15: **North Korea and weapon-ready plutonium:** Glen Kessler, "North Korea Displays 'Nuclear Deterrent,'" *Washington Post,* p. A1.

p. 16: **North Korea "not a crisis":** CBS News Transcripts, *Face the Nation,* "Secretary Colin Powell Discusses North Korea," December 29, 2002.

p. 17: **Iran in nuclearized neighborhood:** Glenn Kessler, "IAEA Cites Iran on Uranium Work," *Washington Post,* p. A9.

p. 17: **European negotiations with Iran:** Glenn Frankel, "Iran Vows to Curb Nuclear Activities; Europeans Win Deal on Rules," *The Washington Post,* October 22, 2003, p. A1.

p. 18: **Pakistan...world's most dangerous proliferators:** BBC Worldwide Monitoring, "Pakistani Paper Says Arrest to Break Al Qa'idah's Backbone," March 3, 2003.

p. 19: **Krauthammer:** Charles Krauthammer, "No Turning Back Now," *Washington Post,* January 24, 2003, p. A27.

p. 22: **Jaswant Singh:** Jaswant Singh, "Against Nuclear Apartheid," *Foreign Affairs,* September 1998, p. 41.

p. 24: **Niels Bohr:** Richard Rhodes, "The Genie Is Out of the Bottle," *The Guardian,* August 6, 2002, p. 16.

p. 24: **Albert Einstein:** On the letterhead of Emergency Committee of Atomic Scientists, Princeton, NJ, January 22, 1947, cited by Howard Morland, in "The Holocaust Bomb, a Question of Time" at www.fas.org.

Chapter Three: A New Global Bargain

p. 28: **Come to a fork in the road:** Address by Secretary General Kofi Annan to the General Assembly, September 2003.

p. 29: **A group of far-sighted leaders:** Ibid.

p. 29: **Whether radical changes are needed:** Ibid.

p. 31: **On the Situation in Afghanistan:** UN Security Council Resolution 1378, November 14, 2001.

p. 34: **The Nunn-Lugar Act:** Jessica Reaves, "The Nunn-Lugar Act: Old Fears, New Era," *Time,* October 1, 2001.

p. 34: **Secretary General's Address to U.N. General Assembly:** Address by Secretary General Kofi Annan to the General Assembly, September 2003.

p. 36: **Secretary Rumsfeld Media Stakeout in Washington:** Secretary of Defense Donald H. Rumsfeld, Department of Defense News Transcript, September 23, 2001, available at www.defenselink.mil/news/Sep2001/ +09242001_+0923so.html.

p. 37: **The Atlantic Charter:** The Atlantic Charter, August 14, 1941.

Chapter Five: An Economy, Not an Empire

p. 53: **Eight million still unemployed:** This number is evidently sharply understated, relative to past experience, due to a dramatic increase in recent years in those classified as disabled rather than unemployed.

p. 57: **Households in fiscal trouble:** This argument has been laid out in a series of strategic analyses prepared by Wynne Godley for the Levy Institute. (An important caveat may be that American households have considerably higher tolerance for the acquisition of debts than any other population in the world, in part because of more extensive experience with debt-friendly public policy. My Levy Institute paper "What Is the American Model Really About?" discusses these issues in detail.)

p. 63: **Social Security and Medicare:** These two great entitlement programs are solvent from Trust Fund resources on their own assumptions until 2042 and 2028. After those dates, the Treasury will be obliged to cover the shortfall between payroll tax receipts and benefits due. This can be financed, like any other obligation, by taxes or further borrowing. It is possible that the overall financial situation of the government will require higher income taxes to meet the obligations to retirees at that time. But since these obligations are full faith and credit bonds held by the Trust Funds, to fail to honor them would constitute a default on United States Government debt. That is unimaginable, and for this reason Social Security and Medicare are as solvent as the government itself, even beyond the dates given. See Weisbrot and Baker, *Social Security: The Phony Crisis* (1999), for further discussion.

p. 63: **Repeal of tax cuts:** Whether the middle-class measures in the Bush tax cuts should eventually be repealed is a secondary question, on which judgment can be made later. The answer should depend on the strength of the economy and the demands of an alternative strategy for growth and security. On the other hand, if the recovery flags again, temporary relief from payroll taxes may be a useful step in promoting private purchasing power. To offset the cosmetic effects of such a holiday, future revenues from a restored estate tax or other revenue sources could be credited to the Trust Funds.

p. 63-64: Tax rates on corporate profits, capital gains, and individuals: These measures were long recommended by the late Nobel laureate in economics, William Vickrey, who provided forceful arguments in their favor. Their purpose would be to foster bona fide business investment out of retained profits, while raising the tax take from the individual wealthy—including predatory CEOs. It is true that reduction of the corporate income tax rates would require strict rules and rigorous auditing of corporate accounts to assure that benefits accruing mainly to individuals (perks) are properly credited to individual incomes. But such reviews would be relatively easy to carry out in the cases of highest ranking officers of major companies, and would be an extremely good use of auditing resources. See William Vickrey, "An Updated Agenda for Progressive Taxation," *American Economic Review,* Volume 82, Issue 2, Papers and Proceedings of the Hundred and Fourth Annual Meeting of the American Economics Association (May 1992), pp. 257–262 and the forthcoming Aaron W. Warner, Mathew Forstater, and Sumner N. Rosen, *Commitment to Full Employment: The Economics and Social Policy of William S. Vickrey,* for further discussion.

p. 65: World oil reserve: For an accessible discussion of the future of oil, see Kenneth Deffeyes, *Hubbert's Peak* (2001). The date by which total oil production will begin to decline remains contested, but the evidence fairly strongly suggests that present growth rates of demand cannot be sustained much beyond the present decade. This problem would thus become urgent even were political condition in the Middle East completely benign. There is a remarkable unwillingness in the public arena to discuss this issue, perhaps due in part to superficially similar, fallacious predictions made in the 1970s by the "Club of Rome." However, geophysical knowledge has advanced since then, and the methods described in Deffeyes are very different than those of that earlier period.

p. 66: Energy alternatives: Should it also include a revival of nuclear power? That issue should be raised and reviewed dispassionately, taking into account economics, safety, and the environment. We know that the model of private corporate control of nuclear generating plants is untenable, having already led to unacceptable safety problems and to economic failure. This issue should not be settled either way without a comprehensive review of technical and organizational alternatives.

p. 66: Alternate energy strategy: Use of the Arctic National Wildlife Refuge (ANWR) can be excluded on two grounds: the important environmental considerations, and also the fact that the ANWR does not contain enough oil to make a major long-term difference to our energy prospects. Pressures to drill in the ANWR appear to be mainly a matter of oil companies seeking new territories to conquer, rather than a fundamental contribution to long-term energy supply.

p. 66: **Stabilize oil prices:** One way to do this is through a variable import fee. Without such a measure, low-cost producers can reduce oil prices temporarily, making domestic investments in alternatives unprofitable, and defeating alternative energy strategies. A variable import fee should be implemented so as to take effect with a delay, allowing for the benefits of a restructuring to be felt before the costs are incurred. It might also be a sensible way to dedicate revenues to the financing of the capital investments required.

Chapter Six: A Broken Federal Fiscal Policy... and How to Fix It

p. 68: **Change in the long-term budget forecast:** The first Bush administration budget, submitted in February 2001, projected budget surpluses every year through about 2035. By contrast, the Bush budgets submitted in February 2003 and February 2004 projected deficits every year in perpetuity under administration policies.

p. 69: **Projections that deficits will total $5 trillion over the next decade:** These forecasts were designed to capture the effect of remaining on the current policy course; they assume extension of the Bush tax cuts, full funding of the President's defense program, and maintenance of funding for other non-entitlement programs at today's levels, adjusted for inflation and population growth. Center on Budget and Policy Priorities, the Committee for Economic Development, and the Concord Coalition, "The Developing Crisis—Deficits Matter" and "Mid-Term and Long-Term Deficit Projections," September 29, 2003; Ed McKelvey, "The Federal Deficit: A $5.5 Trillion Red Elephant," Goldman Sachs, September 9, 2003; William G. Gale and Peter R. Orszag, "The Budget Outlook: Baseline and Adjusted Projections," *Tax Notes*, September 22, 2003.

p. 69: **Magnitude of the policy changes needed to balance the budget by 2013:** CBPP, CED, and the Concord Coalition, *op. cit.*

p. 70: **Tax revenue over the next decade, relative to the 1970s, 1980s, and 1990s, and on the size of the long-term deficits:** CBPP, CED, and the Concord Coalition, *op.cit.*

p. 71: **Possibility of fiscal disarray:** Robert E. Rubin, Peter R. Orszag, and Allen Sinai, "Sustained Budget Deficits: Longer-Run U.S. Economic Performance and the Risk of Financial and Fiscal Disarray," Paper presented at the AEA-NAEFA Joint Session, "National Economic and Financial Policies for Growth and Stability," January 4, 2004.

p. 71: **$9 trillion swing:** CBPP, CED, and the Concord Coalition, *op. cit.*

p. 72: **Causes of the fiscal deterioration:** Richard Kogan, "Swelling Deficits: Increased Spending Is Not the Principal Culprit," Center on Budget and Policy Priorities, October 27, 2003.

p. 72: **Relative size of the tax cuts:** Calculations by Richard Kogan, Center on Budget and Policy Priorities.

p. 73: **Studies of the economic effects of the 2001 tax cut:** The Congressional Budget Office has concluded that "the revenue measures enacted since 2001...will probably have a negative effect on saving, investment, and capital accumulation over the next 10 years." Similarly, William Gale and Samara Potter of the Brookings Institution have estimated that the 2001 tax cut is more likely to reduce than to increase the size of the economy over the long run, because the negative effect of the decline in national saving that will result from the enlarged budget deficits that the tax cut will engender will outweigh the positive effect of reduced marginal tax rates, Douglas Elmendorf and David Reifschneider of the Federal Reserve, Alan Auerbach of the University of California at Berkeley, and Peter Orszag have all found similar results. See Joint Committee on Taxation, *Macroeconomics Analysis of H.R. 2, The "Jobs and Growth Reconciliation Tax Act of 2003,"* 108th Congress, 1st session, 2003; Congressional Budget Office, *The Budget and Economic Outlook,* August 2003. Douglas W. Elmendorf and David L. Reifschneider, "Short-Run Effects of Fiscal Policy with Forward-Looking Financial Markets," prepared for the National Tax Association's 2002 Spring Symposium; William G. Gale and Samara R. Potter, "An Economic Evaluation of the Economic Growth and Tax Relief and Reconciliation Act of 2001," *National Tax Journal* 54 No. 1 (March 2002), pp. 133–86; Peter R. Orszag, "Marginal Tax Rate Reductions and the Economy: What Would Be The Long-Term Effects of the Bush Tax Cut?" Center on Budget and Policy Priorities, March 2001; and Alan Auerbach, "The Bush Tax Cut and National Saving," prepared for the 2002 Spring Symposium of the National Tax Association, May 2002.

p. 73: **Rhetorical claims about tax cuts paying for themselves:** Even the President's own economists have acknowledged that the tax cuts will not pay for themselves. Council of Economic Advisers, *Economic Report of the President* (Washington, D.C.: United States Government Printing Office), February 2003.

p. 74: **Medicare prescription drug legislation:** For example, the legislation prohibits the federal government from using Medicare's vast purchasing power to negotiate lower prices for drugs, as the Department of Veteran's Affairs does. And in an effort to draw more private health care plans into Medicare, the bill subsidizes HMOs to the point that they will be paid over 25 percent more than it costs the traditional Medicare program to provide the same types of services. See Jeanne Lambrew, "Medicare Legislation: Think Twice," Center for American Progress, November 14, 2003; and Transcript of the Medicare Payment Advisory Commission Meeting, October 9, 2003.

p. 74: **LSAs and RSAs:** The estimate provided here of the long-term cost of LSAs and RSAs, relative to the size of the Social Security deficit, is based on the proposal in the administration's FY 2005 budget.

p. 75: **Effects of the proposal to block-grant Medicaid:** See Cindy Mann, Melanie Nathanson, and Edwin Park, "Administration's Medicaid Proposal Would Shift Fiscal Risks to States," Center on Budget and Policy Priorities, April 22, 2003; and John Holahan and Alan Weil, "Block Grants Are the Wrong Prescription for Medicaid," Urban Institute, May 27, 2003.

p. 75: **State cuts related to welfare reform:** See Sharon Parrott and Nina Wu, "States Are Cutting TANF and Child Care Programs," Center on Budget and Policy Priorities, June 3, 2003.

p. 76: **Income disparities:** See Congressional Budget Office, *Effective Federal Tax Rates, 1997–2000*, August 2003.

p. 76: **Recent tax cuts and inequality:** Analysis by the Urban Institute-Brookings Tax Policy Center finds that extending the tax cuts enacted in the past three years will raise after-tax income in 2011 by an average of 9 percent for the top 1 percent of households but only 0.1 percent for the bottom fifth of households.

p. 76: **State revenue losses:** Most state income tax codes use the federal definition of taxable income; shielding more income from the federal income tax therefore tends to have a parallel result at the state level. See Iris J. Lav, "Federal Policies Contribute to the Severity of the State Fiscal Crisis," Center on Budget and Policy Priorities, October 17, 2003.

p. 77: **Extending the budget rules beyond ten years:** Long-term revenue losses are typically estimated by assuming a constant share of GDP after the tenth year, although other procedures will be needed in cases where tax or entitlement changes are designed in such a way that significant increases in revenue losses or entitlement costs will result *after* the tenth year. The long-term revenue losses and entitlement costs would be measured in "present value," which is the immediate amount that, with interest, matches the future flow of revenue losses or entitlement cost increases each year in the future. The offsets also would be measured in present value.

p. 78: **Social Security reform:** See Peter A. Diamond and Peter R. Orszag, *Saving Social Security: A Balanced Approach* (Washington, D.C.: Brookings Institution, 2004).

p. 80: **Medicare subsidies to teaching hospitals:** See Henry J. Aaron and Peter R. Orszag, "Social Security, Medicare, and Medicaid," in Alice Rivlin and Isabel Sawhill, *Restoring Fiscal Sanity* (Washington, D.C.: Brookings Institution, 2004).

p. 81: **Securing savings in the Pentagon:** See Testimony of Lawrence J. Korb before the House Budget Committee, February 12, 2002; Michael E. O'Hanlon, "Limiting the Growth of the U.S. Defense Budget" (Washington, D.C.: Brookings Institution, 2002); and Testimony of Steven Kosiak, Center for Strategic and Budgetary Assessments, before the House Budget Committee, February 27, 2003.

p. 81: **Tax reforms:** See Henry Aaron, William Gale, and Peter Orszag, "Meeting the Revenue Challenge," in Rivlin and Sawhill, *op. cit.*

p. 83: **IRS enforcement:** Leonard Burman, "Tax Evasion, IRS Priorities, and EITC Precertification," Statement before the United States House of Representatives Committee on Ways and Means, July 17, 2003.

p. 83: **Other tax changes:** Another desirable tax policy change would be to repeal the provision of the Medicare drug bill that establishes Health Savings Accounts (HSAs). These accounts represent an unprecedented and fiscally dangerous type of tax shelter, since deposits into the accounts are tax deductible *and* withdrawals from the accounts are tax free. HSAs also represent ill-advised health policy. Healthier, more affluent workers may elect to enroll in HSAs in substantial numbers in coming years and to withdraw from comprehensive health insurance. (HSAs may be used only in conjunction with high-deductible health insurance; people with comprehensive health insurance policies may not use HSAs.) If healthier workers withdraw from comprehensive insurance, the pool of workers remaining in comprehensive insurance will become older and sicker, on average, thereby forcing premiums for comprehensive insurance to rise. That could lead to erosion in the affordability, and even the availability, of comprehensive employer-based insurance. See Robert Greenstein and Edwin Park, "Health Savings Accounts in Final Medicare Conference Agreement Pose Threats Both to Long-Term Fiscal Policy and to the Employment-Based Health Insurance System," Center on Budget and Policy Priorities, December 1, 2003.

p. 84: **U.S. spending for international assistance:** Nancy Birdsall, Isaac Shapiro, and Brian Deese, "How Significant are the Administration's Proposed Increases in Foreign Development Aid?" Center for Global Development and Center on Budget and Policy Priorities, May 20, 2003. The 0.6 percent of the budget level, proposed in the President's fiscal year 2004 budget, will be temporarily exceeded as a result of the costs of reconstruction in Iraq.

p. 85: **Households with "worst case housing needs":** U.S. Department of Housing and Urban Development, *A Report on Worst Case Housing Needs in 1999: New Opportunities Amid Continuing Challenges* (Washington, D.C.: United States Government Printing Office, January 2001).

Chapter Seven: Corporate Accountability

p. 87: **Value of stocks:** Joel Seligman, *The Transformation of Wall Street: A History of the Securities and Exchange Commission* (New York: Aspen Publishers, 2003).

p. 88: **Wilshire Index:** Id. at 623–624.

p. 89: **$80 billion in annual fees:** Arthur Levitt, Jr. and Richard C. Breeden, "Our Ethical Erosion," *Wall Street Journal*, December 3, 2003, p. A16.

p. 89: **Public Utility Holding Company Act:** See SELIGMAN, supra n.1, at chs. 4-8

p. 90-91: **Class action apogee:** Id. at 657–658.

p. 91: ***Central Bank*** **decision:** 511 U.S. 164 (1994).

p. 91: **Justice Stevens:** 511 U.S. at 192. See generally Joel Seligman, "The Implications of *Central Bank*," 49 *Business Law* 1429 (1994).

p. 92: **Motions to dismiss:** A. C. Pritchard and Hillary A. Sale, "What Counts as Fraud? An Empirical Study of Motions to Dismiss under the Private Securities Litigation Reform Act," MTDArticle15.doc (July 8, 2003).

p. 92: **Ovitz:** *Brehm v. Eisner*, 746 A.2d 244, 249 (Del. 2000).

p. 92: ***Disney:*** In re Walt Disney Co. Deriv. Litig., 825 A.2d 275 (Del. Ch. 2003).

p. 92: **CEO compensation:** Susan J. Stabile, "One of A, Two for B, and Four Hundred for C: The Widening Gap in Pay Between Executives and Rank and File Employees," 36 *Journal of Law Reform* 115, 115–116 (2002).

p. 92: **Expensing stock options:** SELIGMAN, supra n.1, at 714–717.

p. 93: **Ball and strikes:** Id. at 722–728.

p. 95: **Independent budgetary process:** Joel Seligman, "Self-Funding for the Securities and Exchange Commission," Nova L. Rev. (forthcoming 2004).

p. 98: **WorldCom:** Richard C. Breeden, Restoring Trust: Report to Hon. Jed S. Rakoff and Corporate Governance for the Future of MCI, Inc. Esp. 21–22, 30–34 (S.D.N.Y. Aug. 2003).

Chapter Eight: Out of the Quagmire

p. 101-102: **U.S. labor market structure:** Frank Levy and Richard Murnane, *The New Division of Labor: How Computers are Creating the Next Job Market* (Princeton, N.J.: Princeton University Press, forthcoming, May 2004).

p. 102: **"regulatory federalism":** James Cibulka, *The Reform and Survival of the American Public School: An Institutional Perspective* (Washington, D.C.: Falmer Press, 1996); Paul Peterson, Barry Rabe, and Kenneth Wong, *When Federalism Works* (Washington, D.C.: Brookings Institution, 1986).

p. 107: **Over-reliance and false precision:** "The Testing Trap," *Harvard Magazine*, September/October 2002; previously published as "Unwarranted Intrusion," in *EdNext*, Spring 2002.

p. 108: **Misclassification of schools:** See Thomas Kane and Douglas Staiger, "Volatility in School Test Scores: Implications for Test-Base Accountability Systems," in Diane Ravitch, ed., *Brookings Papers on Education Policy* (Washington, D.C.: Brookings Institution, 2002).

p. 108: **"logistical nightmare for schools":** See Jimmy Kim and Gail Sunderman, "Does NCLB Provide Good Choices for Students in Low-Performing Schools," Harvard Civil Rights Project Report, February 2004, available at www.civilrightsproject.harvard.edu.

p. 109: **more difficult to improve:** See Richard Elmore, "Knowing the Right Thing to Do: School Improvement and Performance-Based Accountability," Washington, D.C.: National Governors Association, 2003, available at www.nga.org/center/divisions/1,1188,C_ISSUE_BRIEF^D_5843,00.html.

p. 111: **government will maximize interests:** A more extended version of this analysis is in Terry M. Moe, "The Politics of Bureaucratic Structure," in John E. Chubb and Paul E. Peterson, *Can the Government Govern?* (Washington, D.C.: The Brookings Institution, 1989), pp. 267–329.

Chapter Nine: Making Health Care Affordable and Accessible

p. 118: **Census Bureau survey:** Robert J. Mills and Shailesh Bhandari, *Health Insurance Coverage in the United States: 2002, Current Population Reports* (Washington, D.C.: U.S. Census Bureau, September 2003).

p. 118: **43.6 million Americans:** Ron Pollack, *Census Bureau's Uninsured Number Is Largest Increase in Past Decade,* Familes USA website, September 30, 2003, available at www.familiesusa.org/site/PageServer?pagename=Media_Statement_Census_Bureau.

p. 118-119: **Survey and uninsured during portions of the year:** Robert J. Mills and Shailesh Bhandari, *Health Insurance Coverage in the United States: 2002, Current Population Reports* (Washington, D.C.: U.S. Census Bureau, September 2003). By interviewing people in March about their insurance coverage the previous calendar year, the CPS is intended to yield an estimate of the number of people who are uninsured all year. However, controversy exists over whether the CPS actually accomplishes this goal. Some researchers argue that the CPS only provides an estimate of the number of people uninsured at the point in time when they are contacted. See Lyle Nelson et al., *How Many People Lack Health Insurance and For How Long?* (Washington, D.C.: Congressional Budget Office, May 2003).

p. 119: **All or a portion of 2001–2002:** Kathleen Stoll, *Going Without Health Insurance, Nearly One in Three Non-Elderly Americans,* A report released by the Robert Wood Johnson Foundation and prepared by Families USA for Cover the Uninsured Week 2003 (Washington, D.C.: Families USA, March 2003).

p. 119: **"a perfect storm":** Joel E. Miller, *A Perfect Storm: The Confluence of Forces Affecting Health Care Coverage* (Washington, D.C.: National Coalition on Health Care, November 2001).

p. 119: **Prescription drug costs:** Families USA, *Prescription Drug Cost Sharing and Low-Income People: Five Good Reasons to Keep It Minimal,* Families USA Health Policy Memo, September 12, 2003; Dee Mahan, *Out-of-Bounds: Rising Prescription Drug Prices for Seniors* (Washington, D.C.: Families USA, July 2003). *Health Care Costs: Why Do They Increase? What Can We Do?* Workshop sponsored by Agency for Healthcare Research and Quality, U.S. Department of Health and Human Services, for its User Liaison Program (ULP), Los Angeles, California, May 21–23,

2001. Materials available at www.ahcpr.gov/news/ulp/costs/ulpcosts.htm. David Gross, *Medicare Beneficiaries and Prescription Drugs: Costs and Coverage*, AARP, September 2002, available at research.aarp.org/health/dd77_rx.html#Prescription.

p. 119: **Consolidation of hospital systems:** Kelly J. Devers et al., "Hospitals' Negotiating Leverage with Health Plans: How and Why Has It Changed?" *Health Services Research* 38:1, Part II (February 2003), pp. 419–446.

p. 119: **Expensive technology:** J. W. Hay, "Hospital Cost Drivers: An evaluation of 1998–2001 State-Level Data," *American Journal of Managed Care* Special No. 1 (June 9, 2003), pp. SP13-24; K. Hearle et al., "Drivers of Expenditure Growth in Outpatient Care Services," *American Journal of Managed Care* Special No. 1 (June 9, 2003), pp. SP25–33; M. M. Goetghebeur, S. Forrest, and J. W. Hay, "Understanding the Underlying Drivers of Inpatient Cost Growth: A literature review," *American Journal of Managed Care* Special No. 1(June 9, 2003), pp. SP3–12; M. Siegler, A. Weisfeld, and D. Cronins, "Is Medical Research Cost Effective? Response to Murphy and Topel," *Perspectives in Biology and Medicine* 46 (3 Suppl) (Summer 2003), pp. S129–37; S. Glied and S.E. Little, "The uninsured and the benefits of medical progress," *Health Affairs* 22 (July–August 2003), pp. 210–219.

p. 119: **Increased profits by insurance companies:** Ian Reed, "U.S. Health Insurance Midyear Outlook 2003: Enjoying the Payday Heyday…While it Lasts," *Ratings Direct*, Standard & Poor's, May 24, 2003, reprinted at www2.standardandpoors.com. "Five Key Trends Predicted to Drive Health Insurance Industry in 2003," *Managed Care Week*, December 23, 2002, reprinted at AISHealth.com, www.aishealth.com.

p. 119: **Relaxation of managed care approval systems:** J. Lee Hargraves, "Patients Concerned About Insurer Influences," *Center for Studying Health System Change Data Bulletin No. 17* (June 2000); "Aetna Indicates Relaxation of Policies in Connecticut," *CLASSACTIONREPORTER*, May 12, 2000, Vol. 2, No. 93, available at Internet Bankruptcy Library, www.bankrupt.com/CAR_Public000512.MBX.

p. 119: **Cost increases will continue:** Stephen Heffler et al., "Health Spending Projections for 2001–2011: The Latest Outlook," *Health Affairs* 21:2 (March/April 2002), pp. 207–18; Michael E. Chernew et al., "Increased Spending On Health Care: How Much Can the United States Afford?" *Health Affairs* 22:4 (July/August 2003), pp. 15–25; David Blumenthal, M.D., M.P.P., "Controlling Health Care Expenditures," *The New England Journal of Medicine*, 344:10, (March 2001), pp. 766–76910; John K. Inglehart, "Changing Health Insurance Trends," *The New England Journal of Medicine*, 347:12 (September 19, 2002), pp. 956–962.

p. 119: **Workers paying larger share:** Gary Claxton et al., Employer Health Benefits: *2003 Employer Health Benefits Survey* (Menlo Park, Calif.: Henry J. Kaiser Family Foundation, 2003), p. 1; Cover the Uninsured Week, *Key Findings: Survey of Small, Medium and Large Businesses*, March 13, 2003, available at covertheuninsuredweek.org/media/BusinessSurveyReport.pdf; Judy Silber, "Health Care Pre-

miums on the Rise," *Contra Costa Times,* June 19, 2003, available at
www.bayarea.com/mld/cctimes/content_syndication/local_news/6122242.htm.

p. 119: **Health coverage shrinking:** The Commonwealth Fund, "Improving
Insurance Coverage and Access to Care," *2002 Annual Report* available at
www.cmwf.org/annreprt/annreport.asp?link=7.

p. 119: **Health coverage for dependents is diminishing:** Gary Claxton et al.,
Employer Health Benefits: 2003 Employer Health Benefits Survey (Menlo Park, Calif.:
Henry J. Kaiser Family Foundation, 2003), pp. 51–56; Frank McArdle et al., *The
Current State of Retiree Health Benefits: Findings from the Kaiser/Hewitt 2002 Retiree
Survey* (Menlo Park, Calif.: Henry J. Kaiser Family Foundation and Hewitt
Associates, December 2003); John Perry, "Employer Sponsored Health Insurance:
Examining Kentucky," *Kentucky Annual Economic Report 2003.* Lexington, Ky.:
Center for Business and Economic Research, University of Kentucky, 2003, avail-
able at www.gatton.uky.edu/CBER/Downloads/annrpt03.html.

p. 120: **COBRA costs:** Gary Claxton et al., *Employer Health Benefits: 2003
Employer Health Benefits Survey* (Menlo Park, Calif.: Henry J. Kaiser Family
Foundation, 2003), p. 1.

p. 120: **Four out of five eligible for COBRA do not receive it:** Kaiser
Commission on Medicaid and the Uninsured, *COBRA Coverage for Low-Income
Unemployed Workers* (Washington, D.C.: Kaiser Commission on Medicaid and the
Uninsured, October 2001); Stephen Zuckerman, Jennifer Haley, and Matthew
Fragale, *Could Subsidizing COBRA Health Insurance Coverage Help Most Low-Income
Unemployed?* (Washington, D.C.: Urban Institute, October 2001).

p. 120: **Cutbacks in state public health programs:** Donna Cohen Ross and
Laura Cox, *Preserving Recent Progress on Health Coverage for Children and Families:
New Tensions Emerge* (Menlo Park, Calif.: Henry J. Kaiser Family Foundation, July
2003). National Council of State Legislatures, *The State of SCHIP Budgets and
Programs,* March 2003, available at www.ncsl.org/programs/health/
webcastsurvey.htm. Academy Health, *State of the States: Bridging the Health Coverage
Gap,* January 2003, available at www.statecoverage.net/pdf/stateofstates2003.pdf.

p. 120: **18,000 a year die because uninsured:** Institute of Medicine, *Hidden
Costs, Value Lost: Uninsurance in America* (Washington, D.C.: National Academies
Press, 2003), p. 107.

p. 120: **Uninsured less likely to have usual source of care:** *Ibid,* p. 41;
American College of Physicians—American Society of Internal Medicine, *No
Health Insurance? It's Enough to Make You Sick* (Philadelphia: American College of
Physicians—American Society of Internal Medicine, November 1999).

p. 120: **Uninsured often go without preventive care:** Institute of Medicine,
Care Without Coverage: Too Little, Too Late (Washington, D.C.: National Academies
Press, 2002), p. 48. Genevieve M. Kenny, Jennifer M. Haley, and Alexandra Tebay,

Children's Insurance Coverage and Service Use Improve (Washington, D.C.: Urban Institute, July 31, 2003).

p. 120: **Uninsured often delay or forego care:** Institute of Medicine, *Care Without Coverage: Too Little, Too Late*, (Washington, D.C.: National Academies Press, 2002), pp. 47–88; Cheryl Fish-Parcham, *Getting Less Care: The Uninsured with Chronic Health Conditions* (Washington, D.C.: Families USA, February 2001).

p. 120: **Uninsured likely to become bankrupt if they need significant care:** Martha Shirk, *In Their Own Words: The Uninsured Talk About Living Without Health Insurance* (Washington, D.C.: Kaiser Family Foundation, 2000).

p. 120: **Uninsured charged more for health services:** Institute of Medicine, *Hidden Costs, Value Lost: Uninsurance in America* (Washington, D.C.: National Academies Press, 2003), p. 44; Irene Wielawski, "Gouging the Medically Uninsured: A Tale of Two Bills," *Health Affairs* 19 (September/October 2000), pp. 180–185.

p. 121: **Estimates of number of underinsured:** Karen Donelan, Catherine M. DesRoches, and Cathy Schoen, "Inadequate Health Insurance: Costs and Consequences," *Medscape General Medicine* 2 (2000), available at www.medscape.com/viewarticle/408069.

p. 121: **Underinsured estimates range up to more than 30 million:** P.F. Short and J. S. Banthin, "New Estimates of the Underinsured Younger than 65 Years," *Journal of the American Medical Association* 274 (October 25, 1995), pp.1302–1306; Gail Shearer, *Hidden from View: The Growing Burden of Health Care Costs* (Washington, D.C.: Consumers Union, 1998); Robert Kuttner, "The American Health Care System: Health Insurance Coverage," *The New England Journal of Medicine* 340 (January 14, 1999), pp. 165–166.

p. 121: **Effectiveness of Medicare:** Marilyn Moon, "Health Policy 2001: Medicare," *New England Journal of Medicine* 344:12 (March 22, 2001), pp. 928–931; Jonathan Oberlander, *The Political Life of Medicare* (Chicago: University of Chicago Press, 2003), p. 165.

p. 121: **Seniors without drug coverage:** Bruce Stuart, Dennis Shea, and Beck Briesacher, *Prescription Drug Costs for Medicare Beneficiaries: Coverage and Health Status Matter* (Washington, D.C.: Commonwealth Fund, January 2002).

p. 121: **Seniors' coverage for long-term care:** Joshua Wiener, Jane Tilly, and Susan M. Goldenson, "Federal and State Initiatives to Jump Start the Market for Private Long-Term Care Insurance," *The Elder Law Journal* 8 (2000), p. 60.

p. 121: **Senior spending on prescription drugs:** Dee Mahan, *Out-of-Bounds: Rising Prescription Drug Prices for Seniors* (Washington, D.C.: Families USA, July 2003) p. 14.

p. 121: **Seniors spending over $5000 a year:** Henry J. Kaiser Family

Foundation, *Medicare and Prescription Drug Spending Chartpack, High Drug Utilizers,* (Menlo Park, Calif.: Henry J. Kaiser Family Foundation, June 2003), available at www.kff.org/medicare/6087-index.cfm.

p. 121: **Average drug prices for seniors rising faster than inflation:** Dee Mahan, *Out-of-Bounds: Rising Prescription Drug Prices for Seniors* (Washington, D.C.: Families USA, July 2003).

p. 121: **Price increases throughout decade:** *Ibid;* Amanda McCloskey, *Bitter Pill: The Rising Prices of Prescription Drugs for Older Americans* (Washington, D.C.: Families USA, June 2002); Kathleen Haddad, *Hard to Swallow: Rising Drug Prices for America's Seniors* (Washington, D.C.: Families USA, November 1999).

p. 121: **Annual cost of nursing home care:** "What nursing homes cost: Annual average rises 7 percent to $57,700, report finds," *Reuters,* November 13, 2003, available at msnbc.msn.com/Default.aspx?id=3076978&p1=0.

p. 122: **Comprehensive reform may be a political impossibility:** Charles N. Kahn and Ronald F. Pollack, "Building a Consensus for Expanding Health Insurance Coverage," *Health Affairs* 20 (January/February 2001), pp. 40–48; Haynes Johnson and David S. Broder, *The System: The American Way of Politics at the Breaking Point* (Boston: Little Brown, 1996).

p. 123: **Children below poverty level receive coverage:** Donna Cohen Ross and Laura Cox, *Preserving Recent Progress on Health Coverage for Children and Families: New Tensions Emerge* (Washington, D.C.: Kaiser Commission on Medicaid and the Uninsured, July 2003), p. 2. Thirty-nine states currently have open programs covering children up to 200 percent of the federal poverty level.

p. 123: **Participation in SCHIP:** Centers for Medicare and Medicaid Services, *Fiscal Year 2002 Number of Children Ever Enrolled in SCHIP,* January 30, 2003, available at www.cms.gov/schip/enrollment/schip02.pdf.

p. 123: **8.5 million uninsured children:** Robert J. Mills and Sailesh Bhandari, *Health Insurance Coverage in the United States: 2002* (Washington, D.C.: U.S. Census Bureau, September 2003), p. 2.

p. 123: **20.2 million children uninsured in 2001–2002:** Kathleen Stoll, *Going Without Health Insurance: Nearly One in Three Non-Elderly Americans,* (Washington, D.C.: Families USA, March 2003), p. 7.

p. 123: **Failure to reach lower income children with SCHIP coverage:** Families USA, *Promising Ideas in Children's Health Insurance: Simplifying Eligibility Reviews* (Washington, D.C.: Families USA, May 2001).

p. 123: **More than 80 percent of workers eligible for COBRA do not receive it:** Stephen Zuckerman, Jennifer Hale, and Matthew Fragale, *Could Subsidizing COBRA Health Insurance Coverage Help Most Low-Income Unemployed?* (Washington, D.C.: Urban Institute, October 2001).

p. 123: **Grassley and Baucus legislation:** 108th Congress, S. 1693.

p. 123: **1.4 million more could receive COBRA:** Statement of Senator Baucus, *Congressional Record*, October 1, 2003, p. S12282.

p. 124: **Previous attempt at COBRA expansion defeated by Bush and Congressional Republicans:** Robin Toner, "A Stubborn Fight Revived," *The New York Times*, December 20, 2001, p. A34.

p. 125: **New legislation prohibits Medicare from bargaining with drug companies for lower prices:** Medicare Prescription Drug Improvement, and Modernization Act of 2003, 108th Congress, H.R. 1, Section 1860D-11(i).

p. 125: **Senior prohibited from purchasing drugs from Canada:** *Ibid,* Section 1121.

p. 126: **Bush proposal to alter Medicaid:** U.S. Department of Health and Human Services, "Bush Administration Will Propose Innovative Improvements in States' Health Coverage for Low-Income Americans," January 31, 2003, available at www.hhs.gov/news/press/2003pres/20030131d.html.

p. 126-127: **Reduction in state funding for Medicaid:** Rachel Klein, *Slashing Medicaid: The Hidden Effects of the President's Block-Grant Proposal* (Washington, D.C.: Families USA, May 2003).

p. 127: **Almost all states implementing program cuts:** Vernon Smith, et al., *States Respond to Fiscal Pressure: State Medicaid Spending Growth and Cost Containment in Fiscal Years 2003 and 2004, Results from a 50-State Survey* (Washington, D.C.: Kaiser Commission on Medicaid and the Uninsured, September 2003), pp. 21–32.

p. 127: **Eight of nine seniors:** Only 11 percent of Medicare beneficiaries are enrolled in Medicare+Choice plans and that number has been declining. Henry J. Kaiser Family Foundation, *Medicare+Choice Fact Sheet* (Menlo Park, Calif.: Henry J. Kaiser Family Foundation, April 2003); Marsha Gold and John McCoy, *Choice Continues to Errode in 2002* (Washington, D.C.: Mathematica Policy Research, Inc., 2002).

p. 128: **Problems with private plans:** Jeanne M.Lambrew and Becky Briesacher, *Medicare Prescription Drug Legislation: What it Means for Rural Beneficiaries,* (Washington, D.C.: Center for American Progress, September 2003); Marsha Gold and John McCoy, *Choice Continues to Errode in 2002* (Washington, D.C.: Mathematica Policy Research, Inc., 2002).

p. 128: **Private plans more restrictive and expensive:** Brian Biles, Geraldine Dallek, and Andrew Dennington, *Medicare+Choice After Five Years: Lessons for Medicare's Future* (New York: The Commonwealth Fund, September 2002), pp. 11–15.

p. 128: **Private plans "cherry pick":** General Accounting Office,

Medicare+Choice: Payments Exceed Costs of Fee-For-Service Benefits, Adding Billions to Spending (Washington, D.C.: General Accounting Office, August 2000, report number: GAO/HEHS-00-161).

p. 128: **Private plans more costly:** Congressional Research Service, memo from Paulette Morgan, Jim Hahn, and Hinda Chaikind to House Ways and Means Committee, July 22, 2003; Medicare Payment Advisory Commission, *Report to the Congress: Medicare Payment Policy* (Washington, D.C.: MedPAC, March 2003), Chapter 5, available at www.medpac.gov/publications/ generic_report_display.cfm?report_type_id=1&sid=2&subid=0.

p. 128: **Annual tax credits will not help:** Kathleen Stoll and Erica Molliver, *A 10-Foot Rope for a 40-Foot Hole: Tax Credits for the Uninsured, 2002 Update* (Washington, D.C.: Families USA, May 2002).

p. 129: **20 million people would pay more:** Congressional Budget Office, *Increasing Small-Firm Health Insurance Coverage Through Association Health Plans and HealthMarts* (Washington, D.C.: Congressional Budget Office, January 2000).

p. 130: **51 million lower-income people:** John Holahan and Brian Bruen, *Medicaid Spending: What Factors Contributed to the Growth Between 2000 and 2002?* (Washington, D.C.: Kaiser Commission on Medicaid and the Uninsured, September 2003), p. 4.

p. 130: **Child eligible for coverage in four of five states:** Donna Cohen Ross and Laura Cox, *Preserving Recent Progress on Health Coverage for Children and Families: New Tensions Emerge* (Washington, D.C.: Kaiser Commission on Medicaid and the Uninsured, July 2003), p. 2.

p. 130: **Parental eligibility very different:** Families USA calculations based on eligibility limits as of June 2003.

p. 130: **Kennedy and Snowe legislation:** The Family Care Act of 2001, 107th Congress, S. 1244, H.R. 2630.

p. 131: **Immigrant families often ineligible:** 8 U.S.C. §§ 1631–1632.

p. 131: **Institute of Medicine:** Janet M. Corrigan, Ann Greiner, and Shari M. Erickson, eds., *Fostering Rapid Advances in Health Care: Learning from System Demonstrations* (Washington, D.C.: National Academies Press, 2002).

p. 131: **Ideologically diverse think tanks:** Henry J. Aaron and Stuart M. Butler, "Four Steps to Better Health Care," *The Washington Post,* July 6, 2003, p. B7; Henry J. Aaron and Stuart Butler, *How Federalism Could Spur Bipartisan Action on the Uninsured,* paper presented to The Council on Health Care Economics and Policy, November 3, 2003, available at sihp.brandeis.edu/council/.

p. 132: **Federal rules need to be established:** Henry J. Aaron and Stuart Butler, *How Federalism Could Spur Bipartisan Action on the Uninsured,* paper presented to The Council on Health Care Economics and Policy, November 3, 2003, available at sihp.brandeis.edu/council/.

p. 132: **Proposal different from Bush "waiver" initiative:** Center for Medicare & Medicaid Services, *Guidelines for States Interested in Applying for a HIFA Demonstration,* May 23, 2002, available at www.cms.hhs.gov/hifa/hifagde.asp.

p. 133: **Seventy percent of health costs consumed by 10 percent of population:** Karen Davis and Cathy Schoen, "Creating Consensus on Coverage Choices," *Health Affairs,* Web Exclusive (April 23, 2003), p. W3-206, available at content.healthaffairs.org/cgi/content/full/hlthaff.w3.199v1/DC1.

p. 133: **Cost-containment regimens:** Jonathan Oberlander and Jim Jaffe, "Next Step: Drug Price Controls," *The Washington Post,* December 14, 2003, p. B7.

Chapter Ten: Stop Environmental Darwinism

p. 135: **Captain John Smith:** John Smith on Chesapeake Bay: The Proceedings of the English Colonie in Virginia (1612).

p. 137: **Urban lead concentrations:** EPA, quoted in Greenwire, February 25, 2003.

p. 137: **Percent of waterways cleaned up:** EPA, "Quality of the Nation's Rivers and Streams," 2000, available at www.epa.gov/owow/monitoring/nationswaters/quality.htm.

p. 138: **Reduction in value of human life:** Katherine Q. Seelye and John Tierney, "By the Numbers," *The New York Times,* May 8, 2003.

p. 140: **John Graham on hypochondria:** Steve Weinberg, "Mr Bottomline: John D. Graham," *OnEarth,* NRDC, no. 1, vol. 25, March 22, 2003.

p. 141: **Scientists bounced from NIH advisory panels:** Rick Weiss, "HHS Seeks Science Advice to Match Bush Views," *The Washington Post,* September 17, 2002; also Jonathan Cohn, "The Lead Industry Gets Its Turn," *The New Republic Online,* December 23, 2002.

p. 141: **Elimination of NEPA jurisdiction over the oceans:** John McQuaid, "Bush Seeks to Limit NEPA Use Outside U.S. Waters," *Greenwire,* August 12, 2002.

p. 141: **Sue and be settled examples:** "Three Cases Speak Volumes About New EPA Choice," *Earthjustice,* August 13, 2003.

p. 142: **Priority to funding timber industry over small town protection:** "President Acts to Fund Healthy Forest Initiative," *The Forestry Source,* March 2003. See www.safnet.org/archive/0303_budget.cfm.

p. 142: **Oil savings from freedom package:** "Building a Better SUV," Union of Concerned Scientists, September 2003.

p. 143: **Apollo project data:** See www.apolloalliance.org.

p. 144: **Greenberg poll:** See www.greenbergresearch.com/campaigns_us/index.html.

p. 144: **Number of prevented asthma attacks:** "Power to Kill," Clean Air Task Force report, July 2001.

p. 146: **Needed reduction in Co2 emissions:** Dr. Margo Thorning, "Kyoto Protocol and Beyond: 'Whither the Targets?'" International Council Capital Formation, November 2002.

Chapter Twelve: Terrorism and the Rule of Law

Some portions of this chapter are drawn from David Cole, *Enemy Aliens: Double Standards and Constitutional Freedoms in the War on Terrorism* (New York: New Press, 2003), in which these ideas are developed more fully.

p. 167: **Louis Post quote:** Louis F. Post, *The Deportations Delirium of Nineteen-Twenty: A Personal Narrative of an Historic Official Experience* (New York: Da Capo Press, 1923), p. 307.

p. 170: **5,000 detentions:** See David Cole, *Enemy Aliens: Double Standards and Constitutional Freedoms in the War on Terrorism* (New York: New Press, 2003), p. 25.

p. 170: **For details on preventive detention campaign:** See Cole, *Enemy Aliens, supra,* 17–46.

p. 175: **As Stuart Taylor has pointed out...:** Stuart Taylor, "False Alarm: Overblown Fears about Patriot Act Searches Obscure Real Liberties Abuses at Guantanamo," *Legal Times,* November 10, 2003, p. 60.

p. 176: **Bush speech:** "A Nation Challenged: President Bush's Address on Terrorism Before a Joint Meeting of Congress," *New York Times,* September 21, 2001, p. B4.

p. 176: **Tom Ridge quote:** Elizabeth Becker, "One Year Later, Ridge Sees a Country Better Prepared," *New York Times,* September 6, 2002, p. A1.

p. 177: **David Carr quotes:** David Carr, "The Futility of 'Homeland Defense,'" *The Atlantic Monthly,* January 2002, available at www.theatlantic.com/issues/2002/01/carr.htm.

p. 177: **bipartisan commission of national security experts...:** Markle Foundation, "Creating a Trusted Network for Homeland Security," December 2003, available at www.markle.org/news/Report2_Full_Report.pdf.

p. 177: **In addition, as drug smugglers have shown:** Mike Gray, *Drug Crazy: How We Got into This Mess and How We Can Get Out* (New York: Random House, 1998), pp. 148–49.

p. 177: **Daniel Benjamin and Steven Simon:** *The Age of Sacred Terror* (2002), p. 403.

p. 178: **Markle Foundation:** "Protecting America's Freedom in the Information Age: A Report of the Markle Foundation Task Force" (2002).

p. 179: **before Ashcroft relaxed the FBI guidelines:** David Cole and James X.

Dempsey, *Terrorism and the Constitution: Sacrificing Civil Liberties in the Name of National Security* 2d ed., (New York: New Press, 2002).

p. 179: **Jessica Stern:** See Jessica Stern, *The Ultimate Terrorists* (Cambridge, Mass.: Harvard University Press, 1999), pp. 128-48.

p. 181: **We are the richest nation in the world…:** "Ranking the Rich," *Foreign Policy*, May/June 2003.

Chapter Thirteen: From Affirmative Action to Affirmative Opportunity

p. 183: **The Supreme Court's University of Michigan decisions on affirmative action:** *Grutter v. Bollinger*, 123 S. Ct. 2325 (2003). *Cf. Gratz v. Bollinger*, 123 S. Ct. 2411 (2003).

p. 183: **President Bill Clinton, Address at the National Archives:** George Stephanopoulos and Christopher Edley Jr., Affirmative Action Review: Report to the President, (July 19, 1995). See generally, Christopher Edley Jr., *Not All Black and White: Affirmative Action, Race, and American Values* (1996).

p. 184: **President Clinton and Justice O'Connor on the transitional quality of affirmative action:** Clinton, *supra* note 2; *Grutter*, 123 at 322.

p. 184: **Unresolved legal questions after *The Michigan Cases*:** The Civil Rights Project, Post-*Grutter* and *Gratz* legal and research questions (posted Jan. 07, 2004) at http://www.civilrightsproject.harvard.edu/policy/legal_docs/legal_memos.php.

p. 185: **Developments in the courts on school desegregation:** See generally, John C. Boger, Education's "Perfect Storm"? Racial Resegregation, High-Stakes Testing, and School Resource Inequities: The Case of North Carolina, 81 N.C. L. Rev. 1375 (2003); *Belk v. Charlotte-Mecklenburg Bd. of Educ.*, 269 F.3d 305 (U.S. App., 2001); Gary Orfield and Susan E. Eaton, Dismantling Desegregation: The Quiet Reversal of *Brown v. Board of Education* (1996), pp. 1–2.

p. 185: **The "founding document" of standards-based school reform:** The National Comm'n on Excellence in Educ., United States Dep't of Educ., *A Nation at Risk: The Imperative for Educational Reform* (1983).

p. 186: **Crucial school desegregation cases:** *Brown v. Board of Educ.*, 347 U.S. 483 (1954); *Green v. County School Board*, 391 U.S. 430 (1968); Orfield & Eaton, *supra* note 5.

p. 186: **The dynamics surrounding passage of the 1964 Civil Rights Act:** See generally, Hugh Davis Graham, *The Civil Rights Era: Origins and Development of National Policy 1960–1972* (1990), p. 134.

p. 187: **Census trends mid-century:** Gary D. Sandefur et. al., "An Overview of Racial and Ethnic Demographic Trends," in National Research Council (2001) America Becoming: Racial Trends and Their Consequences, Vol. 1 (Neil Smelser et. al. eds.) National Research Council (2001), p. 43.

p. 187: **Immigrant flows in metro areas:** John R. Logan, Lewis Mumford Center for Comparative Urban and Regional Research, University at Albany, "America's Newcomers," June 18, 2003.

p. 187: **Declining proportion of Whites nationally and in metro regions:** John Logan and John Mollenkopf, SUNY Lewis Mumford Center for Comparative Urban and Regional Research, "People and Politics in America's Big Cities," May 15, 2003.

p. 187: **Black immigration:** John Logan and Glenn Deane, Lewis Mumford Center for Comparative Urban and Regional Research, University at Albany, "Black Diversity in Metropolitan America," August 15, 2003.

p. 187: **School demography and resegregation trends:** Erica Frankenberg, Chungmei Lee, Professor Gary Orfield, "A Multiracial Society with Segregated Schools, Are We Losing the Dream?" January 16, 2003.

p. 188: **State and district minority majorities:** Frankenberg, Erica, Lee, Chungmei, and Orfield, Gary. *A Multiracial Society with Segregated Schools? Are we Losing the Dream?* (Cambridge, Mass.: The Civil Rights Project, Harvard University; (2003). Data Source: U.S. Department of Education, National Center for Education Statistics, 1988–89; 2000–2001 Common Core of Data.

p. 188: **Income disparities in Census 2000:** John Logan, Lewis Mumford Center for Comparative Urban and Regional Research, "Separate and Unequal: The Neighborhood Gap for Blacks and Hispanics in Metropolitan America," October 13, 2002.

p. 188-189: **Health care disparities and discrimination:** Report by the Institute of Medicine, "Unequal Treatment: Confronting Racial and Ethnic Disparities in Healthcare," 2003; Report by Physicians for Human Rights, "The Right to Equal Treatment: An Action Plan to End Racial and Ethnic Disparities in Clinical Diagnosis and Treatment in the United States," 2003.

p. 189: **Ballot spoilage disparities by congressional district:** Harvard Civil Rights Project, "Democracy Spoiled: National, State, and County Disparities in Disenfranchisement Through Uncounted Ballots," July 12, 2002.

p. 189: **Youth sentencing disparities:** Eileen Poe-Yamagata and Michael Jones, "And Justice for Some" (Building Blocks for Youth, 2000).

p. 189: **Projected incarceration rates for children born today:** Alfred Blumstein, "An Overview of Racial and Ethnic Demographic Trends," in America Becoming: Racial Trends and Their Consequences, Vol. 1 (Neil Smelser et. al. eds.) National Research Council (2001), p. 22.

p. 189: **Disproportionate minority youth incarceration:** Harvard Civil Rights Project & Northeastern University's Institute on Race and Justice, "Defining and Redirecting a School to Prison Pipeline," May 2003.

p. 189: **Racial disparities in special education:** Harvard Civil Rights Project

& Northeastern University's Institute on Race and Justice, "Defining and Redirecting a School to Prison Pipeline," May 2003.

p. 188-190: **Disparities in drop out rates:** Harvard Civil Rights Project & Northeastern University's Institute on Race and Justice, "Defining and Redirecting a School to Prison Pipeline," May 2003.

p. 190: **Achievement disparities in education:** U.S. Department of Education, National Assessment of Educational Progress, 1990–2003.

p. 190: **Drop out trends and disparities:** U.S. Department of Education, National Center for Education Statistics, *Digest of Education Statistics*, 2000, Table 106.

p. 190: **Civil rights and transportation equity:** Thomas W. Sanchez et al., "Moving to Equity: Addressing Inequitable Effects of Transportation Policies on Minorities," Joint Report of the Harvard Civil Rights Project and Center for Community Change, June 2003.

p. 190: **Discrimination shown in resume study:** "Are Emily and Greg More Employable than Lakisha and Jamal? A Field Experiment on Labor," Market Discrimination, Marianne Bertrand and Sendhil Mullainathan, NBER Working Paper No. 9873 (July 2003), JEL No. J7, J71, J23, J24, J63, J82, C93.

p. 190: **Summarizing housing discrimination evidence:** Douglas Massey, "Residential Segregation and Neighborhood Conditions," in America Becoming: Racial Trends and Their Consequences, Vol. 1 (Neil J. Smelser et al., eds.) (National Research Council, 2001), p. 419. George Galster, Margery Austin Turner, Stephen L. Ross, John Yinger, "Discrimination in Metropolitan Housing Markets: National Results from Phase I of HDS 2000" (Urban Institute, November, 2002).

p. 191: **Cognitive psychology and discrimination:** Maddox and Gray, Cognitive Representations of Black Americans: Reexploring the Role of Skin Tone, *Personality and Social Psychology Bulletin* 28 (2) (Feb. 2002).

p. 191: **Racial profiling research literature:** Randall Kennedy, "Racial Trends in the Administration of Criminal Justice," in America Becoming: Racial Trends and Their Consequences, Vol. 1 (Neil J. Smelser et. al eds.) (National Research Council 2001), p. 3.

p. 192: **Voting rights caselaw and implications:** *Shaw v. Reno*, 509 U.S. 630 (1993). *See generally*, Pamela S. Karlan, The Fire Next Time: Reapportionment After the 2000 Census, 50 Stan. L. Rev. 731 (1998).

p. 192: **Supreme Court restriction on congressional remedial powers under the Fourteenth Amendment:** *City of Boerne v. Flores*, 521 U.S. 507 (1997).

p. 192: **Supreme Court ruling on state immunity to civil rights suits for money damages:** *Kimel v. Florida Board of Regents*, 528 U.S. 62 (2000) (striking down Congress' attempt to abrogate states' sovereign immunity under the Age Discrimination in Employment Act); *Board of Tr. of the Univ. of Ala. v. Garrett*, 121 S. Ct. 955 (2001) (similar, under the Americans with Disabilities Act); *Seminole Tribe v. Florida*, 517 U.S. 44 (1996).

p. 192: **High court ruling limiting private right of action on disparate impact discrimination under Title VI of the 1964 Civil Rights Act:** *Alexander v. Sandoval*, 532 U.S. 275, 280 (2001).

p. 193-194: **Citations to cases threatening civil rights progress:** *Buckhannon Bd. & Care Home v. W. Va. Dep't of Health & Human Res.*, 532 U.S. 598 (2001); *Alexander v. Sandoval*, 532 U.S. 275 (2001); *Hoffman Plastic Compounds, Inc. v. NLRB*, 535 U.S. 137 (2002); *Circuit City Stores v. Adams*, 2002 U.S. LEXIS 4060 (2002); *Gilmer v. Interstate/Johnson Lane Corp.*, 500 U.S. 20 (1991); *Kimel v. Fla. Bd. of Regents*, 528 U.S. 62 (2000); *Alden v. Maine*, 527 U.S. 706 (1999); *Barnes v. Gorman*, 536 U.S. 181 (2002); *Gebser v. Lago Vista Indep. Sch. Dist.*, 524 U.S. 274 (1998); *Hazen Paper Co. v. Biggins*, 507 U.S. 604 (1993); *West Virginia Univ. Hosps. v. Casey*, 885 F.2d 11 (U.S. App. 1989).

p. 195: **Post 9/11 racial profiling and civil liberties:** See C. Edley in, *The War on Our Freedoms: Civil Liberties in an Age of Terrorism* (Richard C. Leone, Greg Anrig Jr., eds.) (*Public Affairs*, 2003).

p. 195: **Doubts concerning contribution of high incarceration rates to crime reduction:** See Paul D. Butler, Symposium: The Role of Race-Based Jury Nullification in American Criminal Justice: Race-based Jury Nullification: Case-in-Chief, 30 J. Marshall L. Rev. 911, 915–16 (1997).

p. 196: **Problems of reentry and the "back end" of the incarceration systems:** Jeremy Travis, Amy L. Solomon, and Michelle Waul, "From Prison to Home: The Dimensions and Consequences of Prisoner Reentry" (2001), pp. 1–2. Ed Koch, "Give Some Ex-Convicts Another Chance," *Newsday* (August 17, 2001), p. A49.

p. 196: **Felon disfranchisement:** Christopher Uggen, Jeff Manza, "Democratic Contraction? Political Consequences of Felon Disenfranchisement in the United Sates," *American Sociological Review*, Vol. 67, (2002), pp. 777–803; Jamie Fellner and Marc Mauer, "Losing the Vote: The Impact of Felony Disenfranchisement Laws in the United States," Sentencing Project and Human Rights Watch (1998).

p. 197: **NCLB implementation and civil rights:** See Orfield, G. (2004). *No Child Left Behind: A Federal-, State- and District-Level Look at the First Year, An Introduction.* Cambridge, MA: The Civil Rights Project at Harvard University. Kim, J., & Sunderman, G. L. (2004). *Does NCLB Provide Good Choices for Students in Low-Performing Schools?* Cambridge, Mass.: The Civil Rights Project at Harvard University. Sunderman, G. L., & Kim, J. (2004). *Increasing Bureaucracy or Increasing Opportunities? School District Experience with Supplemental Educational Services.* Cambridge, Mass.: The Civil Rights Project at Harvard University. Kim, J., & Sunderman, G. L. (2004). *Large Mandates and Limited Resources: State Response to the*

No Child Left Behind Act and Implications for Accountability. Cambridge, Mass.: The Civil Rights Project at Harvard University. Sunderman, G. L., & Kim, J. (2004). *Expansion of Federal Power in American Education: Federal-State Relationships Under the No Child Left Behind Act, Year One*. Cambridge, Mass.: The Civil Rights Project at Harvard University.

Chapter Fourteen: A Progressive Agenda for Women's Rights

p. 204: **First Lady Laura Bush:** Fact Sheet, Office of International Women's Issues, Washington, D.C. January 12, 2004, available from the listserv statelists@state.gov.

p. 205: **Statistics on household composition and incomes:** Julianne Malveaux and Deborah Perry, *Unfinished Business: A Democrat and a Republican Take on the 10 Most Important Issues Women Face* (2003), pp. 1–7 and *in passim*. Also see Karen Gerber, Amy Beacom, Emily Palmer, *Women and the Economy: Mapping a Field*, Report of the Winds of Change Foundation, 2003. Also see Jillian Jonas, "In the Courts, Female Leaders Hail Affirmative Action Ruling, Women's E-News, June 27, 2003, at www.womensnews.org.

p. 206-207: **Bush and de-funded women's programs:** A review of Department of Justice enforcement is at www.watchingjustice.org, a new website sponsored by the Open Society Institute.

p. 207: **Second Bush term:** Letter to the author from the National Women's Law Center, July 23, 2003; Frank Litsky, "Bush Administration Decides Title IX Should Stay as It Is," *The New York Times*, July 12, 2003.

p. 208: **Health benefits:** Karen Kornbluh, "The American Family: Indicators of Economic Stress," January, 2004, Work & Family Program, New America Foundation, www.newamerica.net. Karen Kornbluh, "The Parent Gap," *Washington Monthly*, October, 2002, pp. 13–17.

p. 208: **Survey by Lifetime Television:** *Ibid.*, p.17, and Karen Kornbluh, "The Mommy Tax," *The Washington Post*, January 5, 2001. The Lifetime poll, taken just before the New Hampshire Presidential Primary, is at www.lifetimetv.com.

p. 209: **Independent Women's Forum:** www.justicewatch.org.

p. 209-210: **Bush on reproductive rights:** For the Bush domestic record on reproductive rights see "A Planned Parenthood Report on the Bush Administration and Its Allies: The Assault on Birth Control and Family Planning Programs," October 2003, at www.plannedparenthood.org; *NFPHRA Report*, the newsletter of the National Family Planning and Reproductive Health Association, February 11, 2004 at www.nfprha.org. Also see James Wagoner, "President Seeks to Double Abstinence-only Funding Despite New Research Showing Programs Don't Work," January 21, 2004, a memo to the press prepared by Advocates for Youth. On gag rule impact, also see "Access Denied: U.S. Restrictions on

International Family Planning," A Report of Population Action International, The Planned Parenthood Federation of America, IPAS, and Engender Health, 2003; or Rachel Pine and Christina Wypijewska, "Exposing the Impact of the Global Gag Rule," *Focus,* the newsletter of Engender Health, Winter 2003, www.engender-health.org; Center for Reproductive Rights, "Breaking the Silence: The Global Gag Rule's Impact on Unsafe Abortion" 2003.

p. 212: **U.S. unilateralism on women:** Women's Edge Coalition, "Overview of International Women's Issues and U.S. Spending in 2004," January 23, 2004; "International Women's Programs and the Bush 2005 Budget," February 2, 2004, and "International Women's Issues Highlights, Legislative Prospectus for the 108th Congress, February 20, 2004, all at www.womensedge.org.

p. 212: **Nixon's Labor and Justice Departments:** Cynthia Harrison, *On Account of Sex: The Politics of Women's Issues 1945–1968* (1988), pp. 69–89; Ellen Chesler, *Woman of Valor; Margaret Sanger and the Birth Control Movement in America* (1992, 1993), pp. 465–466. Ruth Bader Ginsburg and Deborah Jones Merritt, "Affirmative Action: An International Human Rights Dialogue," *Cardozo Law Review* (1999), p. 264.

p. 213: **George Lakoff:** See www.berkeley.edu/news/media/releases/2003/10/27_lakoff.shtml.

p. 214: **U.S. not an official party to U.N. agreement on women's rights:** Caren Grown, Geeta Rao Gupta, Zahia Kan, *Promises to Keep: Achieving Gender Equality and the Empowerment of Women,* Background Paper of the Task force on Education and Gender Equality, U.N. Millenium Project, available at www.icrw.org. Also see Elaine Zuckerman and Ashley Garrett, *Do Poverty Reduction Strategy Papers Address Gender? A Gender Audit of PRSPs,* a publication of Gender Action, 2003, at www.genderaction.org.

p. 215: **CEDAW review process:** Leila Milani, ed, *Human Rights for All, CEDAW: Working for Women Around the World and at Home* (2001), compiled by the Working Group on Ratification of the U.N. Convention on the Elimination of All Forms of Discrimination Against Women. For more on the treaty, also see www.WomensTreaty.org.

p. 216: **Remarks of Senator Jesse Helms:** The Honorable Jesse Helms, Remarks on the occasion of International Women's Day, March 8, 2000, quoted in Ambassador Linda Tarr-Whelan, "An Update on CEDAW," a memo prepared for the Open Society Institute, January 31, 2002, p. 4. Other details of the ratification history are also taken from this memo. For examples of the committee's most recent review see "Women's Anti-Discrimination Committee Holds Thirtieth Session in New York," January 12–30, at www.un.org/news/press/docs/wom1421.doc.htm.

p. 216: **U.N. Resolution on "Women and Political Participation":** The resolution is U.N. General Assembly, Fifty-eighth Session, Third Committee, Agenda

Item 110, Advancement of Women, October 30, 2003, or (A/C.3/58/L.17/
Rev.1/Corr.1). Also see remarks to the U.N. General Assembly of Ambassador
Ellen Sauerbrey, U.S. Representative to the Commission on the Status of Women,
October 24, 2003 on statelists@state.gov, October 27, 2003. For criticism of the
resolution, see Letter to the Hon. Colin Powell and the Hon. John Ashcroft,
November 18, 2003, posted at the website of the Women's Environment and
Development Organization, www.wedo.org.

p. 216-217: **Ambassador Linda Tarr-Whelan:** Memo, p. 5.

p. 217: **Percentages of women legislators:** Ginsburg and Merritt, p. 257;
Milani, pp. 32–37.

p. 218: **Ford Foundation:** Larry Cox and Dorothy Q. Thomas, eds, *Close to
Home: Case Studies of Human Rights Work in the United States* (The Ford
Foundation, 2004), p. 11.

Chapter Fifteen: No Compromise on Crime

p. 220: **Preliminary figures for 2003:** For a thorough discussion of the weak-
nesses of both of these measures of crime, and an argument for strengthening the
Crime Victimization Survey as the primary measure, see Henry Ruth and Kevin
R. Reitz, *The Challenge of Crime: Rethinking Our Response* (Cambridge, Mass.:
Harvard University Press, 2003).

p. 220: **Figure 1:** Source: National Crime Victimization Survey for years indicated, U.S. Department of Justice, Bureau of Justice Statistics, available at
www.ojp.usdoj.gov/bjs/cvictgen.htm.

p. 221: **Figure 2:** Uniform Crime Reports for years indicated, U.S. Department
of Justice, Federal Bureau of Investigation, available at www.fbi.gov/ucr/ucr.htm.

p. 221: **Figure 3:** Source: Sourcebook of Criminal Justice Statistics Online, Table
2.13, U.S. Department of Justice, Bureau of Justice Statistics. Results based on
polling by the Gallup Organization, Inc., June 24, 2003, available at www.
gallup.com/poll/releases/pr030619.asp. Question: "I am going to read you a list of
institutions in American society. Please tell me how much confidence you, yourself,
have in each one—a great deal, quite a lot, some, or very little?" Graph shows percentage responding "a great deal" or "quite a lot." Data for 2001 are not available.

p. 222: **Crime in American neighborhoods:** Data from the *Sourcebook of
Criminal Justice Statistics Online*, U.S. Department of Justice, Bureau of Justice
Statistics, Tables 2.39, and 2.41, available at www.albany.edu/sourcebook.

p. 222: **Americans do not trust police:** Data for 2001–2003 from the
Sourcebook of Criminal Justice Statistics Online, U.S. Department of Justice, Bureau of
Justice Statistics, Table 2.30, available at www.albany.edu/sourcebook.

p. 222: **Americans do not believe more policing is the way to reduce
crime:** Survey by the Gallup Organization, conducted October 6–8, 2003. The

same question was asked in eight different polls from 1989 through 2003. The wording of the question was: "To lower the crime rate in the United States, some people think additional money and effort should go to attacking the social and economic problems that lead to crime through better education and job training. Others feel more money and effort should go to deterring crime by improving law enforcement with more prisons, police, and judges. Which comes closer to your view?" Available at www.gallup.com. Accessed on January 1, 2004.

p. 223: **Figure 4:** Source: Uniform Crime Reports for years indicated, U.S. Department of Justice, Federal Bureau of Investigation, available at www.fbi.gov/ucr/ucr.htm. Data for 2001 do not include those killed as the result of terrorist attacks on September 11. Data for 2003 are based on preliminary figures for January through June compared with the same period in 2002, available at www.fbi.gov/ucr/2003/03semimaps.pdf.

p. 223: **1994 Crime Act:** I am dealing here only with crime policy, and not the still uncertain effects of counter-terrorism legislation on state and local law enforcement. For an early review of the dangers in this related realm, see David Cole and James X. Dempsey, *Terrorism and the Constitution: Sacrificing Civil Liberties in the Name of National Security* (New York: The New Press, 2002). Before the 1994 Crime Act, crime policy had been used by many politicians and commentators to differentiate candidates or parties. For an account of the most notorious instance of such posturing out of which the current bipartisan consensus grew, see David C. Anderson, *Crime and the Politics of Hysteria: How the Willie Horton Story Changed American Justice* (New York: Random House, 1995).

p. 224: **Crime between people who know each other:** According to the latest national victimization survey, 51.2 percent of violent victimizations were between non-strangers. The percentage has remained relatively constant for the last several years. About two-thirds of violent crimes against women are committed by people known to their victims. See Bureau of Justice Statistics, *National Criminal Victimization Survey, 2002,* Tables 27 and 43a.

p. 224: **Statistics on husbands/boyfriends and homicide:** *Crime in the United States, 2002,* U.S. Department of Justice, Federal Bureau of Investigation, available at www.fbi.gov/ucr/cius_02/html/web/offreported/02-nmurder03.html#t212.

p. 225: **Figure 5:** Source: U.S. Department of Justice, Bureau of Justice Statistics, National Crime Victimization Survey, Table 2, for years indicated, available at www.ojp.usdoj.gov/bjs/abstract/cvusst.htm. "Completed violent victimizations" exclude attempts and threats.

p. 227: **Federal efforts to improve prevention programs:** See U.S. Department of Education, *Wide Scope, Questionable Quality: Three Reports from the Study on School Violence and Prevention, Executive Summary,* August 2002, available at www.ed.gov/offices/OUS/PES/studies-school-violence/3-exec-sum.pdf.

p. 228: **Figure 6:** Source: U.S. Department of Justice, Bureau of Justice Statistics, National Crime Victimization Survey, Table 64, for years indicated, available at www.ojp.usdoj.gov/bjs/abstract/cvusst.htm. Figure shows total violent victimizations reported as occurring "on the way to or from school" or while "attending school."

p. 229: **Racial profiling still debated by police:** Racial profiling is only one of several areas of the administration of criminal justice where racial inequality threatens the legitimacy of the police and law enforcement generally. See both David Cole, *No Equal Justice: Race and Class in the American Criminal Justice System* (New York: The New Press, 1999); and Randall Kennedy, *Race, Crime, and the Law* (New York: Pantheon Books, 1997). In the latter, Kennedy argues that racial profiling is illegitimate, even if it may, in some circumstances, seem rational to the police. The argument that racial profiling is irrational as well as illegitimate is made particularly powerfully in David A. Harris, *Profiles in Injustice: Why Racial Profiling Cannot Work* (New York: The New Press, 2002).

p. 229: **Institutional and individual racial profiling:** For several eloquent statements about the difficulty of purging race from individual assessments of suspicion, see Linn Washington, *Black Judges on Justice* (New York: The New Press, 1994).

p. 230: **United States and local approach to policing:** The connection between the decentralized nature of American policing and the difficulty of controlling the use of force is made particularly clearly in Jerome H. Skolnick and James J. Fyfe, *Above the Law: Police and the Excessive Use of Force* (New York: The Free Press, 1993). James Fyfe is presently deputy commissioner in the New York Police Department.

p. 231: **Policing standards of U.S. Department of Justice and cities and states around the country:** All of the agreements and the monitoring reports from the jurisdictions where agreements have been implemented are available from the Police Assessment Resource Center at www.parc.info.

p. 231: **Statewide obmudsmen:** For an up-to-date review of the mosaic of civilian oversight of police in the United States, see: Samuel Walker, *Police Accountability: The Role of Citizen Oversight* (Belmont, Calif.: Wadsworth/Thompson Learning Professionalism in Policing Series, 2000).

p. 231-232: **"Invisible Punishments":** The phrase, "invisible punishment" is coined and discussed by Jeremy Travis in his essay, "Invisible Punishment: An Instrument of Social Exclusion" in Marc Mauer and Meda Chesney-Lind, *Invisible Punishment: The Collateral Consequences of Mass Imprisonment* (New York: The New Press, 2002) pp. 15–36.

p. 232: **American and international policing:** The movement for more "restorative justice" is a recent example of issues on which American crime policy has borrowed from innovations developed in other countries. See Roger Graef, *Why Restorative Justice? Repairing the Harm Caused by Crime* (London: Calouste Gulbenkian Foundation, 2000).

p. 233: **Police oversight in the United States:** In order to share experience in the improvement of justice systems, the Vera Institute of Justice has recently joined with five other non-governmental organizations and research centers to form Altus, a global alliance of institutions on five continents. See www.altus.org.

Chapter Sixteen: Beyond Money

p. 235: **Which some have not hesitated to use aggressively:** A study released in October 2003, by the Program on International Policy Attitudes at the University of Maryland found that among people who got most of their news from the Fox stations, four-fifths believed at least one of the common misperceptions about the U.S. war in Iraq, such as that Saddam Hussein had ties to al-Qaeda, while only 55 percent of NBC and CNN viewers, and just 27 percent of PBS viewers held these erroneous beliefs.

p. 236: **Family income of the average voter:** Richard B. Freeman, "What, Me Vote?" NBER Working Paper No. w9896, National Bureau of Economic Research, August 2003.

p. 236-237: **"If you want to be part of our revolution...":** David Maraniss and Michael Weiskopf, *Tell Newt to Shut Up: Prize-winning* Washington Post *Journalists Reveal How Reality Gagged the Gingrich Revolution* (New York: Touchstone Books, 1996), p. 111.

p. 239: **Westar:** Scott Rothschild, "Westar Raises Campaign Finance Questions," *Lawrence Journal-World,* May 17, 2003.

p. 239: **Soft money actually weakened the parties:** Jonathan S. Krasno and Frank Sorauf, "Why Soft Money Has Not Strengthened Parties," in Anthony Corrado, Thomas E. Mann, and Trevor Potter, eds, *Inside the Campaign Finance Battle* (Washington, D.C.: Brookings Institution Press, 2003).

p. 249: **Brownstein:** Ronald Brownstein, "Washington Outlook: In the Political Arena, the Gladiators Are Now Engaged in Total War," *Los Angeles Times,* July 28, 2003.